Friends, Lovers and Groups

160901

Friends, Lovers and Groups
Key Relationships in Adolescence

Edited by

Rutger C. M. E. Engels
Behavioural Science Institute, Radboud University, The Netherlands

Margaret Kerr
Örebro University, Sweden

Håkan Stattin
Örebro University, Sweden

BICENTENNIAL
1807
WILEY
2007
BICENTENNIAL

John Wiley & Sons, Ltd

Other Wiley Editorial Offices

John Wiley & Sons Inc., 111 River Street, Hoboken, NJ 07030, USA
Jossey-Bass, 989 Market Street, San Francisco, CA 94103-1741, USA
Wiley-VCH Verlag GmbH, Boschstr. 12, D-69469 Weinheim, Germany
John Wiley & Sons Australia Ltd, 42 McDougall Street, Milton, Queensland 4064, Australia
John Wiley & Sons (Asia) Pte Ltd, 2 Clementi Loop #02-01, Jin Xing Distripark, Singapore 129809
John Wiley & Sons Canada Ltd, 6045 Freemont Blvd, Mississauga, ONT, L5R 4J3, Canada

Wiley also publishes its books in a variety of electronic formats. Some content that appears in print may
not be available in electronic books.

Library of Congress Cataloging-in-Publication Data

Friends, lovers, and groups : key relationships in adolescence / edited
by Rutger C.M.E. Engels, Margaret Kerr, Håkan Stattin.
   p. cm.
 Includes index.
 ISBN-13: 978-0-470-01885-9 (alk. paper)
 1. Interpersonal relations in adolescence. 2. Friendship in adolescence.
I. Engels, Rutger C.M.E. II. Kerr, Margaret, 1915- III. Stattin, Håkan.
 BF724.3.I58F75 2007
 155.5′18–dc22

                                               2006032498

British Library Cataloguing in Publication Data

A catalogue record for this book is available from the British Library

ISBN 978-0-470-01885-9

Typeset in 10/12 pt Palatino by Thomson Digital
Printed and bound in Great Britain by Antony Rowe Ltd, Chippenham, Wiltshire
This book is printed on acid-free paper responsibly manufactured from sustainable forestry
in which at least two trees are planted for each one used for paper production.

Contents

About the Editors

Rutger C.M.E. Engels, Ph.D., is Professor in Family Psychology at the Behavioural Science Institute, Radboud University Nijmegen, the Netherlands since 2001. He obtained his Ph.D. at the Department of Medical Sociology, Maastricht University in 1998. Since then he has worked for three years as a post-doc and assistant professor at the Department of Child and Adolescent Studies, Utrecht University. Currently, he is involved in fundamental research on the link between (social) environmental influences on adolescent and young adult substance use and delinquency.

Margaret Kerr is Professor of Psychology at Örebro University, Sweden, and Co-director of the Center for Developmental Research. She earned her Ph.D. at Cornell University, U.S.A., and then completed a post-doctoral research fellowship with Richard Tremblay at the University of Montreal, Canada. She is an associate editor of the *Journal of Research on Adolescence*. Her research focuses on internal and external adjustment in adolescents and its role in the life course. Her current research interests include adolescents' choices of developmental contexts and parent-child relationships and their role in the development of delinquency.

Håkan Stattin is Professor of Psychology at Uppsala and Örebro Universities, Sweden. He earned his Ph.D. at Stockholm University. He directs the Center for Developmental Research at Örebro University and has served as President of the European Association for Research on Adolescence and associate editor for the *British Journal of Developmental Psychology*. He is probably best known for his research in three areas: delinquency development, pubertal maturation in adolescent girls, and parental monitoring. His works include an authored book (with David Magnusson in 1990), *Pubertal Maturation in Female Development*. In addition to his continued basic research in these areas, he is conducting prevention trials to reduce alcohol drinking and delinquency among adolescents.

Contributors

Roy F. Baumeister, Department of Psychology, Florida State University, Tallahassee, FL 32306-1270, USA

Ginnette C. Blackhart, Florida State University, Tallahassee, FL 32306-1270, USA

Sander M. Bot, Behavioural Science Institute, Radboud University Nijmegen, P.O. Box 9104, 6500 HE Nijmegen, The Netherlands

William Bukowski, Department of Psychology and Centre for Research in Human Development, Concordia University, 7141 rue Sherbrooke Ouest, Montreal, Quebec, Canada H4B 1R6

Antonius H. N. Cillessen, Behavioural Science Institute, Radboud Universiteit Nijmegen, and Department of Psychology, University of Connecticut, P.O. Box 9104, 6500 HE Nijmegen, The Netherlands

Thomas J. Dishion, Ph.D., Child and Family Center, University of Oregon, 195 West 12th Avenue, Eugene, OR 97401-3408, USA

Rutger C. M. E. Engels, Behavioural Science Institute, Radboud University Nijmegen, P.O. Box 9104, 6500 HE Nijmegen, the Netherlands.

Wyndol Furman, Department of Psychology, 2155 S. Race Street, Frontier Hall, University of Denver, Denver, CO, USA 80208, USA

Isabela Granic, The Hospital for Sick Children, 555 University Ave. Toronto, Ontario, Canada, M5G 1X8

Martin J. Ho, 2155 S. Race Street, Frontier Hall, Department of Psychology, Denver, Colorado 80209, USA

Margaret Kerr, Center for Developmental Research, BSR: Psychology, Örebro University, 701 82 Örebro, Sweden

Jeff Kiesner, Università di egl Studi di Padova, Dipartimento di Psicologia dello Sviluppo e della Socializzazione, Via Venezia 8, 35131 Padova, Italy

Brett Laursen, Professor of Psychology, Florida Atlantic University, 2912 College Avenue, Fort Lauderdale FL 33314, USA

Carolina Lisboa, Universidade Federal do Rio Grande do Sul-UFRGS, Porto Alegre, Brazil

Sabina M. Low, Human Services Policy Center, University of Washington, Box 354804, 1107 NE 45th Street, Suite 205, Seattle, WA 98105-4804, USA

Lara Mayeux, Department of Psychology, University of Oklahoma, 455 W. Lindsey, Room 714, Norman, OK 73019, USA

Karen S. Mooney, Florida Atlantic University, 2912 College Avenue, Fort Lauderdale FL 33314, USA

Sarah E. Nelson, Division on Addictions, Harvard Medical School, USA

Richard J. Rose, Indiana University, Department of Psychology, 1101 East Tenth Street, Bloomington, IN 47405, USA

Ron H. J. Scholte, Behavioural Science Institute, Radboud University Nijmegen, P.O. Box 9104, 6500 HE Nijmegen, the Netherlands

Rainer K. Silbereisen, Friedrich-Schiller-Universitaet Jena Lehrstul fu Entwicklungspsychologie Am Steiger 3, Haus 1, 07743 Jena, Germany

Håkan Stattin, Center for Developmental Research, BSR: Psychology, Örebro University, 701 82 Örebro, Sweden

Peter Titzmann, Friedrich-Schiller-Universitaet Jena, Lehrstul fur, Entwicklungspsychologie, Am Steiger 3, Haus 1, 07743 Jena, Germany

Introduction and Overview

Rutger C. M. E. Engels, Margaret Kerr, and Håkan Stattin

Few would disagree with the assertion that peers are important in adolescence. The literature on peer relationships is large, but for the most part, it is not extremely innovative. Recently, however, there have been some noteworthy advances in peer research, and in this volume we gather some of these innovative lines of research. This volume highlights four areas of peer research. One is the discovery of a 'deviancy training' mechanism of peer influence, in which antisocial pairs have been observed rewarding each other with approval for deviant or antisocial talk, and this has been linked to escalations in antisocial behavior. A second is the use of designs that capture both in-school and out-of-school peers in order to understand their relative influences on problem behavior. A third area of innovative research is the study of romantic partners as important peer relationships in adolescence. This is a newly emerging field of research with only a dozen or so studies published as of 2004, but many are now being presented at conferences and added to the literature in a seeming explosion of interest. A fourth area of innovative research is the application of behavioral genetic analytical techniques to understanding peer selection and peer and environmental influences on problem behavior. For each of these areas of innovative research, this volume contains contributions from the leading figures and comments and elaborations from other leading peer researchers.

DYNAMICS IN FRIENDSHIPS

Beginning with the study of the relative influence of peers on the development of problem behaviors: internalized problems such as depression and anxiety, and externalized problems such as delinquency and substance abuse, have dramatically changed from cross-sectional designs with adolescents themselves as single sources of information to sophisticated, prospective, multi-informant designs. These designs apparently permit us to draw conclusions from the complex reciprocal influence processes between friends. Most recent prospective studies focus on the interplay between individual characteristics, such as initial behavioral states, the development of problem behaviors, or personality and relationship characteristics, such as time spent together or quality of relationships and how they impact on the development of friendships and individual adjustment. This is achieved by assessing these characteristics at multiple moments during adolescence. According to some scholars, observational designs are especially able to show how peers influence each other in real time. In other words, using longitudinal survey designs with substantial intervals between waves may not allow one to fully understand how young people affect one another. Observational designs in which dyads or groups are monitored in their real-time social interactions may help to show the processes through which peers influence each other's behavior and adjustment in the long term.

In their chapter, Dishion and Nelson address the issue of friendship dynamics by examining data from a longitudinal sample of boys. Their basic assumption is that deviancy training in friendship through talk about deviant activities, and lack of talk about normative behaviors, may result in patterns of deviant friendship processes, which will lead to engagement in deviant and delinquent behaviors over time, as well as affiliation with deviant peers. A sample of 206 boys was followed from age 9–10 to age 23–24. Besides interviews with the parents and children themselves, the authors invited these boys to come to the laboratory with the friend with whom they spent the most time, to engage in some tasks. These sessions, which mainly consisted of discussing free-time activities, were videotaped and coded. They used a method to code the topics of the conversations (e.g., drug talk, rule-breaking talk, prosocial talk), but more interestingly, also a coding system of the unfolding dynamics in interactions – both in terms of verbal and nonverbal positive and negative engagement – between the boys. In their analyses, they linked these adolescent social interaction processes to young adult positive and problematic development. Their main findings indicate that negative interactions – and getting involved in talk about deviant and rule-breaking behaviors are related to negative adjustment, such as engagement in deviant behavior later in life, whereas positive friendship dynamics are not at all linked with positive or negative adjustment outcomes many years later.

Influence between peers can be studied on the individual, dyadic, and group levels. After discussing some of the recent works on the significance of peer relations for positive and negative adjustment of adolescents, Mayeux and Cillessen elaborate on some unresolved issues. First, with respect to the assessment of peer influences, they distinguish the various ways peers can passively or deliberately coerce others into becoming engaged in deviant behaviors. The use of experimental designs, vignette studies, self-reports on peer influences, and comparisons of peer and self-reports will be discussed. Then, more insight has to be gained into the identities of the individuals most prone to be affected by peers and the identities of those who are most likely to affect others. As researchers, we sometimes overgeneralize the effects of peers and ignore individual differences in susceptibility to peer influences.

According to Mayeux and Cillessen, laboratory observational studies have the potential to uncover the more fundamental processes underlying peer influences, especially if combined with short and long-term behavioral and socio-cognitive outcomes. Experimental studies in which status and behavior of peers are manipulated may be helpful in more rigorously testing assumptions on directions and magnitudes of influences and the effects of moderating variables such as personality and sociometric status. In terms of a developmental perspective, the authors stress that processes occurring in the short-term, particularly when they are repeated and occur in different relationships, may not be so negative at first, but the effects might be delayed. As such, the effects on individual development could be prolonged. They argue that dynamic system approaches might help researchers understand how these friendship processes unfold over time.

Engels, Bot, Scholte, and Granic respond to the leading chapter by Dishion and Nelson by first elaborating on the problems associated with measuring peer influences using exclusively survey methods in longitudinal designs. In their contribution they focus on the specific issue of peer influences on adolescent substance use. They argue that examining the peer relationship dynamics concerning the use of substances such as cigarettes, alcohol, and drugs use should preferably be done in contexts in which substance use is actually taking place. So, when it comes to alcohol consumption, for example, a party, disco or pub should be the natural context of study. Observational studies on interactions between friends or within peer groups in naturalistic settings are fairly rare. Engels et al. report on the findings of research in their bar lab at the university campus in which they observed real-time social interactions in existing peer groups. They found robust evidence for the existence of direct and indirect peer influences. Furthermore, in response to the approach of Dishion and Nelson, who followed existing friendships, the issue of selective peer affiliation is discussed. This refers to the fact that similarities in behavioral patterns between friends, as well as reciprocal influence processes, may be the result of peers flocking together at first. In order to avoid this interpretational problem, Engels et al. suggest using experimental, observational designs with peers who are unacquainted when they meet in order to unravel the influence processes.

PEERS IN DIFFERENT CONTEXTS

Research on how peers influence problematic adjustment in adolescence has been dominated by school-based surveys in which teenagers and their friends at school are included and followed over time. In most of these studies, the responses of young people are related to those of their classmates or other friends at school, assuming that by using this method, the vast majority of peer influences on adolescents are captured. This is quite a convenient way of assessing peer influences, and it might be accurate in childhood. However, in the teenage years this might not be the case. In most western societies, young people spend time in various social environments besides school and home, such as clubs, sports, bars, discos, parties, friends' homes, and so on. This implies that asking adolescents solely about their friends at school might be too limited and might result in a distorted view of ongoing peer influences. This problem is underscored by research showing that: (a) out-of-school friends' behaviors over and above the behaviors of in-school friends explain a unique part of the variance in adolescent deviant behaviors, (b) many deviant behaviors predominantly occur in out-of-school contexts with a mix of peers, (c) not only close friends – who are mostly the focus of school-based surveys – but also other peers, such as siblings or romantic partners, may affect individual adolescents, and (d) when engaging in extracurricular activities such as unstructured neighborhood activities adolescents may come in contact with, and get affected by, older adolescents, who are normally not included in school-based research.

Kerr, Stattin and Kiesner employed a new approach to overcome some of the limitations of surveys conducted in school classrooms. They assessed all 10 to 18-year-old adolescents in a small, relatively closed community in central Sweden (population of approximately 36,000). In this whole-city design, adolescents were asked about their peers but were not restricted to only their classmates or even their friends at school, but were asked about peers in general, irrespective of whether they were siblings, close friends or romantic partners, or at the same school as the respondent. Further, the design created the opportunity to gather data from the peers themselves, so it was not necessary to rely on the perceptions of the respondents in terms of the behavior exhibited by the peers. Instead of asking friends to name their most important friends – which is the most common way of gathering data on peer relations – they asked adolescents to mention their Very Important Peers. Their findings showed for the first time that the people whom adolescents mention as their most important peers change substantially through the course of adolescence. In early adolescence, a classmate was most often mentioned as the most important peer, while late adolescents more often mentioned a romantic partner as their most important peer. Furthermore, they showed that the friendship groups in which adolescents engaged across contexts – school, home, clubs, sports, and so on – most strongly affected individual behavior, that is, more than friendships in school. In sum, Kerr, Stattin and Kiesner made a strong point that in order to study peer influences in adolescence, one should try to capture the complexity of relationships over social contexts.

To underscore the relevance of studying the links between peer relations and engagement in problem behaviors from a holistic approach, in which all kinds of peer relationships are acknowledged and included, Silbereisen and Titzmann stress that the most important finding of Kerr, Stattin and Kiesner's work is that depending on the phase in adolescence, different types of peers affect juvenile delinquency. Silbereisen and Titzmann, however, suggest that young people are constrained in their selection of peers with whom to affiliate. In a way, in a small city in central Sweden the possibilities for young people to become engaged in a large variety of relationships are restricted, in contrast with adolescents growing up in metropolitan areas. Silbereisen and Tizmann raise the issues of assimilation and separation, especially relevant for immigrants. When young people reach the age and therefore the opportunity to enter new social contexts, do they want to maintain their own social roots – and therefore restrict the possibilities for all kinds of peer relationships – or do they look for new social contexts? The authors had analyzed data from a German study of immigrant youths, mainly from Russia and Kazakhstan, and reported that the number of intra-ethnic friends was positively related with delinquency. They also showed that if immigrants had relatively more friends from the local German population they were less likely to suffer from depression. As a result, the composition and size of the peer network were associated with adjustment, although in a more complex manner than expected. The concentration of intra-ethnic peers in the school and, to a lesser degree, in the neighborhood, played a moderating role. Concerning the research of Kerr et al., the authors stress that when immigrants are able to find friends in the local community, in school and out-of-school contexts they are more likely to integrate successfully and protect themselves against maladjustment. On the other hand, the authors also argue that there might be substantial constraints on the type of peer relationships individual youngsters can establish.

'Understanding the Place of Place' is the intriguing title of the chapter by Bukowski and Lisboa. They argue that, sometimes implicitly and at other times explicitly, place has its role in theories of development. Although theories have always acknowledged the environment in which individuals function, in empirical testing researchers often disregard the complexity of the various contexts in which young people function. Observing individuals in multiple social contexts should receive much attention from our methods and statistics analytic approaches. Moreover, the authors distinguish levels of analyses of the environment, focusing on very proximal ones, from the specific context in which a child is playing (e.g., school, home, kindergarten, friend's home) to the more abstract one, such as the organization of environment (e.g., ecological system theory, Bronfenbrenner, 1979). According to Bukowski and Lisboa, the work of Kerr et al. builds a bridge between the proximal multiple contexts adolescents operate in and the broader social systems Bronfenbrenner distinguishes, by aiming to include everyone of every context in their study. They emphasize the opportunities this kind of design provides to understand the changes and stability in influences of specific peers in the course of adolescence.

LOVERS IN ADOLESCENCE

The teenage years are characterized by considerable shifts in orientation from family to peers. Contrary to the childhood period, during teenage years adolescents spend much more time with their peers, and build longer-lasting, stronger relationships with them. Further, characteristics of peer relationships, such as getting social support, sharing big and small life events, and establishing intimate bonds more strongly affect young people's adjustment in this period of life than in perhaps any other phase in life. Adolescence is also the period of life in which persons get experienced with new kinds of relationships such as romantic and sexual relationships. Young people can have hedonistic or social goals when they engage in romantic relationships – hedonistic, in the sense that the relationship provides them with sexual experiences, offers higher status in the peer group, and fulfils basic personal needs, or social in the sense that the relationship provides them with a safe haven in which they can give and receive warmth and support.

There is substantial evidence that romantic relationships become increasingly important for young people's functioning over time. When adolescents are asked who the most important person for them is, most late adolescents will mention their romantic partner. The support provided by romantic partners outweighs that of other peers and family members, especially in late adolescence. In a longitudinal study, Overbeek et al. (2005) showed that the quality of romantic relationships in adolescence affect adjustment in young adulthood, even more strongly than support provided by parents. All in all, this would recommend a strong line of international research on the development of intimate relationships in adolescence, and on the negative and positive effects of these relationships on adjustment of young people in the short and long term. Oddly enough, however, there has traditionally been rather limited attention paid to romantic peer relationships. Furthermore, despite all the positive features of romantic relationships, the vast majority of studies in this area have focused on the downsides of romantic and sexual relationships, such as teenage pregnancy, sexually transmitted diseases, rape and violence in date contexts, and emotional problems following relationship break-ups.

Furman, Ho and Low took a different approach in their studies. They focused in their longitudinal research projects on the advantages as well as the disadvantages of romantic relationships. Furthermore, in doing so, they took a developmental perspective and tested whether the pros and cons of relationships depended on the timing and nature of dating. In their chapter they describe the findings of studies in which they followed 14 to 16-year-olds in their dating and sexual experiences over time. They were one of the first, who not only gathered data through questionnaires about relationship experiences and personal development, but also conducted observations of a series of interactions of these adolescents with close friends, mothers, and romantic partners (if they had one at the moment of administration). This of course offered not only multi-informant data on adolescents functioning in romantic relationships, but also provided the opportunity to look at the cross-relational continuity of behaviors. Concerning the quality of romantic relationships, Furman et al. distinguished support and negative interactions as key elements. They found that the impact of these elements on individual competence and engagement in risk behaviors became stronger with age. Moreover, the authors focused on the cognitive representations of the romantic relationship (views), and found that primarily for late adolescents (compared with early and middle adolescents) and for girls, these representations were linked to individual adjustment. The authors further express the need to focus on sexual and romantic relationships starting from the assumption that they might not be two sides of the same coin. For instance, many youngsters have light sexual experiences with close friends. Finally, they stress that the timing of dating and sexual experiences strongly determine whether these experiences have positive or negative consequences, and ingenious designs are required in future studies to fully capture the micro-development of romantic relationships in adolescence.

In their contribution, Laursen and Mooney build upon the work of Furman and colleagues on the advantages and disadvantages of romantic relationships in terms of individual adjustment. They start from the assumption that whether romantic relationships are beneficial depends on the experiences of young people in previous kinds of social relationships, like those with parents and friends. They tested three theoretical perspectives. The first postulates that involvement in romantic relationships as such will affect the adolescent's development in a positive manner as it provides a context to learn new forms of socially desirable behaviors; the second postulates that adolescent outcomes are not affected by engagement in romantic relationships per se, but that this depends on the quality of this relationship; and the third assumes that whether romantic relationships function beneficially depends on how individuals operate in other social relationships. Their findings strongly support the last perspective in a way that, according to Laursen and Mooney, the effects of participation in and the quality of romantic relationships should be considered in the broader context of relationships which adolescents have. They finish by stressing that the impact of experiences in romantic relationships on mental well-being can be easily misinterpreted if romantic relationships are solely examined without paying attention to the network of social relationships in which romantic relationships are a part.

Baumeister and Blackhart offer three perspectives on sexual transitions and experiences in adolescence from a gender perspective. They start by addressing the topic of erotic plasticity, or the degree to which the sex drive is shaped by social, cultural and biological factors (Baumeister, 2000). Women experience stronger plasticity in sex drive than men. This suggests that when females enter the period of adolescence (and in the phases after) they experience greater changes and subsequently flexibility in their sexuality. Furthermore, the authors discuss evidence for the assumption that environmental influences, ranging from cultural norms in a broad sense to peer group norms in a narrow sense, affect female sexuality stronger than that of males. Moreover, the immediate context women are in more strongly influences their sexual responses (Baumeister, 2000). A second perspective Baumeister and Blackhart discuss is that men and women differ in their sex drives, and that this difference is already visible early in adolescence. These gender differences in sex drive may affect the attitudes of young people when they first enter romantic relationships. The third perspective deals with the theory of sexual economics (Baumeister & Vohs, 2004). This theory starts from the assumption that in most societies female sexuality is a valued resource and forms the basis for social exchange. The authors address empirical evidence for the existence and operating mechanisms beyond the sexual marketplace. Implications for understanding the development of the adolescent's sexual and romantic relationships are discussed.

GENES AND PEERS

In recent decades, substantial attention has been given to the relative effects of genes versus shared and unique environmental influences on children's and adolescents' development. Behavioral genetic research, in particular twin designs, has provided fascinating food for thought in terms of understanding the changes and stability in social and problematic development. Years ago, some scholars suggested that shared environmental influences, such as parental upbringing and sibling behaviors have little effect on a variety of outcomes in young people, such as personality, school performance, psycho-pathology, and social development. In addition, if parents do little to shape their offspring's behaviors, it is often assumed that peers will be the primary influences. This is underscored with evidence of studies showing that peer influences are strongly related to adolescent development (Petraitis et al., 1995). In the past decade, however, this opinion has substantially changed, as many finely grained longitudinal analyses showed that substantial variance in behavioral outcomes can be explained by environmental influences (Rutter, 2002). To give a simple example, there is now compelling evidence that the initiation of smoking and alcohol consumption cannot be explained very well by genetic factors, but substantially by shared environmental factors (e.g., Koopmans & Boomsma, 1996). Moreover, the most widely held assumption now is that, when it comes to behavioral outcomes in adolescence such as socio-emotional development and problem behaviors, theoretical models that include gene-environmental interactions are most helpful.

In the final chapter of this book, Rose reviews the influence of peers and parents on adolescent problem behavior and decides to focus on alcohol use as the primary behavioral outcome. He uses data from a Finnish longitudinal twin study to test his assumptions. Rose starts by clearly arguing that the onset age of drinking is primarily affected by environmental (familial) factors shared by twins and not by heritability. Concerning peer relationships, part of the environment siblings share is related to the peer relationships they have. Shared genes cannot explain resemblances in the behaviors of friends, as they grew up in different families; however, processes of selective affiliation and mutual influence may affect this resemblance. Indeed, there is evidence for the operation of both selection and influence processes. Rose, however, takes this type of research one step further by examining whether adolescents' genetic dispositions affect selective peer affiliation. In prospective research on Finnish 11 to 12-year-old twins and their classmate friends, there is apparent evidence that adolescent friendships are partly conditioned by genetic factors. After discussing the relative influence of peers – as peer selection strongly affects homogeneity of behaviors in friendships – Rose focuses on the broader role of the social environment, namely the neighborhood, arguing that besides the family members and peers in a young person's immediate environment, neighborhood characteristics may explain additional variance in adolescent substance use. Finally, some recent findings concerning the direct and indirect influence of parenting practices (e.g., monitoring and supervision) on adolescent substance use are addressed. Their data show that despite the very small immediate effects of monitoring on adolescent substance use, the moderating role of parental monitoring is strong: especially in families where monitoring is high, genetic effects are substantially lower than in families where monitoring is low. It is essential to not only examine the direct influences of parental practices like support and monitoring, but also not to overlook potential strong moderating effects. In sum, Rose essentially argues that selection of friends in adolescence is affected by gene-environment interactions; young people affiliate with those who have similar attitudes and behaviors, creating opportunities and contexts that encourage expression of genetic dispositions as well as social reinforcement.

WHAT YOU CAN EXPECT

In your hands you have a book that focuses on a hot issue in adolescent research today – *which* peers are important in young people's lives and *how* they affect and are affected by them. This book gathers the freshest views on these issues. We have gone to great length to recruit some of the strongest, most active researchers to present their current thinking and research on this hot topic. We have enjoyed reading this book on friends, lovers and groups, and we have learned much. We are convinced that you will, too. Perhaps most important, we are convinced that you will develop new ideas from the contributions in this volume that will ultimately take research on adolescent peer relationships to the next level.

REFERENCES

Baumeister, R. F. (2000). Gender differences in erotic plasticity: The female sex drive as socially flexible and responsive. *Psychological Bulletin, 126*, 347–374.

Baumeister, R. F. & Vohs, K. D. (2004). Sexual economics: Sex as a female resource for social exchange in heterosexual interactions. *Personality and Social Psychology Review, 8*, 339–363.

Engels, R. C. M. E., Knibbe, R. A., & Drop, M. J. (1999). Why do late adolescents drink at home? A study on psychological well-being, social integration and drinking context. *Addiction Research, 7*, 31–46.

Koopmans, J. R. & Boomsma, D. I. (1996). Familial resemblances in alcohol use: Genetic or cultural transmission? *Journal of Studies on Alcohol, 57*, 19–28.

Overbeek, G. J., Vollebergh, W., Engels, R. C. M. E., & Meeus, W. (2003). Parental attachment and romantic relationships: Associations with emotional disturbance during late adolescence. *Journal of Counseling Psychology, 50,* 28–39.

Petraitis, J., Flay, B. R., & Miller, T. Q. (1995). Reviewing theories of adolescent substance use: Organizing pieces in the puzzle. *Psychological Bulletin, 117,* 67–86.

Rutter, M. (2002). The interplay of nature, nurture, and developmental influences: The challenge ahead for mental health. *Archives of General Psychiatry, 59,* 996–1000.

CHAPTER 1

Male Adolescent Friendships: Relationship Dynamics that Predict Adult Adjustment

Thomas J. Dishion
Child and Family Center and Department of Psychology, University of Oregon, USA

Sarah E. Nelson
Division on Addictions, Harvard Medical School, USA

INTRODUCTION

One of the most compelling questions in social developmental research is what role peers play in social and emotional adaptation (Hartup, 1983; Piaget, 1954; Sullivan, 1953). The question can be divided into two, more specific inquiries. First, to what extent does acceptance by peers influence social development? Second, do friendship dynamics shape individual social development trajectories?

With respect to the first inquiry, there is evidence that rejection by peers uniquely undermines children's social development (e.g., Nelson & Dishion, 2004). We have found that peer rejection seems to structure peer networks, with respect to the aggregation of deviant youth into peer groups (Dishion, Patterson, Stoolmiller, & Skinner, 1991). In fact, we recently found that peer rejection was uniquely predictive of gang involvement two years later, controlling for academic skills and antisocial behavior (Dishion, Nelson, & Yasui, 2004).

Thus, the inquiries into the unique role of peer acceptance and the influence of friendships in the social development of youth are not unrelated.

Friends, Lovers and Groups: Key Relationships in Adolescence. Edited by Rutger C.M.E. Engels, Margaret Kerr and Håkan Stattin. Copyright © 2007 John Wiley & Sons, Ltd.

Extensive research supports the idea that deviant friendships can promote delinquent and problem behavior (Brendgen, Vitaro, & Bukowski, 2000; Elliott, Huizinga, & Ageton, 1985; Tremblay, Masse, Vitaro, & Dobkin, 1995; Vitaro, Gendreau, Tremblay, & Oligny, 1998). In fact, as youth become involved in groups such as gangs, even the most antisocial escalate their deviant behavior (Cadwallader & Cairns, 2002; Cairns, Cadwallader, Estell, & Neckerman, 1997; Craig, Vitaro, Gagnon, & Tremblay, 2002; Hill, Howell, Hawkins, & Battin-Pearson, 1999).

Over the past ten years, we have been interested in studying the social interaction mechanism that drives the formation of deviant friendships. Specifically, we tested the proposition that friends' contingent positive reactions to deviant talk influence the development of adolescent problem behavior (Dishion, Spracklen, Andrews, & Patterson, 1996); we referred to this as *deviant friendship process*, or more simply, *deviancy training*. Formal testing of this idea requires the collection of direct observations of friendship interactions that capture antecedents and consequences, such as deviant talk and laughter. Contingencies between two repeating events can be quantified by a Z score (Bakeman & Gottman, 1986; Bakeman & Quera, 1995; Gottman & Roy 1990; Sackett, 1979). When two events reliably covary in time, the Z-score index is somewhere above 1.96. It is often the case that research on relationships examines a sequence of lag 1, examining the contingency between events that are contiguous in time (t_n and t_{n+1}).

Using this approach, we found support for the hypothesis that friends mutually influence one another through contingent laughter to deviant talk. We also discovered that not only did antisocial boys respond more positively to deviant talk, they also *did not reinforce* normative talk. In general, adolescents tended to match their level of deviant talk to the relative rate of reinforcement, a principle referred to as *matching law* (for a review, see McDowell, 1988).

This deviant friendship process has been found to contribute to escalations in drug use, delinquency, and violent behavior (Dishion, Andrews, & Crosby, 1995; Dishion, Eddy, Haas, Li, & Spracklen, 1997; Dishion et al., 1996). Patterson, Dishion, and Yoerger (2000) examined the link between early involvement in deviant peer groups and young adult problem behavior (i.e., substance use, high-risk sexual behavior, and repeated offending), and found that deviancy training in adolescent friendships mediated the relation between early adolescent involvement in a deviant peer group and young adult problem behavior. More recently, we examined the relation between deviancy training in early and late adolescence and the progression from substance use exploration to young adult substance abuse (Dishion & Owen, 2002). These data suggested that it was the deviancy friendship process in the early adolescent friendship that seemed to be prognostic of a pathogenic progression in substance use. Friendship dynamics in late adolescence (age 17–18) did not predict young adult substance use, once controlling for earlier substance use.

What is surprising is the lack of longitudinal research documenting interpersonal transactions associated with *positive* adjustment, despite the strong theoretical framework for suggesting such a role for peers (e.g., Piaget, 1954; Sullivan, 1953). For years, peer relationship research focused on the lack of social skills as a characteristic of delinquent and behavior problem children. However, research revealed that social skill deficits were best conceptualized as a proxy for a general pattern of social maladaptation associated with early-onset antisocial behavior and arrested socialization (Moffitt, 1993; Patterson, 1982). By and large, we know that delinquent, aggressive youth are less socially skilled in their friendships by virtue of being more often coercive and directive (Austin & Draper, 1984; Coie & Kupersmidt, 1983; Dishion et al., 1995; Dodge, 1983).

The study of normative patterns of friendship formation is fundamental for constructing a model of the contribution of peers to social development. Seminal work by Berndt (Berndt, 1981, 1989; Berndt, Hawkins, & Jiao, 1999), for example, documents the growth of sharing, prosocial behavior, and its increasing stability as children get older. Unfortunately, there is scarce evidence to suggest that individual differences in positive dimensions of friendship interactions are predictive of positive developmental trajectories. The best that we can say is that having supportive friendships during adolescence is likely to be associated with positive adult adjustment, even when controlling for childhood indices of adjustment (Bagwell, Newcomb, & Bukowski, 1998). No study yet has identified a dynamic construct from direct observations of friendship interactions that could be developmentally sensitive and explain individual differences in long-term positive outcomes (i.e., a positive counterpart to deviancy training).

One of the more promising constructs defining positive social development is the concept of regulation behavior (Eisenberg, 1998). Intrapersonal mechanisms such as inhibitory control or effortful attention control are linked strongly to advances in prosocial behavior in children (Eisenberg & Fabes, 1998; Rothbart & Bates, 1998). It would make sense that close relationships with conspecifics provide a 'training opportunity' for fine-tuning one's ability to regulate within a relationship dyad. Adjusting one's wants and wishes to accommodate those of a friend, listening and caring about the thoughts and feelings of another, and understanding another's point of view certainly require a certain level of 'self-regulation' in the service of 'dyadic regulation.' One would think that close and enduring friendships provide a unique context for the development of social and relationship skills. It does not seem particularly risky to hypothesize that Dyadic Regulation, as learned in friendships, would be predictive of adjustment and satisfaction in adult work, play, and love; as these three domains demand extensive interpersonal skill and sensitivity.

Given the relative neglect in studying the long-term contributions of positive and negative friendship aspects to child and adolescent social development (Hartup, 1996), we propose to disentangle the unique roles of deviancy training

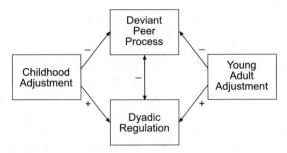

Figure 1.1 Hypothesized mediating link between peer relations in adolescence and young adult adjustment

and Dyadic Regulation in predicting young adult social and emotional adjustment. In this study, we used advanced statistical modeling to examine two dimensions of male adolescents' friendships, as assessed via videotaped observations of participants at 14, 16, and 18 years of age. Figure 1.1 provides a summary of our hypotheses, suggesting that both dimensions of adolescent friendship will be prognostic of young adult outcomes.

The goal of the present study is to determine the extent that friendship processes (i.e., deviant vs. regulated interactions) (a) change across time, and (b) influence adult adjustment. Composite scores of antisocial behavior, drug use, arrests, relationship quality, health/happiness, and success at age 22–23 were used as adult outcome variables. These scores also were combined into metaconstructs: adult maladjustment and adult positive adjustment. Specifically, we hypothesize:

1. Friendships will provide a context for the development of social skills, as evidenced by an increase in Dyadic Regulation over the course of adolescence.
2. Deviant friendship process in adolescence will be predictive of maladjustment in adulthood.
3. Dyadic Regulation in adolescence will be predictive of positive adjustment in young adulthood.
4. Youth who are high in Dyadic Regulation and low in deviancy training will be the most well adjusted with respect to low rates of antisocial behavior and high levels of personal satisfaction and success.

METHOD

Participants

This study used data from the Oregon Youth Study (Capaldi & Patterson, 1987) sample of boys, who were between the ages of 9 and 10 at the time data collection began (the 1983–84 school year) and attended schools in a high-crime area of a medium-sized city in the Pacific Northwest. From all the 4th-grade classes invited to participate, 206 boys were recruited to the study (74.4% of invitees). Capaldi and Patterson (1987) found that the boys who were recruited did not differ significantly from those who did not participate on any of the clinical scales of the teacher version of the Child Behavior Checklist (CBCL; Edelbrock & Achenbach, 1984). Overall, the recruited families were of slightly lower socioeconomic status than average (according to national norms) and predominantly White. More than 20% of parents were unemployed and more than 20% were on some form of welfare or financial assistance in the first year of the study. Initially, 42% of the families had two biological parents, 32% were single-parent families, and 26% were step-parent families (Patterson, Reid, & Dishion, 1992). Data used in this article were collected between 1983 and 1998, when the boys were between the ages of 9 and 24.

Data Collection Procedures

Boys were assessed yearly from age 9 to adulthood using parent and son interviews, questionnaires (completed by the child, parent, peers, and teachers), in-home assessments, school data, and court records. Both parents and teachers completed the CBCL each year. The child and parent interviews, which took place at the research center each year, gathered information about parenting, child behavior, and peer behavior. Table 1.1 provides an overview of the measures and timing of the data collection utilized in the present study.

Videotaped Observations

Boys participated in peer interaction tasks at ages 14, 16, and 18. During the parent and child interview portion of these assessments, the boys and parents

Table 1.1 Overview of the measurement strategy

Wave 1 (Age 9–10)	Wave 5 (Age 13–14)	Wave 7 (Age 15–16)	Wave 9 (Age 17–18)	Wave 15 (Age 23–24)
Multiagent Measure	Videotaped Friendship Interactions			Multiagent Measures
OSLC* Construct				
Antisocial	Deviant Peer Process			Poor Adjustment
Teacher Report	Coder-Dyad Antisocial			Antisocial Behavior
Parent Report	Coder-Dyad Drug Talk			Drug Use
Youth Report	Observed-Dyad Rule-Breaking Talk			Arrests
	Dyadic Regulation			Good Adjustment
	Coder-Dyad Interpersonal Regulation			Achievement
	Observed-Dyad Calm Conversation			Health, Happiness
	Observed-Dyad Directives (Reverse)			Positive Relationships

Note. *OSLC = Oregon Social Learning Center.

independently identified the three male friends with whom the boys spent the most time (rank-ordered). The male friend identified as being the most frequent companion by both the parent and study boy was identified for recruitment into the friendship study. At ages 14, 16, and 18, the recruitment rate averaged 89% across the three assessment waves (91%, age 14; 88%, age 16; 86%, age 18). For all recruited friends, a home visit was made to discuss the study and to obtain informed consent from each friend and his parents.

At each time point, the boys brought a friend to the lab and they were videotaped interacting across a 25-minute session. During that time, the boys were instructed to plan an activity together and discuss four problems (two per boy) they were having with parents and peers. The problem-solving tasks were counterbalanced.

As discussed above, the videotapes were coded by two groups of independent coding teams, focusing on different aspects of the interaction. The Peer Process Code focused on the interpersonal process of the friendship interaction, and the Topic Code focused on the deviance of the discussion topic. Both coding systems relied on coded speakership and used an event recorder to obtain the sequencing and duration of the relationship interaction. *Coded speakership* refers to a process of coding interaction data where the observer makes judgments regarding the person in the interaction who is talking. Occasionally two people in a relationship will speak at the same time, but their data are rendered as sequential when coding speakership. Event recorders are hand-held computers that allow the automatic entry of behavior codes, as well as a record of who is the initiator and recipient of the behavior.

Peer Process Code

The Peer Process Code was developed by Dishion et al. (1989) for the purpose of coding the videotaped friendship interactions studying adolescence (see Dishion et al., 1995). The coding system was developed with a focus on assessing the interpersonal process of a close relationship. Codes were systematically created to represent verbal, nonverbal, and physical interpersonal behaviors as well as those that were deemed to be experienced as positive, neutral, or negative. The positive or negative impact dimension was based on a series of studies that assessed the subjective ratings of behaviors coded within similar coding systems (see Hoffman, Fagot, Reid, & Patterson, 1987). Verbal codes included Positive Verbal, Endearments, Talk, Negative Verbal, Verbal Attack, Commands, Requests, Coercive Commands. Physical codes included Positive Physical, Negative Physical (hit or push), and Object Manipulation (giving or taking of an object in the session). Nonverbal codes were coded as either positive, neutral, or negative.

Behaviors were entered with an event recorder, with each entry defining the initiator (one digit), the content (two digits), the recipient (one digit), and the affective valence. Affective valence was recorded by entering one digit (among six), indicating anger–hostility (two levels), depression, neutral, and positive affect (two levels). The 24 codes used in this system were clustered into four, a priori summary scores: Negative Engagement, Directives, Converse, and Positive Engagement.

Negative engagement represented all codes presumed to have a negative interpersonal impact (e.g., criticisms, verbal attacks, name calling, coercive threats), as well as any neutral or positive content codes recorded in negative affect. A Directives score was indicated by two content codes describing the adolescent's attempt to direct or guide the behavior of his friend. Positive engagement included all positive content codes (compliments, positive nonverbal gestures, endearments), as well as neutral codes recorded in positive affect. Finally, Converse included only one code (talk) recorded in neutral valence. Thus, friendship interactions coded in Converse were typically calm, regulated discussions of mutual interest. Much of the interaction in both families and friendships is coded talk, which was the motivation for creating the Topic Code describing the content of the discourse.

Topic Code

The Topic Code was designed to capture variability in the boys' discussion topics (Poe, Dishion, Griesler, & Andrews, 1990). In contrast to the Peer Process Code, the Topic Code measures the extent to which antisocial boys selectively reinforced deviant talk.

To assess deviant talk, we took a broadband approach to topic classification: if two coders could agree that a discussion was in violation of conventional norms, it was coded as rule-breaking talk, which consisted of any reference to violations of legal or conventional norms, any inappropriate behavior during the taped interaction, and any activities violating the instructions given for the task. All other talk was coded as normative: if two boys were talking about the dangers of drug use, it would be coded as normative talk. In contrast, if the two boys were discussing their own drug use, it would be coded as rule-breaking talk. Because of the contextual nature of such topics, we found it necessary to simplify the coding of discussion topics by having only two possible topics.

For this study, we examined the average duration of rule-breaking talk, incorporating it with two coder impressions scales describing drug use and antisocial talk, to form a deviant peer process construct described below. We also used the proportion of time spent conversing (as defined by the Peer Process Code) and the proportion of time spent issuing directives (reversed) to help define the Dyadic Regulation construct described below.

Coder Impression Scales

Following the Peer Process Coding, observers completed an inventory assessing their global impressions of the friendship interaction from the 25-minute videotaped interaction. As in previous research, two scales were created from this inventory and used for the Deviant Peer Process construct: drug talk and antisocial behavior. One scale used in the Dyadic Regulation construct was created from this inventory measuring coder impression of the dyad's interpersonal regulation.

Constructs

The two constructs, Deviant Peer Process and Dyadic Regulation, were created to describe the friendship interactions at each of the three time points (ages 14, 16, and 18). The Deviant Peer Process score was based on the coding from the Topic Code and the coder impressions of drug talk and antisocial behavior during the friendship interaction. The Dyadic Regulation score was based on the Peer Process Code and coder impressions of interpersonal regulation during the friendship interaction. The psychometric characteristics of each construct are summarized in Table 1.2.

Dyadic Regulation

This score represents the extent to which the two adolescents were normatively engaged with one another with respect to listening, turn taking, politeness, and Dyadic Regulation. Three scores comprised this construct, two from the direct observations of calm conversation and a third from the coder impressions. The construct had a reliability ranging from 0.56 to 0.74 across waves.

An average of 70% of the dyadic interactions were coded in Converse. Being able to hold a conversation is thought to be a key feature of friendship Dyadic Regulation. Thus, the average duration of Converse served as one indicator of Dyadic Regulation. This score reflects the average duration of a Converse episode, coded at the dyad level. Specifically, a study boy Converse (20-s) followed by a peer Converse (20-s) would reflect a 40-s dyadic Converse event.

Being directive with a friend is considered to be a social skill deficit and a sign of a dysregulated friendship. The Directives score reflects the average duration of Directives over the course of the 25-minute videotaped observation. This score reflects the average duration of a Directives episode, coded at the dyad level, as explained above for Converse. For use in the Dyadic Regulation construct, the score was multiplied by -1 so that a high score represents fewer directives.

The interpersonal regulation score reflects the coder's impression of the prosocial nature of the friendship with respect to mutual concern, responsiveness, and regulation. Seven items across the three waves were used: eye contact, social skills, concern, responsiveness, turn taking, derogatory behavior (reversed), and hyperactivity (reversed). Scores were averaged across the target child and his peer. The internal consistency ranged from 0.79 to 0.82

Table 1.2 Internal consistency of peer process constructs

| | Wave 5 | | | Wave 7 | | | Wave 9 | |
	α	Correlations Item-total	Peer	α	Correlations Item-total	Peer	α	Correlations Item-total	Peer
Dyadic Regulation	0.71			0.56			0.74		
Converse		0.45			0.32			0.49	
Coder Impressions		0.63	0.80		0.37	0.85		0.52	0.82
Directives (R)		0.51			0.40			0.62	
Deviant Peer Process	0.70			0.77			0.71		
Drug Talk		0.52			0.64			0.59	
Antisocial Talk		0.46			0.55			0.48	
Rule-breaking		0.51			0.60			0.45	

across waves and the correlation between the target child's scores and the peer's scores ranged from 0.80 to 0.85.

Deviant Peer Process. The Deviant Peer Process construct consisted of three variables from the peer interaction task: drug talk, antisocial talk/behavior, and duration of rule-breaking talk. The construct had a reliability ranging from 0.61 to 0.70 across waves and item-total correlations ranging from 0.45 to 0.64. The construct was developed using methods detailed by Capaldi and Patterson (1989).

A score representing the time a dyad spent either talking or behaving in a rule-breaking fashion was generated using the topic coding system for the peer interaction task. Rule-breaking talk consisted of any reference to violations of legal or conventional norms, any inappropriate behavior during the taped interaction, and any activities violating the instructions given for the task. Coder reliability analyses for the topic code yielded mean agreements over 90% and kappas over 0.65. The actual score used in these analyses was the average duration (in seconds) of a dyad's rule-breaking talk.

We used coder impressions to create a drug talk score. Coders answered 12 questions about whether the adolescent or his peer had referred to use of specific substances during the peer interaction task. Each question asked about a specific substance: alcohol, tobacco, marijuana, cocaine, hallucinogens, and methamphetamine. The six questions for each adolescent were averaged, and the mean of the two boys' scores was taken. Correlations between the two boys' drug talk scores ranged from 0.87 to 0.97.

We also used coder impressions to create an antisocial talk score. Coders answered questions about both the boy and his peer, judging how much the two engaged in antisocial behavior, how much they engaged in prosocial behavior, how much the peer encouraged antisocial behavior from the target boy, and how much the peer encouraged prosocial behavior. The mean of these four items was taken.

Young Adult Outcomes

Young adult (age 23–24) outcomes included measures of adult positive adjustment and adult maladjustment. Because this study investigated both positive and negative early peer experiences, we wanted to measure both adaptive and maladaptive outcomes. Constructs measuring health and happiness, work and school success, and relationship quality combined to form a metaconstruct of adult positive adjustment. Constructs measuring drug use, antisocial behavior, and arrests combined to form a metaconstruct of maladjustment. We created all constructs using a method of including all face valid items within a rating scale (e.g., interviewer impressions), retaining items that did not detract from the reliability of the scale, then combining scales and retaining scales that did not detract from the reliability of the construct. The psychometric properties of the six constructs and their metaconstructs are summarized in Table 1.3.

Table 1.3 Young-adult Outcomes (Wave 15)

Poor Adjustment ($\alpha = 0.62$)	Good Adjustment ($\alpha = 0.79$)
Antisocial Behavior ($\alpha = 0.61$)	Health, Happiness ($\alpha = 0.74$)
Interviewer Report	Interviewer Report
Parent Report	Self-Perception Scale
Self-Report	Self-Report
Drug Use ($\alpha = 0.58$)	Success ($\alpha = 0.76$)
Self-Report	Interviewer Report
	Peer Report
	Self-Report
	Coder Report
	NEO Conscientiousness
	School Completion
	Months in School, Work
Arrests	Positive Relationships ($\alpha = 0.75$)
Criminal Records, Age 19–24	Interviewer Report Social Skills
	Self-Report Verbal Conflict
	Dyad DSS*
	Dyad Verbal Conflict
	Peer Report Relationship
	Self-Report Relationship
	Self-Report Relationship Satisfaction
	NEO* Agreeableness

Note. *DSS = Dyadic Social Skills Scale; NEO = Neuroticism-Extraversion-Openness Personality Inventory.

Adult Health and Happiness

Adult health and happiness was conceptualized as an index of mental health and contentment. The construct consisted of five scales: two self-report scales of life satisfaction and self-report of self-esteem, and interviewer and parent impressions of the target adolescent's happiness. The construct was internally consistent with an alpha of 0.74.

Adult Success

Adult success was conceptualized as an index of engagement in work and education and ratings of conscientiousness. The construct consisted of eight scales: self-report of months spent in school or at work, level of education, engagement in school or work, success, the Neuroticism-Extraversion-Openness (NEO) conscientiousness scale (Costa & McRae, 1985; Saucier & Goldberg, 2003), coder and interviewer impressions of work or school engagement, and peer impressions of school or work involvement. The construct was internally consistent with an alpha of 0.76.

Adult Relationship Quality

Adult relationship quality was conceptualized as an index of social skills, problem-solving and conflict resolution skills, and reports of relationship quality, all derived from the Oregon Youth Study assessment of intimate heterosexual relationships and same gender relationships at age 23–24 (Capaldi, Dishion et al., 2001), as well as a measure of agreeableness. The construct consisted of eight scales: two self-report scales of satisfaction with relationships, self-report of verbal conflict, the NEO self-report Agreeableness scale (Costa & McRae, 1985; Saucier & Goldberg, 2003), interviewer impressions of dyadic social skills, peer report of relationship with the target child, and two dyadic ratings of level of conflict in their relationship. The construct was internally consistent with an alpha of 0.75.

Adult Drug Use

Adult drug use was conceptualized as an index of adult substance-use patterns. The construct consisted of two self-report scales: self-report of alcohol and marijuana use patterns and frequency, and self-report endorsement of using drugs or drinking too much alcohol. The construct was moderately internally consistent with an alpha of 0.58.

Adult Antisocial Bbehavior

Adult antisocial behavior was measured similarly to antisocial behavior in 10th grade. The construct consisted of five scales: one self-report item measuring guilt after breaking rules, the externalizing scale from the young adult self-report, the self-report Elliot Behavior Checklist, the externalizing scale from the parent version of the CBCL, and interviewer impressions of the adolescent's antisocial behavior. The construct was moderately internally consistent with an alpha of 0.61.

Adult Arrests

Adult arrests were measured using court records. All arrests between 11th grade and young adulthood (juvenile and adult) were summed to create this measure.

Analysis Strategy

In order to examine the effect of Deviant Peer Process and Dyadic Regulation on young adult outcomes, we conducted four sets of analyses. First, we ran confirmatory factor analyses of the two peer process constructs to test their internal consistency and independence. Next, we used latent growth modeling to investigate separately the effect of each construct on young adult adjustment. Finally, we tested the relative influence of and interaction between Deviant Peer Process and Dyadic Regulation in predicting outcomes.

RESULTS

Confirmatory Factor Analyses

To test the independence of Deviant Peer Process and Dyadic Regulation, we ran confirmatory factor analyses of the two constructs at each assessment period (age 14, 16, and 18). As can be seen in Figure 1.2, which displays the results for all three assessments, Deviant Peer Process and Dyadic Regulation are not independent, but the models do fit well as specified when the two constructs are allowed to covary. The negative relationship between the two constructs indicates, as one would expect, that boys who have high Deviant Peer Process tend to be low on Dyadic Regulation. Table 1.4 displays the correlation matrix for the two constructs across assessments.

Latent Growth Modeling

To investigate the development of Deviant Peer Process and Dyadic Regulation across time and their effect on young adult outcomes, we used a latent growth modeling procedure. Because we wanted to investigate the two constructs' independent effects on the outcomes, we ran two sets of models: one with Deviant Peer Process and one with Dyadic Regulation. In both cases, we first specified the model for the peer process construct across the three assessment points, testing a linear growth model and setting the intercept at the first assessment point. Next, we added childhood antisocial behavior as a predictor (i.e., to test for peer process' influence above and beyond a known predictor of young adult outcome) and ran two models, one predicting young adult maladjustment (i.e., the metaconstruct of antisocial behavior, drug use, and arrests) and one predicting young adult positive adjustment (i.e., the metaconstruct of success, health and happiness, and relationship quality). Zero-order correlations between the constructs and young adult outcomes are displayed in Table 1.5.

Base Models

Both the Deviant Peer Process and Dyadic Regulation linear growth models fit the data well ($\chi^2(1) = 0.42$ and 1.37, respectively; $p > 0.20$, RMSEA < 0.05). For the Deviant Peer Process model, both the intercept and slope had significant variances and means. Deviant Peer Process increased across time and its mean level and growth varied between participants; intercept and slope were significantly negatively correlated: participants who had low Deviant Peer Process at the first assessment grew more than those who had high Deviant Peer Process at the first assessment (possibly indicating a ceiling effect). For the Dyadic Regulation model, both the intercept and slope had significant means, but only the intercept had significant variance. Participants varied on their

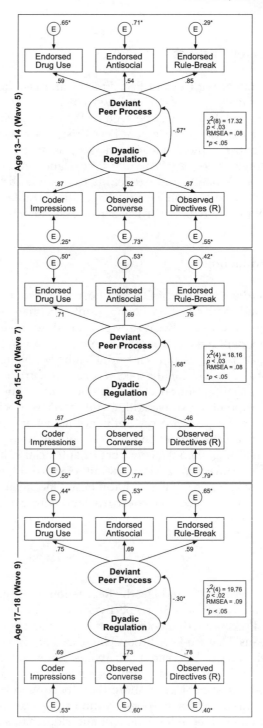

Figure 1.2 Confirmatory factor analyses

Table 1.4 Bivariate Correlations between Deviant Peer Process (DPP), Dyadic Regulation (DR)

	DR 5	DR 7	DR 9	DPP 5	DPP 7	DPP 9
DR 5	1.00			−0.45**		
DR 7	0.46**	1.00			−0.45**	
DR 9	0.27**	0.29**	1.00			−0.36**
DPP 5				1.00		
DPP 7				0.51**	1.00	
DPP 9				0.39**	0.50**	1.00

Note. List-wise deletion; $n=160$ *$p < 0.05$ **$p < 0.01$

initial levels of Dyadic Regulation, but did not vary significantly in that growth across time. Dyadic Regulation slope was significantly negatively correlated. Just as with Deviant Peer Process, participants who had low levels of Dyadic Regulation initially increased their Dyadic Regulation more across time than those who began with higher levels (see Figure 1.3 for both models). This finding is consistent with the notion of arrested social development of anti-social children. It is clear from these data, however, that boys characterized as antisocial 'catch up' to their normative counterparts by late adolescence.

Prediction of Young Adult Positive Adjustment and Maladjustment from Deviant Peer Process

As explained above, we added childhood antisocial behavior (a construct meas-ured via multiple agents and multiple measures at age 9) to the base model as a predictor, and young adult maladjustment or positive adjustment as the

Table 1.5 Bivariate correlations between Deviant Peer Process (DPP), Dyadic Regulation (DR), and Young Adult Adjustment

	Success	Health, Happiness	Positive Relationship	Antisocial	Drug Use	Arrests
DPP 5	−0.19*	−0.06	−0.12	0.22**	0.21**	0.25**
DPP 7	−0.32**	−0.31**	−0.28**	0.32**	0.12	0.33**
DPP 9	−0.32**	−0.23**	−0.26**	0.39**	0.17*	0.24**
DR 5	0.13	0.09	0.06	−0.16*	−0.07	−0.16*
DR 7	0.18*	0.04	00.10	−0.09	0.02	−0.17*
DR 9	0.21**	0.20*	0.19*	−0.19*	0.04	−0.12

Note. Listwise deletion; $n = 157$
*$p < 0.05$ **$p < 0.01$

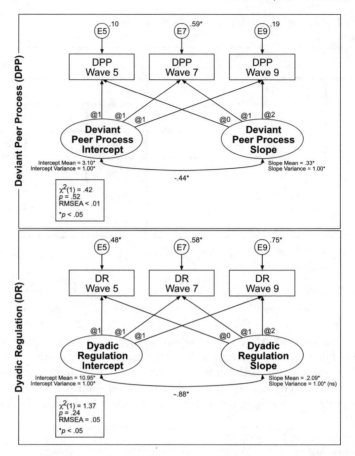

Figure 1.3 Latent growth models

outcome. Paths from antisocial behavior to slope, intercept, and outcome were allowed, as were paths from intercept and slope to outcome (see Figure 1.4).

The model predicting maladjustment from Deviant Peer Process fit the data well, $\chi^2(3) = 3.06$, $p > 0.05$, RMSEA $= 0.01$. Antisocial behavior positively predicted initial levels of Deviant Peer Process; both initial levels and growth across time predicted young adult maladjustment. No other paths were significant, indicating that the relationship between childhood antisocial behavior and negative outcome (zero-order correlation $= 0.36$) was mediated by Deviant Peer Process.

The model predicting positive adjustment from Deviant Peer Process did not fit the data as well, $\chi^2(3) = 11.45$, $p < 0.05$, RMSEA $= 0.13$. In this model, antisocial behavior again positively predicted initial levels of Deviant Peer Process; and both initial levels and growth across time negatively predicted young adult positive adjustment. As before, no other paths were significant, indicating that the relationship between childhood antisocial behavior and

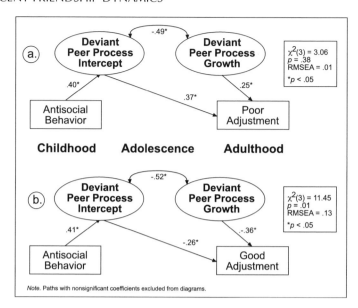

Figure 1.4 Deviant peer process as a mediating link between childhood adjustment and young adult adjustment

positive outcome (zero-order correlation $= -0.32$) was mediated by Deviant Peer Process.

Prediction of Young Adult Adjustment and Maladjustment from Dyadic Regulation

The same models were run using Dyadic Regulation in place of Deviant Peer Process (see Figure 1.5).

The model predicting maladjustment from Dyadic Regulation fit the data well, $\chi^2(3) = 2.02$, $p > 0.05$, RMSEA < 0.01. Antisocial behavior negatively predicted initial levels of Dyadic Regulation and positively predicted young adult maladjustment. Neither initial levels nor growth of Dyadic Regulation across time predicted young adult maladjustment.

The model predicting positive adjustment from Dyadic Regulation also fit the data well, $\chi^2(3) = 3.06$, $p > 0.05$, RMSEA $= 0.01$. In this model, antisocial behavior again negatively predicted initial levels of Dyadic Regulation, but no other paths were significant.

Relationship Between Deviant Peer Process and Dyadic Regulation

To test the relative effects of Deviant Peer Process and Dyadic Regulation on outcomes, we also ran two hierarchical regressions. In the first regression, we predicted young adult maladjustment, entering childhood antisocial behavior in the first step, Deviant Peer Process slope and average in the second step, and Dyadic Regulation slope and average in the third step. Both the first and

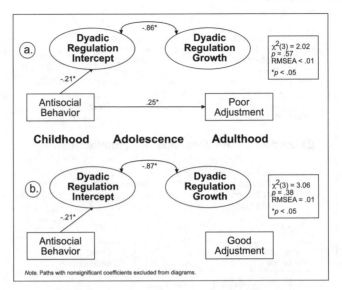

Figure 1.5   Dyadic regulation as a mediating link between childhood adjustment and young adult adjustment

second steps contributed significantly to the model, R^2 change $= 0.09$, F change $(1, 184) = 18.68$, $p < 0.001$; and R^2 change $= 0.06$, F change $(2, 182) = 6.03$, $p < 0.01$, respectively. The third step, in which Dyadic Regulation was added, did not contribute to the model. Specifically, antisocial behavior and average level of Deviant Peer Process significantly predicted young adult maladjustment.

In the second regression, using the same steps to predict young adult positive adjustment, both the first and second steps again contributed significantly to the model, R^2 change $= 0.08$, F change $(1, 180) = 15.32$, $p < 0.001$; and R^2 change $= 0.07$, F change $(2, 178) = 6.76$, $p < 0.01$, respectively. The third step, in which Dyadic Regulation was added, again did not contribute to the model. Specifically, antisocial behavior and average level of Deviant Peer Process again significantly predicted young adult maladjustment.

We ran a final set of models (i.e., the two models predicting maladjustment and positive adjustment, respectively), adding a fourth step predicting outcome from the interaction between average levels of Deviant Peer Process and Dyadic Regulation (standardized prior to creating the interaction term in order to center the interaction). The interaction term did not significantly contribute to either model.

CONCLUSIONS AND FUTURE DIRECTIONS

It was of some surprise to us that we were unable to identify a positive friendship dynamic that uniquely predicted positive or negative adjustment outcomes in young adulthood. Given the extensive measurement strategy, including direct observation, one would think that at least one or two of the prosocial friendship indices would be predictive. It is fundamental to our conceptualization of peer relationships that they occupy a unique 'developmental niche' in which youth have the opportunity to co-regulate with an interactive partner of equal status, and to learn and practice skills that are later crucial for negotiating healthy relationships fundamental to work, love, and play in the adult years.

One potential oversight in our collective thinking about the role of friendship in social and emotional development is the mixing of an individual difference perspective with a developmental one. It is clearly true that friendships over the course of adolescence appear to become increasingly engaging, regulated, and less directive from early to late adolescence. This is perhaps true for everyone, regardless of the quality of the friend. In fact, our data suggest that early-onset antisocial youth have somewhat lower initial levels of prosocial behavior with friends in early adolescence, but completely catch up by late adolescence. Paradoxically, adolescent friendships may be especially important for youth who are lower in social status and in marginal family situations. This seems true in some respects, as we found that early-onset antisocial youth spend increasing amounts of time with friends, whereas well-adapted youth spend less, from early to late adolescence (Dishion, Nelson, Winter, & Bullock, 2004).

What we often have neglected in our thinking about the role of friendship in social and emotional development is the salient role of norms, values, and attitudes. If one thinks of adolescence as a time when youth emerge with an autonomous life course, then it would make sense that an important function of adolescent peer groups is to sort out within a social niche that which resonates with respect to a set of norms and behaviors that define such a trajectory. What is interesting is that deviance, within human culture, appears to be a very salient feature of these friendship dynamics. Nearly all adolescent friendships 'dabble' in deviance, yet some are highly organized in their deviance discussions (see Dishion, Nelson, Winter, et al., 2004). It is as if deviance serves as an alternative path to adulthood, less than the socially sanctioned achievements of school and occupational status. Previous research suggests that friendships high in deviancy training certainly have more fun, if parties, substance use, and sexual activity are defined as fun. Moreover, they predict early mating and prolific parenting.

This broad view of deviance in adolescence as a functional adaptation that has survival value for youth who understand all too well their long-term marginal social status is referred to as the *premature autonomy hypothesis* (Dishion, Nelson, & Bullock, 2004; Dishion, Poulin, & Medici Skaggs, 2000). We assume that in very early adolescence, the public school setting often defines the socially marginal status of many youth. Deviance emerges at this time as a pattern of behavior that brings this heterogeneous group together, hence, the term *confluence* (Dishion, Patterson, Reid, & Griesler, 1994). This process of social augmentation has been documented at the level of network analysis, where we find that initial levels of peer rejection interact with levels of peer liking (multiplicative term) to predict growth in the homogeneity in deviance of one's social clique, which in turn predicts increasing levels of deviance (Dishion, Light, & Yasui, 2004).

With this broader perspective in mind, it is not surprising that we find that these brief, videotaped interactions yield such powerful predictions. In general, we find that both initial level of deviant talk and growth in deviant talk, in the context of friendships, is related to lower levels of achievement and happiness and to higher levels of negative adult outcomes. From this evolutionary point of view, the tension of a paradox is reduced, in that, if deviance is functional from both a microsocial (i.e., elicits laughter) and a macrosocial (i.e., sex and parties) level, then the youths' neglect of potential long-term negative side effects is understandable. Similar decisions are made all the time, when youth and adults develop behavior patterns that are, in the short run, enjoyable, but in the long run, detrimental to health.

AUTHORS' NOTE

We are deeply grateful for the hard work of the Oregon Youth Study staff, directed and managed by Drs. Gerald Patterson and Deborah Capaldi, as well as study families and participating schools; this study would not have been possible without them. Thanks to Chere Di Valero for assistance in preparation of this chapter. This project was supported by grants DA07031, DA13773, and DA16110 to the first author from the National Institute on Drug Abuse at the National Institutes of Health.

REFERENCES

Austin, A. M. B. & Draper, D. C. (1984). Verbal interactions of popular and rejected children with their friends and non-friends. *Child Study Journal, 14*, 309–323.

Bagwell, C. L., Newcomb, A. F., & Bukowski, W. M. (1998). Preadolescent friendship and peer rejection as predictors of adult adjustment. *Child Development, 69*, 140–153.

Bakeman, R. & Gottman, J. M. (1986). *Observing Interaction: An Introduction to Sequential Analysis.* New York: Cambridge University Press.

Bakeman, R. & Quera, V. (1995). Log-linear approaches to lag-sequential analysis when consecutive codes may and cannot repeat. *Psychological Bulletin, 118*, 272–284.

Berndt, T. J. (1981). Age changes and changes over time in prosocial intentions and behavior between friends. *Developmental Psychology, 17*, 408–416.

Berndt, T. J. (1989). Friendships in childhood and adolescence. In W. Damon (ed.), *Child Development Today and Tomorrow* (pp. 332–349). San Francisco: Jossey-Bass.

Berndt, T. J., Hawkins, J. A., & Jiao, Z. (1999). Influences of friends and friendships on adjustment to junior high school. *Merrill-Palmer Quarterly, 45*(1), 13–41.

Brendgen, M., Vitaro, F., & Bukowski, W. M. (2000). Deviant friends and early adolescents' emotional and behavioral adjustment. *Journal of Research on Adolescence, 10*(2), 173–189.

Cadwallader, T. W. & Cairns, R. B. (2002). Developmental influences and gang awareness among African-American inner city youth. *Social Development, 11*(2), 245–265.

Cairns, R. B., Cadwallader, T. W., Estell, D., Neckerman, H. J. (1997). Groups to gangs: Developmental and criminological perspectives and relevance for prevention. In D. M. Stoff, J. Breiling, & J. D. Mader (eds.), *Handbook of Antisocial Behavior* (pp. 194–204). New York: Wiley.

Capaldi, D. M. (1984–). [Oregon Youth Study; addresses broad range of mental health and developmental questions for adolescent and early adult men]. Unpublished raw data.

Capaldi, D. M. & Patterson, G. R. (1987). An approach to the problem of recruitment and retention rates for longitudinal research. *Behavioral Assessment, 9,* 169–177.

Capaldi, D. M. & Patterson, G. R. (1989). *Psychometric Properties of Fourteen Latent Constructs from the Oregon Youth Study.* New York: Springer-Verlag.

Capaldi, D. M., T. J. Dishion, et al. (2001). Aggression toward female partners by at-risk young men: The contribution of male adolescent friendships. *Developmental Psychology, 37,* 61–73.

Coie, J. D. & Kupersmidt, J. B. (1983). A behavioral analysis of emerging social status in boys' groups. *Child Development, 54,* 1400–1416.

Costa, P.T. & McCrae, R.R. (1988). Personality in adulthood: A six-year longitudinal study of self-reports and spouse ratings on the NEO Personality Inventory. *Journal of Personality and Social Psychology, 54,* 853–863

Craig, W. M., Vitaro, F., Gagnon, C., & Tremblay, R. E. (2002). The road to gang membership: Characteristics of male gang and nongang members from ages 10 to 14. *Social Development, 11*(1), 53–68.

Dishion, T. J., Andrews, D. W., & Crosby, L. (1995). Antisocial boys and their friends in early adolescence: Relationship characteristics, quality, and interactional process. *Child Development, 66,* 139–151.

Dishion, T. J., Crosby, L., Rusby, J. C., Shane, D., Patterson, G. R., & Baker, J. (1989). *Peer Process Code: Multidimensional system for observing adolescent peer interaction.* Unpublished training manual. (Available from Oregon Social Learning Center, 160 East 4th Avenue, Eugene, OR 97401-2426.)

Dishion, T. J., Eddy, J. M., Haas, E., Li, F., & Spracklen, K. (1997). Friendships and violent behavior during adolescence. *Social Development, 6,* 207–223.

Dishion, T. J., Light, J. M., & Yasui, M. (2004, July). *A network analysis of the confluence hypothesis in early adolescence.* Poster presented at the 2004 Biennial Meeting of the International Society for the Study of Behavioral Development, Ghent, Belgium.

Dishion, T. J., Nelson, S. E., & Bullock, B. M. (2004). Premature adolescent autonomy: Parent disengagement and deviant peer process in the amplification of problem behavior. *Journal of Adolescence, 27,* 515–530.

Dishion, T. J., Nelson, S. E., Winter, C. E., & Bullock, B. M. (2004). Adolescent friendship as a dynamic system: Entropy and deviance in the etiology and course of male antisocial behavior. *Journal of Abnormal Child Psychology, 32,* 651–663.

Dishion, T. J., Nelson, S. E., & Yasui, M. (2004). Predicting early adolescent gang involvement from middle school adaptation. *Journal of Clinical Child and Adolescent Psychology, 33,* 69–81.

Dishion, T. J. & Owen, L. D. (2002). A longitudinal analysis of friendships and substance use: Bidirectional influence from adolescence to adulthood. *Developmental Psychology, 38*(4), 480–491.

Dishion, T. J., Patterson, G. R., Reid, & Griesler, P. C. (1994). Peer adaptation in the development of antisocial behavior: A confluence model. In L. R. Huesmann (ed.), *Aggressive Behavior: Current Perspectives* (pp. 61–95). New York: Plenum.

Dishion, T. J., Patterson, G. R., Stoolmiller, M., & Skinner, M. (1991). Family, school, and behavioral antecedents to early adolescent involvement with antisocial peers. *Developmental Psychology, 27,* 172–180.

Dishion, T. J., Poulin, F., & Medici Skaggs, N. (2000). The ecology of premature autonomy in adolescence: Biological and social influences. In K. A. Kerns, J. M. Contreras, & A. M. Neal-Barnett (eds.), *Family and Peers: Linking Two Social Worlds* (pp. 27–45). Westport, CT: Praeger.

Dishion, T. J., Spracklen, K. M., Andrews, D. M., & Patterson, G. R. (1996). Deviancy training in male adolescent friendships. *Behavior Therapy, 27*(1), 373–390.

Dodge, K. A. (1983). Behavioral antecedents of peer social status. *Child Development, 54,* 1386–1399.

Edelbrock, C. S. & Achenbach, T. M. (1984). The teacher version of the Child Behavior Profile: I. Boys aged 6–11. *Journal of Consulting and Clinical Psychology, 52,* 207–217.

Eisenberg, N. (1998). The socialization of socioemotional competence. In D. Pushkar, W. M., Bukowski, A. E. Schwartzman, D. M. Stack, & D. R. White (eds.), *Improving Competence Across the Lifespan: Building Interventions Based on Theory and Research* (pp. 59–78). New York: Kluwer.

Eisenberg, N. & Fabes, R. A. (1998). Prosocial development. In W. Damon (ed.), *Handbook of Child Psychology* (5th ed., Vol. 3, pp. 701–778). New York: Wiley.

Elliott, D. S., Huizinga, D., & Ageton, S. S. (1985). *Explaining Delinquency and Drug Use.* Beverly Hills: Sage.

Gottman, J. M. & Roy, A. K. (1990). *Sequential Analysis: A Guide for Behavioral Researchers.* Cambridge, MA: Cambridge University Press.

Hartup, W. W. (1983). Peer relations. In P. H. Mussen (series ed.), E. M. Hetherington (vol. ed.), *Handbook of Child Psychology: Vol. 4. Socialization, Personality and Social Development* (pp. 103–196). New York: Wiley.

Hartup, W. W. (1996). The company they keep: Friendships and their developmental significance. *Child Development, 67,* 1–13.

Hill, K. G., Howell, J. C., Hawkins, J. D., & Battin-Pearson, S. R. (1999). Childhood risk factors for adolescent gang membership: Results from the Seattle Social Development Project. *Journal of Research in Crime and Delinquency, 36*(3), 300–322.

Hoffman, D. A., Fagot, B. I., Reid, J. R., & Patterson, G. R. (1987). Parents rate the family interaction coding system comparisons of problem and nonproblem boys using parent-derived behavior composites. *Behavior Assessment, 9,* 131–140.

McDowell, J. J. (1988). Matching theory in natural human environments. *The Behavior Analyst, 11,* 95–109.

Moffitt, T. E. (1993). Adolescence-limited and life course persistent antisocial behavior: Developmental taxonomy. *Psychological Review, 100,* 674–701.

Nelson, S. E. & Dishion, T. J. (2004). From boys to men: Predicting adult adaptation from middle childhood sociometric status. *Development and Psychopathology, 16,* 441–459.

Patterson, G. R. (1982). *A Social Learning Approach: Vol. III. Coercive Family Process.* Eugene, OR: Castalia.

Patterson, G. R., Dishion, T. J., & Yoerger, K. (2000). Adolescent growth in new forms of problem behavior: Macro- and micro-peer dynamics. *Prevention Science, 1,* 3–13.

Patterson, G. R., Reid, J. B., & Dishion, T. J. (1992). *A Social Learning Approach: Vol. IV. Antisocial Boys.* Eugene, OR: Castalia.

Piaget, J. (1954). *The Construction of Reality in the Child.* New York: Basic Books.

Poe, J., Dishion, T. J., Griesler, P., & Andrews, D. W. (1990). *Topic Code.* Unpublished coding manual. (Available from Child, 195 West 12th Avenue, Eugene, OR 97401-3408).

Rothbart, M. K. & Bates, J. E. (1998). Temperament. In W. Damon (series ed.) & N. Eisenberg (vol. ed.), *Handbook of Child Psychology: Vol. 3. Social, Emotional and Personality Development* (5th ed.) New York: Wiley.

Sackett, G. P. (1979). The lag sequential analysis of contingency and cyclicity in behavioral interaction and research. In J. D. Osofsky (ed.), *Handbook of Infant Development* (pp. 623–649). New York: Wiley.

Saucier, G. & Goldberg, L. R. (2003). The structure of personality attributes. In M. R. Barrick & A. M. Ryan (eds.,) *Personality and Work* (pp. 1–29). San Francisco: Jossey-Bass-Pfeiffer.

Sullivan, H. S. (1953). *The Interpersonal Theory of Psychiatry.* New York: Norton.

Tremblay, R. E., Masse, L. C., Vitaro, F., & Dobkin, P. L. (1995). The impact of friends' deviant behavior on early onset of delinquency: Longitudinal data from 6 to 13 years of age. *Development and Psychopathology, 7,* 649–667.

Vitaro, F., Gendreau, P. L., Tremblay, R. E., & Oligny, P. (1998). Reactive and proactive aggression differentially predict later conduct problems. *Journal of Child Psychiatry and Psychology, 39,* 377–385.

CHAPTER 2

Peer Influence and the Development of Antisocial Behavior

Lara Mayeux
University of Oklahoma, USA

Antonius H. N. Cillessen
University of Connecticut, USA

INTRODUCTION

The developmental significance of peer relations for the social, emotional, cognitive, social-cognitive, and academic development of children and youth has received much attention from developmentalists over the last several decades (see, for reviews, Asher & Coie, 1990; Bierman, 2004; Kupersmidt & Dodge, 2004; Rubin, Bukowski, & Parker, 1998). This chapter addresses the role of peers in the development of antisocial behavior, and specifically focuses on the concept of peer influence. As the review sources above indicate, research on peer relations has grown exponentially over the past 25 years. One of the reasons for the initial interest in research in this area came in the late 1970s and early 1980s. Researchers concerned about aggression and antisocial behavior in underprivileged youth, especially boys, recognized that these behaviors almost never occur in social isolation, but rather in the context of interactions with a friend, clique, or larger peer group (see, e.g., Coie & Dodge, 1998).

This observation inspired much research on the measurement of peer relations at the individual, dyadic, and group levels, and on the associations between those measurements and social behavior. This research demonstrated, for example, important associations between peer rejection and aggression (see, e.g., Newcomb, Bukowski, & Pattee, 1993, for a review), and the clustering of deviant individuals in friendship dyads and cliques (e.g., Cairns, Cairns, Neckerman, Gest, & Gariépy, 1988). Even though these

Friends, Lovers and Groups: Key Relationships in Adolescence. Edited by Rutger C.M.E. Engels, Margaret Kerr and Håkan Stattin. Copyright © 2007 John Wiley & Sons, Ltd.

empirical relationships have been documented extensively, less is known about the specific mechanisms and processes of peer influence underlying these associations. Until recently, those underlying mechanisms have more often been implied than observed explicitly. Beyond documenting the correlates of measures of peer relations, an important goal for the next generation of peer relations researchers is to more explicitly study these processes of peer influence. Several examples of this important goal already exist (e.g., Dishion, this volume; Gardner & Steinberg, 2005), but more research is needed. The goal of this chapter is to examine the status of the concept of peer influence in the larger context of peer relations research.

Towards this end, this chapter is structured as follows. First, we will provide a brief review of the significance of peer influence for the development of antisocial behavior. We then raise three critical questions that reflect important areas of knowledge that are incomplete in our current understanding of peer influence. These questions are: (1) How should peer influence be conceptualized and measured? (2) Who is the influencer and who is the target?, and (3) How exactly does peer influence work? For this latter question, we will address issues such as the role of motivational factors, short-term processes of peer influence, and how short-term processes of peer influence are embedded in a larger developmental perspective. We indicate why these three questions are important, and we will give examples of what is known about each of them. At the same time, we will also emphasize the existing gaps in our current knowledge, and conclude that these three questions represent areas of research that deserve further attention and form an important agenda for future research.

Developmental Significance of Peer Influence

Developmental scientists have long been aware of the importance of peer relations for the socialization of children and adolescents (e.g., Asher & Coie, 1990; Hartup, 1983; Kupersmidt & Dodge, 2004; Rubin et al., 1998). As one of the first developmentalists to address issues of group belonging in youth, Sullivan (1953) stressed the importance of peer groups as vital to the development of a sense of social well-being. He maintained that failing to find a group of peers to associate with could lead to concerns about one's own social competence and desirability as a person. As a result, Sullivan hypothesized that some adolescents who do not find a peer group will develop psychological problems such as severe loneliness or depression that can impair their school functioning. Erikson (1968) theorized that finding a peer group with which to affiliate is a key developmental task of adolescence, leading to a sense of identity and feelings of independence from parents.

Along with the benefits of peer group membership can come certain drawbacks. Developmental researchers interested in social processes have studied peer pressure for several decades. Erikson (1968) addressed the issue of peer pressure in his early writings, hypothesizing that it was the primary channel through which group norms and values are spread. Indeed, the cohesiveness and unity of the group can be strengthened when group members convince each other to conform to certain norms (Newman & Newman, 1976). Problems arise, however, when the pressures adolescents exert on each other encourage behaviors that are dangerous, unhealthy, or illegal, or that interfere with their school performance. Some adolescents form cliques that endorse antisocial behavior and devalue school engagement. Research over the past 20 years has focused on these issues surrounding peer influence for negative behaviors.

Coleman (1961) conducted a classic investigation of the social structure in high school by examining the peer groups that existed in ten midwestern high schools. Coleman found that adolescents were under significant pressure to strive to be 'popular' and become a member of the 'popular' crowd. He also found that these high-status groups, the social goal-states of many youth, were at the same time characterized by a subculture of norms and values that were contrary to teacher expectations. And, even when the culture of these 'popular' crowds was distinctly different from adolescents' own beliefs and behaviors, the youth in these schools often aspired to become part of them anyway. Several important ethnographic studies have since provided evidence that attaining high peer status is a primary goal of many adolescents, and that some youth will employ virtually any means to do so (e.g., Adler & Adler, 1995; Eder, 1985).

Researchers of adolescent development have for some years been interested in factors that contribute to the initiation and maintenance of health risk-taking behaviors such as tobacco, alcohol, and drug use, and antisocial behaviors such as juvenile delinquency and aggression. The need for research that aids our understanding of these behaviors is apparent. The statistics are disturbing. Fifty-four percent of graduating high school seniors has used an illegal drug (American Psychological Society, 2001). Thirty-one percent of new female drinkers are between the ages of 10 and 14 (Substance Abuse and Mental Health Services Administration, 2001). Each day approximately 3000 children become regular smokers; one third of them will eventually die of an illness linked to tobacco use (Center for Substance Abuse Prevention, 2001). Eighty percent of all smokers begin smoking cigarettes before age 20 (Centers for Disease Control, 1999). One in five girls and one in three boys have sex by their 15th birthday and each year one quarter of sexually active teens contract a sexually transmitted disease. Almost one million teenage girls – a full 10% of girls aged 15 to 19 – get pregnant each year (Alan Guttmacher Institute, 1999).

Not surprisingly, maladaptive behaviors tend to co-occur. Two thirds of the adolescents treated for substance abuse problems are also diagnosed with a mental illness such as depression (American Psychological Society, 2001). In one study, youth aged 12 to 16 who had used marijuana were more likely to have sold marijuana (24% vs. 1%), carried a gun (21% vs. 7%), or been a member of a gang (14% vs. 2%) than adolescents who had never used the drug (Centers for Disease Control, 1999). Substance use, risky sexual behavior, and delinquency leading to police arrest form a latent construct that predicts increasing behavioral and academic problems (Patterson, Dishion, & Yoerger, 2000).

What are the factors that underlie these behaviors? One thing is certain: much of adolescents' antisocial behavior occurs in the presence of peers. Global measures of peer relationships strongly predict adolescent maladaptive behavior (Coie & Dodge, 1998). Evidence typically indicates that poor peer relations predict negative outcomes (Coie, Terry, Lenox, Lochman, & Hyman, 1995; Parker & Asher, 1987). However, recent investigations have shown that positive peer relationships may predict antisocial behavior as well (e.g., Rodkin, Farmer, Pearl, & Van Acker, 2000).

Given the emerging findings of a positive association between peer relationships and antisocial behavior, one contributor to these negative behaviors that has received extensive empirical investigation is that of peer influence. Peer influence is considered to be one of the most robust predictors of adolescent maladaptive behaviors (Dishion, McCord, & Poulin, 1999; Kandel, 1980). The power of peer influence has been empirically linked to various types of negative or antisocial behavior, including smoking, drinking, drug use, early and/or risky sexual behavior, and delinquency.

Numerous studies have supported the link between peer influence and antisocial behavior. Patterson's well-known model of the development of delinquency includes the commitment to a deviant peer group and the resulting pressure to commit deviant acts as two of the primary factors predicting antisocial behavior (Patterson, DeBaryshe, & Ramsey, 1989). Although it is difficult to separate the effects of peer selection and peer influence when investigating delinquency, a longitudinal study of adolescent boys found that so-called 'deviancy training,' a style of interaction characterized by positive responses to rule-breaking and other nonnormative behaviors, was more strongly predictive of later delinquent behavior than were current levels of antisocial behavior (Poulin, Dishion, & Haas, 1999). This theory of deviancy training has been applied to other problem behaviors, such as sexual promiscuity, substance use, and relationship violence, with similar findings (Capaldi, Dishion, Stoolmiller, & Yoerger, 2001; Patterson et al., 2000). Furthermore, in interventions in which delinquent youth are grouped together for treatment, levels of delinquency and aggression typically increase rather than decrease during and after the intervention (Dishion et al., 1999), compared to control interventions. In summary, there is ample evidence that peer influence plays an important role in adolescents' initiation and maintenance of problem behaviors.

In spite of the extensive knowledge about the association between peer relations and negative outcomes, relatively little is known about several issues related to peer influence. First, even though much progress has been made regarding the measurement of peer relations, less is known about the best ways to conceptualize and measure peer influence. Second, little is known about the identity of those adolescents who might be most likely to and most successful at influencing others, or about those who are most likely to be influenced by others. Third, more information is needed about the short-term behavioral and social cognitive processes that take place during peer influence events. Fourth and finally, more research is needed to determine how short-term mechanisms and outcomes of peer influence are embedded in long-term developmental trajectories of antisocial behavior. We now turn to each of these four issues.

Conceptualizing and Measuring Peer Influence

Since the 1960s, researchers have sought to measure the processes by which adolescents influence and are influenced by the behavior of peers. Early research focused primarily on conformity to peer group behavior, similar to the Asch (1951) line-judging studies with adults (e.g., LeFurgy & Woloshin, 1969). The phrase *peer pressure* was introduced in the 1980s to explain the new rise in antisocial behaviors by adolescents and prompted field studies of influence and conformity using school-based data (e.g., Brown, Clasen, & Eicher, 1986; Castro, Maddahian, Newcomb, & Bentler, 1987).

Operational definitions of peer influence have varied widely. An important distinction has been made between *peer pressure*, or direct attempts by peers to instigate or prevent behaviors (e.g., Brown et al., 1986), and *peer influence*, or indirect social influence of peer behaviors that occur naturally as part of a particular peer group's norms (e.g., Keefe, 1992). Beyond this distinction, however, little agreement is found among operational definitions of peer influence.

Early studies of peer influence in adolescence were based on the social psychological concepts of Reference Group Theory (Sherif & Sherif, 1964). In a classic experimental manipulation modeled after Asch's paradigm, LeFurgy and Woloshin (1969) established consensus among a group of confederates and measured target adolescents' conformity to that group norm. Although no direct pressure was applied to the target participants, the normative response of the reference group was enough to change the targets' responses.

In other studies, peer influence was defined as occurring within the context of interactions with peers whose opinions are clearly presented and with whom the adolescent identifies (Stone, Miranne, & Ellis, 1979). This indirect view of influence has been implicitly adopted by researchers who see influence as simply the behaviors of the target's close friends or peer network (e.g., Wills & Cleary, 1999). Urberg and colleagues defined influence as the difference between the level of a target's self-reported behaviors and the levels of the same behaviors reported by the target's friends (Urberg, 1992; Urberg, Cheng, & Shyu, 1991). In these studies, peer influence was measured as an indirect phenomenon involving no actual act of pressure or coercion from peers.

More direct, coercive conceptualizations of peer influence are less common. Researchers have sometimes defined peer influence in terms of direct attempts by peers to change, instigate, or prevent specific behaviors. Some investigators have defined direct influence as the strength and valence of peers' reactions to certain behaviors (e.g., Krohn & Lizotte, 1996). Others have focused on verbal encouragement by peers to engage or not engage in certain activities (e.g., Berndt, 1979; Brown et al., 1986). Some researchers have even conceptualized peer pressure simply as the frequency of being offered drugs, alcohol, or cigarettes (e.g., Kung & Farrell, 2000). Given the sometimes opposing roles of parents and peers in adolescence, definitions of influence that emphasize choosing peer-sanctioned behaviors over parent-sanctioned behaviors have also been used (e.g., Berndt, 1979; Emmerich, 1978).

Experimental Methods

Asch's line-judging paradigm to measure conformity sparked interest in the idea of conformity to group norms and provided a promising method by which to investigate the process in children and adolescents. Studies of influence and conformity in this tradition focused on such academic constructs as moralistic reasoning (LeFurgy & Woloshin, 1969), stimulus ambiguity (Hoving, Hamm, & Galvin, 1969), and the attractiveness of the influencer (Dion & Stein, 1978) – variables that were manipulable experimentally. These studies confirmed that influence and conformity occurred in youth and are valid constructs for developmental research.

Hypothetical Vignettes

More recent studies have moved away from laboratory experiments. Hypothetical vignettes have been used to ask adolescents to judge their most likely reaction to a peer pressure situation or provocation. For example, vignettes have been used to ask adolescents to choose between peer-sanctioned and parent-sanctioned activities (Emmerich, 1978). Berndt (1979) used hypothetical vignettes to assess children's responses to peer pressure for positive, negative, and neutral behaviors. Children were asked to indicate their likely course of action (e.g., join friends in the activity vs. do something else) as well as their certainty that they would respond in that way. In this research, developmental changes in susceptibility to peer influence have been found, as well as gender differences, with boys conforming to peer pressure for antisocial behavior more than girls.

Similar measures were used in a study of the relative contributions of conformity and perceived peer pressure to both positive and negative behaviors (Brown et al., 1986). Both contributed significantly to the prediction of misconduct and antisocial behavior. Finally, a study of peer pressure to smoke in adolescence used a short set of vignettes as part of a larger instrument measuring the motivation behind smoking (Covington & Omelich, 1988). The vignettes varied with respect to the composition of the group imposing influence (e.g., one friend vs. several friends), the nature of the relationship between the target and the group (friends vs. strangers), and whether or not the group was already smoking or if the target would have to initiate the smoking.

Comparisons of Target and Peer Behavior

The most common method of studying peer influence, comparisons between the self-reported behaviors of adolescents and the behavior of their best friends or peer group members, has been used in numerous studies, especially of antisocial and health-risk-taking behaviors. Some studies have compared adolescents' self-reported behaviors to their perceptions of their friends' behaviors (e.g., Dobkin, Tremblay, Masse, & Vitaro, 1995) or approval of those behaviors (e.g., Stacy, Sussman, Dent, Burton, & Flay, 1992). Others have compared adolescents' self-reported behaviors with their friends' self-reported behaviors (e.g., Mounts & Steinberg, 1995).

Although determining the similarity between adolescents' own behaviors and that of their peers is important, it does not show conclusively that influence took place. As Urberg (1999) stated, comparisons of target and peer behaviors must be interpreted with caution. First, using target perceptions of peer behavior will inflate the estimation of influence, because adolescents overestimate how similar their peers' behaviors are to their own (see Fisher & Bauman, 1988; Urberg et al., 1991). Second, unless longitudinal designs are used to study behavioral change within stable friendships, similarity in peer behavior may be attributable to friend selection based on existing similarities and shared interests. It is impossible to separate selection from influence unless careful analytical procedures are applied (Fisher & Bauman, 1988; Kandel, 1978).

Self-report Questionnaires

Self-reports of perceived peer pressure, although less common, have also been used in the study of adolescent peer influence (e.g., Barber, Bolitho, & Bertrand, 1999; Brown, 1982; Castro et al., 1987; Kung & Farrell, 2000; Urberg, Shyu, & Liang, 1990). Results with these methods have been mixed. Barber et al. (1999) found self-reports of direct pressure predictive of drug use in mid-adolescence; Urberg et al. (1990) found no association between direct pressure and later smoking. However, these measures reliably predicted behaviors such as cigarette smoking and drug use over and above measures of conformity, stressful life events, or parent influence. They represent a substantial improvement in methodologies for studying influence because, unlike simply comparing target and peer behaviors, they assess what adolescents perceive as influence rather than assuming influence that may actually be due to friendship selection or other factors. They are among the most promising methods of linking influence with conformity, or influence to behavior, in the literature.

Despite a rich tradition of measuring peer influence and establishing links with actual adolescent behaviors, the study of peer influence has been characterized by the use of a variety of measurement techniques, the associations among which are not clear. An important agenda for future research is to investigate these associations and develop a comprehensive measure that can be used in research with a variety of populations, age groups, and designs.

Identity of the Influencer and the Influencee

The influence of peers can be studied at multiple levels. While some investigations have focused on dyadic peer relationships, such as best friend dyads (e.g., Urberg et al., 1990) and romantic partners (Stanton, Currie, Oei, & Silva, 1996), others have focused on the larger context of the peer group. At the group level, a further distinction can be made between a social clique (i.e., the group of friends an adolescent hangs around with or spends the most time with) and the peer group at large, for example all of the adolescent's grade mates.

Even though these distinctions have been made, we know relatively little about the identity of those youth who are most likely to successfully engage others in antisocial behavior and those who are mostly likely to go along with this influence. The question is, what are the social network positions, traits, and behaviors of potential influencers and influencees? We hypothesize that the construct of 'perceived popularity,' used in recent sociometric research (e.g., Cillessen & Mayeux, 2004), may help to answer this question. Specifically, we hypothesize that adolescents who are perceived popular are most likely to be agents of peer influence, as well as among the most successful at influencing others. We also expect that those who aspire to become perceived popular are most likely to be susceptible to that influence.

An adolescent who is an agent of peer influence for antisocial behavior must have two characteristics. First, this person must have a tendency to engage in antisocial behaviors her/himself, even if on a relatively small scale. Second, this person must also have both (1) a sufficient level of social competence to be able to successfully engage others in the same behaviors, and (2) a sufficient level of social power to inspire others to want to emulate him. Thus, successful influencers need to possess the mixture of antisocial and prosocial skills that is exactly characteristic of adolescents labeled as *perceived popular* (e.g., Parkhurst & Hopmeyer, 1998).

Perceived popularity refers to a relatively new distinction in the sociometric literature, although the components of this distinction have existed separately for a long time in different fields (Parkhurst & Hopmeyer, 1998). The majority of past studies focusing on peer status have looked at sociometric status as a measure of likeability. Sociometric status types are typically derived from children's nominations of peers who they like the most and like the least in their classroom or grade (Coie, Dodge, & Coppotelli, 1982). Continuous measures of sociometric status (e.g. social preference) are also based on liking. Alternatively, however, peer status can be measured by asking participants not who they personally like the most or the least, but who they perceive as most and least popular in their classroom or grade. Recent research (e.g., Cillessen & Mayeux, 2004; LaFontana & Cillessen, 2002) indicates that sociometric and perceived popularity are separate dimensions of peer status with unique correlates. Whereas sociometric popularity is traditionally associated with prosocial behaviors and positive social adjustment outcomes, perceived popularity is associated with a combination of both positive and negative behaviors (LaFontana & Cillessen, 1998, 1999, 2002). There is also evidence that perceived popularity is *positively* correlated with health risk behaviors in high school (Mayeux & Sandstrom, 2005). Given their mixture of engagement in antisocial behaviors and social success, we hypothesize that these socially central adolescents are prime candidates to be successful sources of peer influence.

Further, we propose that adolescents who aspire to be like these socially central and perceived popular peers are also the ones most likely to go along with the influence they exert. Based on ethnographic studies of popular adolescents (Adler & Adler, 1995; Eder, 1985), we hypothesize that adolescents who are at the periphery of desirable social groups and desire to become more central members of these groups may be the most susceptible to peer influence. These ethnographic studies indicate that in a clique of popular peers, group members can often be classified into one of three groups: leaders, followers, and wannabes. The primary goal of the leaders is to maintain their dominant position in their group; followers and wannabes, however, are concerned with improving their status in the hierarchy (Adler & Adler, 1985). This observation is consistent with the finding that much of the social behavior of youth of this age is directed at improving their visibility in the peer group (Block, 1976; Eder, 1985). Adolescents often try to improve their visibility by attempting to join popular cliques, often through ingratiation toward group members and conformity to their norms. At the same time, members of popular cliques seek to maintain the exclusivity of their group by controlling who is allowed to join and who must be excluded (Elkin & Handel, 1989). The socially savvy methods used by adolescents to manipulate their groups can be both physically and relationally aggressive (LaFontana & Cillessen, 1998, 2002). Thus, networks of popular peers uniquely influence and regulate the behavior not only of their own members, but also of others who aspire to join them.

While the role of popular networks in influence research is important, additional factors must be considered as well. For example, personality variables (e.g., resilience to resisting peer pressure), social contextual variables (e.g., gender and/or ethnic composition of the peer group), and motivational factors (the desire to be more socially central) may play a role as well as moderators or mediators of influence. We now turn to these additional factors that may further enhance our understanding of peer influence processes among adolescents.

Issues for Further Research

Laboratory studies of peer influence have the potential to further illustrate important fundamental aspects of peer influence processes. These studies could follow a two-step approach. In Step 1, using sociometric methods, multiple indicators of status can be established in naturalistic peer groups (e.g., in the school or neighborhood) to identify adolescents who are particularly likely to be agents or targets of peer influence. Selected participants can then be invited to take part in experimental lab procedures in Step 2. Observations of influence behaviors could be made in paradigms where adolescents are asked to engage each other in antisocial or prosocial behaviors. In addition to varying the valence of the behaviors, manipulations can be made of the perceived status of the influencer and the target, the familiarity of the influencer and target with one another, task structure (cooperative vs. competitive), group size, group gender composition, and the communication medium (unstructured, confederate peer, internet communication). Developmental variation in the associations of interest can be studied by running these procedures with participants of different age groups.

For example, Gardner and Steinberg (2005) recently examined in the effects of peers on adolescents' willingness to make increasingly risky choices in a computer game. The implications of the findings from this research for adolescents' decisions to engage in health risk behaviors are clear. Studies such as these should be conducted more frequently because of their potential to elucidate information about basic processes of peer influence.

From a developmental perspective, short-term processes of peer influence should be seen as embedded in longer-term developmental trajectories. The processes that occur in short-term interactions may have long-term effects in more or less complex ways. For example, exposure to negative influence may have effects only if it occurs repeatedly and at certain ages. The effects of negative influence may not be immediate, but delayed, or their effects may be cumulative over time. Further, such effects may be exacerbated or mitigated by a variety of yet unknown moderators such as personality, motivational, or social contextual variables. The nature of these mechanisms might indeed be quite complex.

Dynamic systems theory may provide an ideal framework to understand the unfolding of these processes over time. Dynamic systems theory has been widely used to explain developmental phenomena (Thelen & Smith, 1996), in particular perceptual and motor development. More recently, researchers have begun to apply its principles to social processes and behaviors (see, e.g., Granic & Dishion, 2003; Granic, Hollenstein, Dishion, & Patterson, 2003). Such studies illustrate several factors of importance for research on peer influence, including studying behavior as it unfolds over time, either short-term (microgenetic) or long-term (longitudinal); being sensitive to how small events can have larger effects on long-term trajectories; and focusing on the self-perpetuating and self-reinforcing behavioral (attractor) states that influence short- and long-term outcomes.

For example, Granic and Dishion (2003) conceptualized the amount of deviant talk between peers during a particular conversation as an attractor state that predicts subsequent problem behaviors. Adolescents who were easily 'sucked in' to deviant talk with a peer and who seemed to find it difficult to disengage from deviant talk were more likely to have behavior problems later. These findings point to processes and mechanisms that may be central to understanding peer influence. Consistent with the ideas expressed above, for adolescents who wish to increase their status in the peer group deviant behaviors of high-status peers may serve as attractor states that pull them towards a trajectory of increasing engagement in deviant behaviors. This example emphasizes the need to study these processes as they unfold over time, with 'time' referring to anything from several minutes in short-term experimental observations in the laboratory to several years in longitudinal studies in naturalistic settings.

CONCLUSION

In this chapter, research on peer influence and the development of antisocial behavior was placed in the context of new and recent developments in peer relations research, specifically focusing on new approaches to measuring peer influence and on research demonstrating an association between new dimensions of peer structure (in particular perceived popularity) and antisocial behavior, concern for status, susceptibility to peer influence, as well as being a powerful source of influence over others. Embedding peer influence in a dynamic context, both short-term and long-term, is critical as well.

REFERENCES

Adler, P. A. & Adler, P. (1995). Dynamics of inclusion and exclusion in preadolescent cliques. *Social Psychology Quarterly, 58*, 145–162.

Alan Guttmacher Institute (1999). *Teenage Pregnancy: Overall Trends and State-by-state Information*. New York: AGI.

American Psychological Society (2001). Fifty-four percent of youth have tried an illicit drug. *Monitor on Psychology, 32*, 17.

Asch, S. E. (1951). Effects of group pressure upon the modification and distortion of judgments. In H. Guetzkow (ed.), *Groups, Leadership and Men: Research in Human Relationships* (pp. 177–190). Oxford, England: Carnegie Press.

Asher, S. R. & Coie, J. D. (1990). *Peer Rejection in Childhood*. New York: Cambridge University Press.

Barber, J. G., Bolitho, F., & Bertrand, L. D. (1999). Intrapersonal versus peer group predictors of adolescent drug use. *Children and Youth Services Review, 21*, 565–579.

Berndt, T. J. (1979). Developmental changes in conformity to peers and parents. *Developmental Psychology, 15*, 608–616.

Bierman, K. L. (2004). *Peer Rejection: Developmental Processes and Intervention Strategies*. New York: Guilford Press.

Block, J. H. (1976). Issues, problems, and pitfalls in assessing sex differences: A critical review of *The Psychology of Sex Differences. Merrill-Palmer Quarterly, 22*, 283–308.

Brown, B. B. (1982). The extent and effects of peer pressure among high school students: A retrospective analysis. *Journal of Youth and Adolescence, 11*, 121–133.

Brown, B. B., Clasen, D. R., & Eicher, S. A. (1986). Perceptions of peer pressure, peer conformity dispositions, and self-reported behavior among adolescents. *Developmental Psychology, 22*, 521–530.

Cairns, R. B., Cairns, B. D., Neckerman, H. J., Gest, S. D., & Gariépy, J.-L. (1988). Social networks and aggressive behavior: Peer support or peer rejection? *Developmental Psychology, 24*, 815–823.

Capaldi, D. M., Dishion, T. J., Stoolmiller, M., & Yoerger, K. (2001). Aggression toward female partners by at-risk young men: The contribution of male adolescent friendships. *Developmental Psychology, 37*, 61–73.

Castro, F. G., Maddahian, E., Newcomb, M. D., & Bentler, P. M. (1987). A multivariate model of determinants of cigarette smoking among adolescents. *Journal of Health and Social Behavior, 28*, 273–289.

Centers for Disease Control (1999). *Youth Risk Behavior Survey*. Washington, DC.

Center for Substance Abuse Prevention (2001). Facts and figures. *Monitor on Psychology, 32*, 11.

Cillessen, A. H. N. & Mayeux, L. (2004). From censure to reinforcement: Developmental changes in the association between aggression and social status. *Child Development, 75*, 147–163.

Coie, J. D. & Dodge, K. A. (1998). Aggression and antisocial behavior. In W. Damon (series ed.) & N. Eisenberg (vol. ed.), *Handbook of Child Psychology: Vol. 3. Social, Emotional, and Personality Development* (5th ed., pp. 779–862). New York: Wiley.

Coie, J. D., Dodge, K. A., & Coppotelli, H. (1982). Dimensions and types of social status: A cross-age perspective. *Developmental Psychology, 18*, 557–570.

Coie, J. D., Terry, R., Lenox, K. F., Lochman, J. E., & Hyman, C. (1995). Childhood peer rejection and aggression as predictors of stable patterns of adolescent disorder. *Development and Psychopathology, 7*, 697–713.

Coleman, J. S. (1961). *The Adolescent Society*. New York: Free Press.

Covington, M. V. & Omelich, C. L. (1988). I can resist anything but temptation: Adolescent expectations for smoking cigarettes. *Journal of Applied Social Psychology, 18*, 203–227.

Dion, K. K., & Stein, S. (1978). Physical attractiveness and interpersonal influence. *Journal of Experimental Social Psychology, 14*, 97–108.

Dishion, T., McCord, J., & Poulin, F. (1999). When interventions harm: Peer groups and problem behavior. *American Psychologist, 54*, 755–764.

Dobkin, P. L., Tremblay, R. E., Masse, L. C., & Vitaro, F. (1995). Individual and peer characteristics in predicting boys' early onset of substance abuse: A seven-year longitudinal study. *Child Development, 66*, 1198–1214.

Eder, D. (1985). The cycle of popularity: Interpersonal relations among female adolescents. *Sociology of Education, 58*, 154–165.

Elkin, F., & Handel, G. (1989). *The Child and Society* (5th ed.). New York: Random House.

Emmerich, H. J. (1978). The influence of parents and peers on choices made by adolescents. *Journal of Youth and Adolescence, 7*, 175–180.

Erikson, E. H. (1968). *Identity, Youth, and Crisis*. New York: Norton.

Fisher, L. A. & Bauman, K. E. (1988). Influence and selection in the friend-adolescent relationship: Findings from studies of adolescent smoking and drinking. *Journal of Applied Social Psychology, 4*, 289–314.

Gardner, M. & Steinberg, L. (2005). Peer influence on risk taking, risk preference, and risky decision making in adolescence and adulthood: An experimental study. *Developmental Psychology, 41*, 625–635.

Granic, I. & Dishion, T. J. (2003). Deviant talk in adolescent friendships: A step toward measuring a pathogenic attractor process. *Social Development, 12*, 314–334.

Granic, I., Hollenstein, T., Dishion, T. J., & Patterson, G. R. (2003). Longitudinal analysis of flexibility and reorganization in early adolescence: A dynamic systems study of family interactions. *Developmental Psychology, 39*, 606–617.

Hartup, W. W. (1983). Peer relations. In E. M. Hetherington (ed.), *Handbook of Child Psychology: Socialization, Personality, and Social Development* (Vol. 4). New York: John Wiley & Sons.

Hoving, K. L., Hamm, N., & Galvin, P. (1969). Social influence as a function of stimulus ambiguity at three age levels. *Developmental Psychology, 1*, 631–636.

Kandel, D. B. (1978). Homophily, selection, and socialization in adolescent friendships. *American Journal of Sociology, 84*, 427–436.

Kandel, D. B. (1980). Drug and drinking behavior among youth. *Annual Review of Psychology, 6*, 235–285.

Keefe, K. (1992). Perceptions of normative social pressure and attitudes toward alcohol use: Change during adolescence. *Journal of Studies on Alcohol*, 46–54.

Krohn, M. D. & Lizotte, A. J. (1996). Reciprocal causal relationships among drug use, peers, and beliefs: A five-wave panel model. *Journal of Drug Issues, 26*, 405–429.

Kung, E. M. & Farrell, A. D. (2000). The role of parents in early adolescent substance abuse: An examination of mediating and moderating effects. *Journal of Child and Family Studies, 9*, 509–528.

Kupersmidt, J. B. & Dodge, K. A. (2004) (Eeds.), *Children's Peer Relations: From Development to Intervention*. Washington, DC: American Psychological Association Press.

LaFontana, K. M. & Cillessen, A. H. N. (1998). The nature of children's stereotypes of popularity. *Social Development, 7*, 301–320.

LaFontana, K. M. & Cillessen, A. H. N. (1999). Children's interpersonal perceptions as a function of sociometric and peer-perceived popularity. *Journal of Genetic Psychology, 160*, 225–242.

LaFontana, K. M. & Cillessen, A. H. N. (2002). Children's perceptions of popular and unpopular peers: A multimethod assessment. *Developmental Psychology, 38*, 635–647.

LeFurgy, W. G. & Woloshin, G. W. (1969). Immediate and long-term effects of experimentally induced social influence in the modification of adolescents' moral judgments. *Journal of Personality and Social Psychology, 12*, 104–110.

Mayeux, L. & Sandstrom, M. J. (2005, April). *Is being popular a risky proposition?* Paper presented at the biennial meeting of the Society for Research in Child Development, Atlanta, GA.

Mounts, N. S. & Steinberg, L. (1995). An ecological analysis of peer influence on adolescent grade point average and drug use. *Developmental Psychology, 31*, 915–922.

Newcomb, A. F., Bukowski, W. M., & Pattee, L. (1993). Children's peer relations: A meta-analytic review of popular, rejected, neglected, controversial, and average sociometric status. *Psychological Bulletin, 113*, 99–128.

Newman, P. R., & Newman, B. M. (1976). Early adolescence and its conflicts: Group identity vs. alienation. *Adolescence, 11*, 261–274.

Parker, J. & Asher, S. (1987). Peer relations and later personal adjustment: Are low-accepted children 'at risk'? *Psychological Bulletin, 102*, 357–389.

Parkhurst, J. & Hopmeyer, A. G. (1998). Sociometric popularity and peer-perceived popularity: Two distinct dimensions of peer status. *Journal of Early Adolescence, 18*, 125–144.

Patterson, G. R., DeBaryshe, B. D., & Ramsey, E. (1989). A developmental perspective on antisocial behavior. *American Psychologist, 44*, 329–335.

Patterson, G., Dishion, T., & Yoerger, K. (2000). Adolescent growth in new forms of problem behavior: Macro- and micro-peer dynamics. *Prevention Science, 1*, 3–13.

Poulin, F., Dishion, T. J., & Haas, E. (1999). The peer influence paradox: Friendship quality and deviancy training within male adolescent friendships. *Merrill-Palmer Quarterly, 45*, 42–61.

Rodkin, P., Farmer, T., Pearl, R., & Van Acker, R. (2000). Heterogeneity of popular boys: Antisocial and prosocial configurations. *Developmental Psychology, 36*, 14–24.

Rubin, K. H., Bukowski, W. M., & Parker, J. G. (1998). Peer interactions, relationships, and groups. In W. Damon (series ed.) & N. Eisenberg (vol. ed.). *Handbook of Child Psychology: Vol. 3. Social, Emotional and Personality Development* (5th ed. pp. 619–700). New York: Wiley.

Sherif, M. & Sherif, C. W. (1964). *Reference Groups*. Chicago: Regnery.

Stacy, A., Sussman, S., Dent, C., Burton, D., & Flay, B. (1992). Moderators of peer social influence in adolescent smoking. *Personality and Social Psychology Bulletin, 18*, 163–172.

Stanton, W. R., Currie, G. D., Oei, T. P. S., & Silva, P. A. (1996). A developmental approach to influences on adolescents' smoking and quitting. *Journal of Applied Developmental Psychology, 17*, 307–319.

Stone, L. H., Miranne, A. C., & Ellis, G. J. (1979). Parent-peer influence as a predictor of marijuana use. *Adolescence, 14*, 115–122.

Substance Abuse and Mental Health Services Administration (2001). Facts and figures. *Monitor on Psychology, 32*, 11.

Sullivan, H. S. (1953). *The Interpersonal Theory of Psychiatry*. New York: Norton.

Thelen, E. & Smith, L. B. (1998). Dynamic systems theories. In W. Damon (series ed.) & R. M. Lerner (vol. ed.), *Handbook of Child Psychology: Vol. 1. Theoretical Models of Human Development* (5th ed., pp. 563–634). New York: Wiley.

Urberg, K. (1992). Locus of peer influence: Social crowd and best friend. *Journal of Youth and Adolescence, 21*, 439–450.

Urberg, K. A. (1999). Some thoughts on studying the influence of peers on children and adolescents. *Merrill-Palmer Quarterly, 45*, 1–12.

Urberg, K. A., Cheng, C., & Shyu, S. (1991). Grade changes in peer influence on adolescent cigarette smoking: A comparison of two measures. *Addictive Behaviors, 16*, 21–28.

Urberg, K. A., Shyu, S., & Liang, J. (1990). Peer influence in adolescent cigarette smoking. *Addictive Behaviors, 15*, 247–255.

Wills, T. A. & Cleary, S. D. (1999). Peer and adolescent substance use among 6th–9th graders: Latent growth analyses of influence versus selection mechanisms. *Health Psychology, 18*, 453–463.

CHAPTER 3

Peers and Adolescent Substance Use

Rutger C. M. E. Engels, Sander M. Bot, Ron H. J. Scholte, and Isabela Granic
Behavioural Science Institute, Radboud University Nijmegen, the Netherlands and the Hospital for Sick Children, Toronto, Canada

INTRODUCTION

Friends are assumed to be of major importance for the development of substance use in young people (Petraitis, Flay, & Miller, 1995). Throughout adolescence, youngsters experience feelings of uncertainty about their self-image, and consider themselves more or less dependent on the opinions and judgments of friends (Engels, Knibbe, Drop, & De Haan, 1997). Meeting the expectations of one's group is crucial for preventing loss of friends, becoming a loner, and eventually losing one's identity. Therefore, associating with friends will be less distressing when one's own behaviors are congruent with others'. People are in general more susceptible to conform to prevailing norms in the teenage years than in any other period (Finkenauer et al., 2003) making them vulnerable to initiate or maintain risky habits such as heavy drinking or smoking. Thus, it is not surprising that from the middle of the twentieth century, scholars started to explore the role of peers in the development of smoking and alcohol consumption.

In general, research conducted in the 1970s shows that adolescents tend to be similar to their friends in their behaviors and attitudes (Cohen, 1977; Kandel, 1978). This homogeneity of health related behavior in peer groups could be caused by two processes: influence and selection. Influence refers to the fact that a friend's or peer's behavior or opinions affects an individual's behaviors and opinions. Selection can be divided into two conceptually different mechanisms. First, adolescents might acquire new friends with similar characteristics, attitudes, and behaviors. In this way they 'select' friends partly on the basis of similarities. Second, they might avoid contacts with friends, or even break off friendships, because of differences in opinions and behaviors (i.e., deselection of friends) (Ennett & Bauman, 1994). Primarily, from research employing longitudinal designs in which changes in substance use and changes in friendships are traced, accurate conclusions can be drawn about (a) the relative contribution of selection processes and (b) the relative effects of friends' behaviors on similarities in individuals' substance use.

In the past decades, several longitudinal studies have examined peer influence and selection processes in relation to adolescent substance use (Engels, Knibbe, & Drop, 1999a; Fisher & Bauman, 1988; Urberg et al., 1997, 2003). For example, a prospective study by De Vries, Engels, Kremers, Wetzels, and Mudde (2003) with 15,705 adolescents in six European countries showed only marginal effects of best friend's smoking and the proportion of smokers in the peer group on individual smoking onset. These findings are comparable with longitudinal studies of youths in the US (Ennett & Bauman, 1994). Further, Wang and colleagues (1999) showed that although both peer influence and selection occurred, selection might play a greater role in affecting homogeneity of smoking within peer groups. Thus, several studies have shown that selection processes are largely responsible for homogeneity of smoking in friendships (see review by Bauman & Ennett, 1996). Concerning alcohol use, longitudinal analyses have shown that alcohol consumption of best friends and peer group members is not strongly related to juvenile drinking (e.g., Andrews, Tildesley, Hops, & Li, 2002; Bauman & Ennett, 1996; Bot, Engels, Knibbe, & Meeus, 2005a; Engels, Knibbe, De Vries, Drop, & Van Breukelen, 1999a; Fisher & Bauman, 1988; Gaughan, 1999; Poelen, Engels, Van Der Vorst, Scholte, & Vermulst, 2006; Urberg et al., 1997, 2003). The small to nonsignificant effects of best friend alcohol use on the development of drinking in adolescence led Jaccard, Blanton, and Dodge (2005, p. 144) to conclude that 'overall, our data do not support the notion of pervasive peer influence on the part of one's friend with respect to adolescent health behaviors.'

We found convincing support for Jaccard et al.'s (2005) conclusion in our own prospective studies. In a five-year three-wave study among 1063 adolescents, Engels et al. (1999a) have demonstrated very small modelling effects of best friend's alcohol and cigarette use on the development of substance use over time: Best friend's use explained only a few percent of the variance in smoking and alcohol use at a subsequent wave. Second, in a prospective study with a full family design, Poelen et al. (2006) showed that sibling and best friend drinking did not affect changes in alcohol use over a 12-month period. Third, we conducted a school-based study in which we included early adolescents as well as their reciprocal best friend (Bot et al., 2005a). In this study we again found only very marginal effects of reciprocal best friend's drinking on adolescent use over a period of six months. In analyses on smoking in early adolescence, we found that reciprocal best friend's smoking hardly predicted individual smoking onset over a period of six and twelve months (Engels, Vitaro et al., 2004). In analyses on data from a full-family study, Harakeh, Engels, Scholte, De Vries, and Vermulst (2006) found, after controlling for the effects of sibling smoking, marginal effects of best friend's smoking on onset and continuation of smoking over a period of twelve months. It should be said that also in other prospective studies on the prediction of regular smoking (Engels et al., 1999b; Vink et al., 2003), heavy drinking and drunkenness (Poelen et al., 2006), continuation of smoking (Van Zundert et al., 2006) and smoking cessation (Engels et al., 1998) we found nonsignificant or very small effects of peer influences. Thus, it seems there is little empirical support for the widely held belief that peers have an enormous influence on their friends' substance use.

However, it is important to ask whether peer influences have an equal impact (or lack of impact) under different circumstances. Peer relations may take many shapes and it seems logical that friendships with different properties may have differential effects on the magnitude of peer influence exercised. Urberg et al. (1997) found that close friends affected initiation and persistence of alcohol use, and that the close friend as well as the friendship group influenced drinking to intoxication. According to Urberg et al., best friends seem to be more influential than the peer group in general. Friendships may be categorized on the basis of 'best friends' and 'other friends,' as Urberg et al. (1997) did, but other friendship aspects may also play a role in the adolescent's susceptibility to peer influence. For example, some adolescents consider themselves to be a friend of a peer, without this peer reciprocating the friendship nomination. Such friendships are called unilateral. When, on the other hand, both adolescents mutually nominate the other one as friend, these friendships are called reciprocal. Aloise-Young, Graham, and Hansen (1994) found that respondents without a reciprocal friend were affected more by the smoking behavior of their desired (unilateral) friends than those with a reciprocal friend. Gaughan (1999) reported that adolescents' frequency of drunkenness was influenced to the highest degree by peers who were to become friends in the future, but were not reciprocal friends initially. In addition, Bot et al. (2005a) showed that young people were most likely to conform to best friend's drinking levels when this friendship was unilateral and this particular friend had a higher social status. Thus, most of the evidence suggests that established, reciprocal friends are less likely to influence their peers, compared to unilateral relationships or relationships characterized by differential status.

Not only relationship characteristics, such as quality of the friendship, but also individual characteristics, such as social status within the group, personality, self-efficacy or psychosocial well-being, may moderate the effect of peer influences (Urberg et al., 2003). Poelen et al. (2006) examined in a longitudinal two-wave sample of 826 early and mid adolescents whether Big Five personality traits would moderate the associations between best friend's drinking levels and individual use. One might expect for instance that adolescents who are extraverted are more susceptible to peer influences than adolescents who are introverted. However, the authors found no evidence what so ever for moderating effects of personality traits. Although normal personality dimensions may not strongly affect peer influences, more extreme personality factors such as psychopathology may have an impact. For example, in another longitudinal study, Engels, Hale, Noom, and De Vries (2005) found that adolescents who suffered from depressive feelings were more likely to be susceptible to peer pressure to start smoking than adolescents who were not suffering from depressive feelings. However, in general it should be stressed that even if moderating effects were found, the absolute effects of these variables were rather small (see Jaccard et al., 2005; Urberg et al., 2003).

Taken together, there are a few studies that have suggested some peer influence processes at work in adolescent friendships, however, the majority of the empirical evidence shows surprisingly small peer effects.

DO PEERS MATTER?

In this chapter we argue that survey methods are not suitable for getting a grip on processes underlying peer influences on adolescent substance use. The vast majority of prospective studies have been using surveys in which adolescents, and sometimes their peers, are regularly interviewed about their own behavior and that of their peers. Subsequently, they aim to predict changes in individual drinking and smoking over time by examining corresponding behaviors of peers. With these methodologies we assume that we are able to test whether young people's smoking and drinking habits are affected by what their peers do. In other words, whether young people imitate (or model) behavior. Survey studies however generally fall short of taking into account how the development of peer interactions affects imitation (Engels & Granic, 2005). Survey designs can not examine the real-time influence processes which are operating in peer relations. Designs that follow adolescents over extended periods of time may not be the most effective way to study directly how peers influence one another. Instead, observational designs that allow examination of the interpersonal processes underlying imitation effects in real time seem to be strongly warranted.

There are very few studies that have employed methodologies other than surveys to test hypotheses regarding peer influence on substance use. First, in the 1970s and 1980s, a relatively small research tradition existed of experimental studies on alcohol use and modeling (see review by Quigley & Collins, 1999). The findings of these studies generally show that when people are in the company of a drinker, the drinking pace of this drinker (a confederate) affects individual drinking rates and consumption levels. However, these types of studies examined processes of imitation in pairs of strangers, while adolescents and young adults mainly drink with friends or other peers (Knibbe, Van De Goor, & Drop, 1993). Also, they mostly carried out the experiments with a taste-test paradigm limiting the ecological validity of the findings. In our opinion, both these limitations strongly impact on the generalizability of these experimental studies.

Second, some scholars have been systematically observing communication in friendships. In a series of studies, Dishion and colleagues demonstrated that the content and structure of communication between close friends are related to development of deviant behaviors including drinking (Dishion et al., 2002, chapter in this book). For example, in a project with 206 boys who were followed from late childhood to young adulthood, videotaped interaction tasks between these boys with their closest friend were coded on the content and structure of their communication. Granic and Dishion (2003) showed that antisocial peers are drawn into deviant conversations and become increasingly 'stuck' in these topics over the course of an interaction. This pattern of becoming more and more locked into these deviant interactions predicted substance abuse and delinquency three years later. In another prospective study, Dishion and Owen (2002) revealed that deviancy talk in friendships – explicitly addressing issues related to substance use – in the teenage years was associated with alcohol abuse in young adulthood.

An important limitation of these studies is that although they focus on observing communication on deviant topics in friendships, they do not observe peer influences as they arise in their natural context. In other words, they are not assessing actual social interaction processes in relation to, for instance, substance use in a bar, pub, disco or at a party.

Only a very limited number of studies have examined peer influence processes in real life settings. Aitken (1985) for example conducted quantitative observations of 200 groups in bars. His findings showed that most drinkers were members of groups in which round-buying procedures were used. Purchasing procedures were good predictors of alcohol consumption among males. Males who purchased rounds tended to consume more alcohol than did males who did not purchase drinks for others. Drinkers with companions who consumed large amounts of alcohol tended to consume more alcohol and tended to have higher drinking rates (see also Aitken, 1983; or for a similar approach, Van Der Goor, 1990). The problem, however, with this type of anthropological-oriented research is that it (a) does not provide insights into the various types of social relations existing within groups and (b) can not reveal how individual characteristics, such as history of substance use, current use, personality traits, or outcome expectancies, are related to susceptibility to peer influences. This makes it very difficult to establish *why* some people imitate other's behaviors and other people do not.

Systematic observations of drinking in existing social groups have rarely been conducted. One of the few exceptions is the seminal work of Kettil Bruun (1959) who observed drinking habits in existing groups and for instance, examined the role of group cohesion and social interactions in alcohol consumption of adults. To our knowledge, no such naturalistic observational studies on peer influences have been conducted with adolescents and young adults. Our research program aims to address this gap. In the next section, we discuss the findings of a few of our observational studies on substance use in peer groups. In all these studies, we make use of observational data of real-time interactions between peers in the context of a bar lab.

OBSERVATIONAL STUDIES ON PEERS AND ALCOHOL USE

In a first report on our observational study among 238 late adolescents, we aimed to examine the functionality of alcohol expectancies in predicting drinking behavior in existing peer groups of young adults in a 'naturalistic' setting (Bot, Engels, & Knibbe, 2005). In other words, we aimed to examine whether people's expectations of the outcomes of drinking affect their drinking levels in a social situation. If peer influences are operating, they might overshadow the impact of people's more rationally-based cognitions regarding alcohol on their drinking levels. Young adults were invited to join an experiment with their peer group in a bar annex laboratory. During a 'break' of 50 minutes in this experiment, their activities, social behavior and drinking behavior were observed with digital video and audio equipment. A total of 28 peer groups were involved in this study. A peer group consisted of seven–nine persons and the type of relations within these groups ranged from intimate relations and close friendships to acquaintances. Information on drinking behavior from direct observations, together with questionnaire data on alcohol expectancies, provided the opportunity to look at how and which expectancies are related to actual drinking patterns.

We showed that individual drinking levels in a bar lab among peers who normally go out together were strongly related to the average drinking levels of the group. Further, the findings convincingly showed that expectancies regarding the positive and arousing effects of alcohol predicted alcohol consumption in the bar lab above and beyond the group effects of drinking. Expectancies of the negative and sedative effects of drinking, however, did not predict drinking levels. In sum, these findings show that people's actual drinking behavior, as observed in a bar lab context, seems to be affected by peer group drinking levels as well as their expectations of the positive outcomes of drinking.

In a follow-up of these analyses, we tested whether men and women differ in the extent to which they are affected by drinking by peers (Engels, Bot, Van Der Vorst, & Granic, 2006). There is evidence that in particular among boys, alcohol use is related to better social functioning and relational competence. This suggests that not conforming to the group norm has more social consequences for boys than for girls (e.g., Pape & Hammer, 1996). This is in contrast with longitudinal findings from surveys showing no gender differences in the extent to which peer drinking affects individuals' alcohol consumption. Again, we used the observational data from the bar lab study (N = 238; in 28 groups). The constellation of the groups differed from all men (7%) and all women (7%) to mixed gender (86%). In our observational data, multilevel analyses showed robust gender differences in susceptibility to peer drinking; men appear to be strongly affected by the average drinking levels in the group, but women do not. To find out why women are not strongly affected by peer drinking, we tested a series of hypotheses. The first is that women's drinking is less context-dependent; so adjust their drinking less to that of other group members. We found evidence for that. Analyses showed that women's drinking in the bar is more strongly affected by what they normally drink (questionnaire data) than men's drinking. The second is that women are more strongly affected by their own expectancies on how alcohol affects them than by the specific social context. However, we found no gender differences in the associations between participant's expectations that alcohol makes them more sociable, energetic, sexually aroused or powerful and actual alcohol consumption. The third hypothesis is that when group members are high on sexual and power expectancies, women are more careful and stop drinking after having had a very few drinks. Women might do this to maintain an acceptable level of control, especially around heavy drinking men. Multi-level analyses indeed showed that in groups where peer group members are high on sexual expectancies, women, but not men, limit their drinking. Social enhancement as well as power expectancies by group members did not affect individual drinking. These strong gender differences in susceptibility to peer pressure strongly suggest that more attention should be paid to the development of gender-specific theoretical models of peer modeling and alcohol use.

Alcohol consumption typically takes place in a recreational, time-out situation, and a time-out can be spent by engaging in several leisure time activities (Bot, Engels, Knibbe, & Meeus, 2006). Contextual circumstances like arrangement of a drinking setting might just as strongly affect people's tendencies to consume alcohol as individual characteristics (like alcohol expectancies, intentions to drink, or implementation intentions) or group characteristics (norms and behaviors of the company). In a bar, conversation is the dominant pastime, but this may take place during other activities, like watching TV or playing games. These activities might inhibit drinking because of the physical difficulties of combining drinking with other activities. In a third study, we tracked the drinking behaviors as well as the type of activities of peer groups (consisting of seven–nine persons) during a one-hour period. Findings indicated that (1) selection of activities is not related to initial drinking level or personality characteristics; (2) in males, active pastimes (e.g., playing billiards, cards, table soccer) is related to slower drinking than passive pastimes (e.g., conversations); (3) male problem drinkers appear to compensate for the 'lost' time drinking after an active pastime phase by drinking more heavily afterwards ; and (4) involvement in active pastimes is unrelated to total alcohol consumption. In other words, in general, people's drinking levels are indeed affected by the activities they undertake in a bar; but for a specific group, namely heavy drinking males, this is not the case because they catch up in terms of drinking after refraining from consumption in more active pastimes.

FURTHER STUDIES

So far, we have not focused on how the various types of relationships existing in groups affect social influence processes. It is very likely that whether people adopt the prevailing drinking norms within their peer group depends on the types of relationships within the group. Some groups consist, like in real life, of weak ties and people hardly know each other, while other groups consist of friends who have known each other for a long time. One might assume that within long-lasting peer groups – in which selection processes already have taken place – it will be more likely that deviation from the norm by individual members will be more readily accepted than in groups that have just formed. In the latter groups, there are more social risks (e.g., exclusion, rejection) associated with deviations from the norm and therefore higher levels of conformity might be expected. In addition, within each group different types of relationship exist. Some members are more popular than others, and some are seen as more dominant than others. It would be interesting to examine whether social positions within the peer group are related to people's tendency to adopt certain drinking behaviors. One might assume that popular and dominant members are more likely to set the stage when it comes to drinking as this is also partly expected by the others (see Engels, Scholte et al., 2006). The less popular and more passive and permissive members might be more likely to follow the popular and dominant ones, and might feel more pressured to drink when the others are drinking. This aspect, which is in our opinion, one of the most interesting features of group processes to study in relation to substance use, will be the topic of further analyses.

Apart from the role of different types of relationships within peer groups, it is fascinating to analyze what kind of social influence processes are unfolding in real-time interactions within groups. This, of course, depends to a large extent on the history of the group, the specific set of relationships within the group, the specific context people are in at the moment, the individual expectations people have about what alcohol (or smoking) does to them, and on their regular substance use patterns. These all form conditions for the starting point of the interaction processes, but it is also the process itself within that one-hour in our bar lab which is interesting to study. For instance, our findings on women drinking less when they are in a group with members who think that drinking leads to sexual arousal suggests that women may go through different phases of drinking and stop drinking at a certain moment. Specifically, when they perceive that a situation might be too dangerous or risky, they may stop drinking (see Suls & Green, 2003). This leads to the question of what some women do in this particular context; do they try to avoid the heavy drinking males and seek company of other men, do they seek company of other females to get some support, or do they attempt to withdraw from the situation to be alone? Perhaps what they undertake depends on the group constellation; when girls are with only girls less control is needed, whereas when a group is dominated by males, they may feel obliged to control their drinking rate. All of these questions point to the need for a different lens through which to study group interaction processes. What has been missing so far in our work is a methodology that can tap the temporal patterns that emerge over time in peer interactions. A method to investigate these interactions in more detail is State-Space Grid analysis, a method developed to examine sequences of nonverbal and verbal interactions in individuals (Lewis,

Lamey, & Douglas, 1999) or dyads with real-time quantitative data (Granic & Lamey, 2002). Recently this methodology was adapted to trace systematically interactions of individuals in groups. With this method, the behavioral trajectory (i.e., the sequence of behavioural states) is plotted as it proceeds in real time on a grid representing all possible behavioral combinations (Granic et al., 2003). This technique will enable us to track drinking behaviors over the course of the session, measure interpersonal interactions that promote or dampen further drinking, and identify the conditions under which individuals switch from conforming to refusing to behave according to group norms.

EXPERIMENTAL STUDIES

Non-experimental observational studies suffer from shortcomings that limit the understanding of peer influence processes. Research on alcohol use in peer groups (Bot et al., 2005b, 2006a) and deviancy in friendships (e.g., Dishion et al., 2002; Dishion et al., this book; Granic & Dishion, 2003) examine influence processes in existing networks of friends. Their findings leave us with the alternative explanation that similarities in drinking, smoking or drug use can be explained by selective peer affiliation. This problem can be solved by using an experimental design and using confederates (peers who are unfamiliar to the participant). As mentioned above, there is a small experimental research tradition in the field of alcohol, though there are problems with many of these studies as they use a so-called taste-test paradigm or conduct experiments in an artificial lab setting (for an exception see Caudill & Kong, 2001). Processes of imitation might be better understood using an approach that combines a confederate and a naturalistic smoking or drinking context (without the taste-test paradigm). To enhance the ecological validity of the studies conducted with adolescents or young adults, smoking and drinking should probably be examined where it most often naturally occurs, a pub, disco or bar.

Recently, we conducted an experimental observational study on imitation by peers and smoking (Harakeh et al., 2006). To observe participants in a naturalistic setting, we invited them to our bar lab at the university. A total of 125 participants conducted two tasks in which they had to rate advertisements shown on a television screen together with a confederate. These two tasks were 30 minutes apart and in the break we observed and recorded smoking and social behavior of the participants with digital video and audio equipment. Male and female daily smokers were exposed to same-gender confederates who differed on smoking and social behavior during the observed session (i.e., the break). An experimental design with a three (smoking behavior of confederate) by two (type of social interaction) factorial design was used. The smoking conditions were 'non smoking,' 'light smoking (i.e. one cigarette),' and 'heavy smoking (i.e. four cigarettes).' Type of interaction during the break included a 'warm model condition' in which the confederate was open and sociable, and a 'cold model condition' in which the confederate was distant, quite silent and unsociable. Participants were asked before each session to fill in a questionnaire and at the end of the session to fill in an evaluation form. Just before each session started, confederates were told which condition they were to act out.

Findings indicated that the participants imitated the smoking behavior of the confederate. Even after controlling for young people's urge to smoke, the confederate's smoking explained a large proportion of the variance in number of cigarettes smoked by the participant. Further, in a warm, sociable interaction, participants were more likely to continue smoking. Both the confederate's smoking and the urge to smoke influenced participants to light up their first cigarette. Concerning the second cigarette smoked, we found that participants in the heavy smoking condition and in the warm model condition were more likely to light up a second one. With regard to the third cigarette, only in the heavy smoking condition, participants lit up a third one. Thus, the findings of this observational experimental study showed that young adults imitate smoking behavior of complete strangers, and the imitation effects also substantially explain why individuals start and continue smoking. Further, young people are more likely to continue smoking if this takes place with a warm and sociable person.

Future Research

In experimental alcohol research and in our experimental study on smoking, the hypothesis has been tested that people imitate their same-sex partner's behavior more strongly when they like him or her (see also Van Baaren et al., 2004). This has been tested by using a 'warm' and 'cold' model, showing that imitation effects are strongest in the case a confederate acts warmly (i.e., friendly, open, responsive) (Collins et al., 1985). But this probably does not explain why people continue imitation or even do it more strongly over time. Thus, a question remains how the real-time unfolding of peer interactions affects imitation. We propose that whether imitation will continue or even accelerate depends on the quality of dyadic interactions and how it develops over time (see Engels & Granic, 2005). Similarly, we expect that imitation not only depends on initial levels of liking, but also on how interactions progress moment to moment. We suspect that after the initial meeting phase, if people are mutually engaged in warm conversations they will be more likely to imitate the other's behaviors than when conversations are variable in nature over time, or decrease in liveliness and reciprocal engagement over time (see Granic & Hollenstein, 2003). So, compared to previous scholars who focused on initial imitation effects, we assume that the duration of imitation depends upon the quality of the social interaction as it develops in real time.

Another, related question is whether the quality of past peer interactions impacts on future drinking imitation? It may be that the poor predictive power of peer imitation found in previous longitudinal studies can be explained by the variability in the types of interactions adolescents have had with various peers. The quality and temporal patterns of *past* peer interactions may strongly affect *future* imitation. A way to test how people are affected by previous interactions with (until then) unfamiliar peers is to conduct a second session together with the same confederate. Our general hypothesis is that the behavioural patterns displayed in this second session will be partly based on the previous interactions with the confederate. A number of more specific hypotheses can also be put forward. First, participants who show strong mutually positive engagement patterns with confederates in the first session will show even stronger imitation effects in the second session. Conversely, participants who were disengaged from their confederates are expected to show significantly less imitation in the second session. Second, one might expect that dyads that ended up in a strong, mutual engagement pattern by the end of the first session will take significantly less time to become mutually engaged in the second session; and this temporal pattern will be related to earlier and more persistent imitation of smoking or drinking behaviors.

   In sum, we argue that to study peer influence processes thoroughly, experimental designs in which young people are confronted with an unfamiliar peer have the advantage of excluding the possibility that similarities in behavioral patterns in dyads are due to selective peer affiliation or by previous mutual influence processes. The obvious disadvantage of this approach is that it is difficult to estimate to what extent the unfolding social interactions as well as imitation effects in these dyads can be extrapolated to ongoing processes in existing peer groups or friendships. There is no simple answer to this question. Probably the best way to proceed is to combine insights from observational studies conducted with existing friends and peer groups with experimental observational studies conducted with unfamiliar confederates. A second question is whether the imitation effects assessed in a singular session in a (experimental) setting are long-lived. In other words, it is a question whether these effects are (a) truly exemplary for how some individuals are susceptible to substance use by peers, and (b) whether the imitation pattern exhibited in these experiments are affecting young people's patterns of substance use on the long run.

CONCLUSION

We have discussed the role of peer substance use on adolescent substance use. Based on the evidence we reviewed, longitudinal survey studies do not provide convincing evidence for a strong modeling effect of substance use by peers. We argue that survey designs are less suitable to gain insights into the conditions under which people actually imitate others' drinking or smoking behaviors or are susceptible to explicit peer pressure. We propose that longitudinal studies that combine survey and observational data may be more successful in shedding light on the intriguing matter of how friends actually affect individual differences in substance use. We argue that observational studies, especially, that measure real-time microsocial interactions between peers in the natural contexts in which the behaviors take place will provide insight into not only whether peers actually have an impact on individual use but, more importantly, the mechanisms underpinning imitation of peer behaviors.

AUTHORS' NOTE

Rutger Engels was supported by a fellowship of the Dutch Organization of Scientific Research during the preparation of this manuscript.

REFERENCES

Aitken, P. P. (1985). An observational study of young adults' drinking groups II. Drink purchasing procedures, group pressures, and alcohol consumption by companions as predictors of alcohol consumption. *Alcohol & Alcoholism, 20*, 445–457.

Aitken, P. P. & Jahoda, G. (1983). An observational study of young adults' drinking groups I. Drink preferences, demographic and structural variables as predictors of alcohol consumption. *Alcohol & Alcoholism, 18*, 135–150.

Aloise-Young, P. A., Graham, J. W., & Hansen, W. B. (1994). Peer influence on smoking initiation during early adolescence: A comparison of group members and group outsiders. *Journal of Applied Psychology, 79*, 281–287.

Andrews, J. A., Tildesley, E., Hops, H., & Li, F. (2002). The influence of peers on young adult substance use. *Health Psychology, 21*, 349–357.

Bauman, K. E. & Ennett S. E. (1996). On the importance of peer influence for adolescent drug use: Commonly neglected considerations. *Addiction, 91*, 185–198.

Bot, S. M., Engels, R. C. M. E., Knibbe, R. A., & Meeus, W. (2005a). Friend's drinking and adolescent alcohol consumption: The moderating role of friendship characteristics. *Addictive Behaviors, 30*, 929–947.

Bot, S. M., Engels, R. C. M. E., & Knibbe, R. A. (2005b). The effects of alcohol expectancies on drinking behaviour in peer groups: Observations in a naturalistic setting. *Addiction, 100*, 1270–1279.

Bot, S. M., Engels, R. C. M. E., Knibbe, R. A., & Meeus, W. (in press). *Pastime in a pub: Observations of young adults' activities and alcohol consumption.* Addictive Behaviors.

Bruun, K. (1959). *Drinking Behaviour in Small Groups.* Helsinki: Uudenmaan Kirjapaino.

Caudill, B. D. & Kong, F. H. (2001). Social approval and facilitation in predicting modeling effects in alcohol consumption. *Journal of Substance Abuse, 13*, 425–441.

Cohen, J. M. (1977). Sources of peer group homogeneity. *Sociology of Education, 50*, 227–241.

Collins, R. L., Parks, G. A., & Marlatt, G. A. (1985). Social determinants of alcohol consumption: The effects of social interaction and model status on the self-administration of alcohol. *Journal of Consulting and Clinical Psychology, 53*, 189–200.

De Vries, H., Engels, R. C. M. E., Kremers, S., Wetzels, J., & Mudde, A. (2003). Influences of parents and peers on adolescent smoking behavior in six European countries. *Health Education Research, 18*, 617–632.

Dishion, T., Bullock, B. M., & Nelson, S. (2002, July). *A dynamic system analysis of developmental trajectories: Prosocial and deviant adaptation as an attractor process.* 17th Biennial ISSBD meeting, Ottawa, Canada.

Dishion, T. J. & Owen, L. D. (2002). A longitudinal analysis of friendships and substance use: Bidirectional influence from adolescence to adulthood. *Developmental Psychology, 38*, 480–491.

Engels, R. C. M. E., Bot, S. M., Van Der Vorst, H., & Granic, I. (2005). *Smells like teen spirit. Gender differences in susceptibility to peer influences concerning alcohol consumption.* Under Review.

Engels, R. C. M. E. & Granic, I. (August, 2005). *Experimental observational studies on peer influence processes and alcohol consumption.* Research proposal NWO.

Engels, R. C. M. E., Knibbe, R. A., De Vries, H., & Drop, M. J. (1998). Antecedents of smoking cessation among adolescents: Who is motivated to change? *Preventive Medicine, 27*, 348–357.

Engels, R. C. M. E., Knibbe, R. A., De Vries, H., Drop, M. J., & Van Breukelen, G. J. P. (1999a). Influences of parental and best friends' smoking and drinking on adolescent use: A longitudinal study. *Journal of Applied Social Psychology, 29*, 338–362.

Engels, R. C. M. E., Knibbe, R. A., & Drop, M. J. (1999b). Predictability of smoking in adolescence: Between optimism and pessimism. *Addiction, 94*, 115–124.

Engels, R. C. M. E., Knibbe, R. A., Drop, M. J., & De Haan, J. T. (1997). Homogeneity of smoking behavior in peer groups: Influence or selection? *Health Education and Behavior, 24*, 801–811.

Engels, R. C. M. E., Noom, M., Hale III, W. W., & De Vries, H. (2005). Self-efficacy and emotional adjustment as precursors of smoking in early adolescence. *Substance Use and Misuse, 40*, 1883–1893.

Engels, R. C. M. E., Scholte, R., Van Lieshout, C., Overbeek, G., & De Kemp, R. (2006). Peer group reputation and alcohol and cigarette use. *Addictive Behaviors, 31*, 440–449.

Engels, R. C. M. E., Vitaro, F., Den Exter Blokland, A., De Kemp, R., & Scholte, R. (2004). Parents, friendship selection processes and adolescent smoking behavior. *Journal of Adolescence, 27*, 531–544.

Finkenauer, C., Engels, R. C. M. E., Meeus, W., & Oosterwegel, A. (2002). Self and identity in early adolescence. In: T. M. Brinthaupt & R. P. Lipka (eds.). *Understanding the Self of the Early Adolescent.* State University of New York Press.

Fisher, L. A. & Bauman, K. E. (1988). Influence and selection in the friend-adolescent relationship: findings from studies of adolescent smoking and drinking. *Journal of Applied Social Psychology, 18*, 289–314.

Gaughan, M. (1999). *Predisposition and Pressure: Getting Drunk in Adolescent Friendships.* UMI PROQuest Digital Dissertations.

Goor, L.A.M. van de (1990). *Situational Aspects of Adolescent Drinking.* Maastricht: Datawyse.

Granic, I. & Dishion, T. J. (2003). Deviant talk in adolescent friendships: A step toward measuring a pathogenic attractor process. *Social Development, 12*, 314–334.

Granic, I. & Hollenstein, T. (2003). Dynamic systems methods for models of developmental psychopathology. *Development and Psychopathology, 15*, 641–669.

Granic, I., Hollenstein, T., Dishion, T. J., & Patterson, G. R. (2003). Longitudinal analysis of flexibility and reorganization in early adolescence: A dynamic systems study of family interactions. *Developmental Psychology, 39*, 606–617.

Granic, I. & Lamey, A.V. (2002). Combining dynamic-systems and multivariate analyses to compare the mother-child interactions of externalizing subtypes. *Journal of Abnormal Child Psychology, 30*, 265–283.

Harakeh, Z., Engels, R. C. M. E., Van Baaren, R., & Scholte, R. (in press). *Imitation of smoking behavior in dyads: An experimental observational study. Drug and Alcohol Dependence.*

Harakeh, Z., Engels, R. C. M. E., Scholte, R., De Vries, H., & Vermulst, A. A. (in press). Best friend's smoking influences on adolescent smoking. *Psychology and Health.*

Jaccard, J., Blanton, H., & Dodge, T. (2005). Peer influences on risk behavior: An analysis on the effects of a close friend. *Developmental Psychology, 41*, 133–147.

Kandel, D. B. (1978). Homophily, selection and socialization in adolescent friendships. *American Journal of Sociology, 84*, 427–436.

Lewis, M. D., Lamey, A. V., & Douglas, L. (1999). A new dynamic systems method for the analysis of early socioemotional development. *Developmental Science, 2*, 457–475.

Pape, H. & Hammer, T. (1996). Sober adolescence: Predictor of psychosocial maladjustment in young adulthood? *Scandinavian Journal of Psychology, 37*, 362–377.

Petraitis, J., Flay, B. R., & Miller, T. Q. (1995). Reviewing theories of adolescent substance use: organizing pieces in the puzzle. *Psychological Bulletin, 117*, 67–86.

Poelen, E., Engels, R.C. M. E., Van Der Vorst, H., Scholte, R., & Vermulst, A. A. (in press). The role of close friends in adolescent drinking: A within family analysis. *Drug and Alcohol Dependence.*

Poelen, E. A. P., Scholte, R. H. J., Willemsen, G., Boomsma, D. I., & Engels, R. C. M. E. (2006). *The effects of familial and peer drinking on development of drinking in Dutch adolescent and young adult twins.* Submitted for publication.

Quigley, B. M. & Collins, R. L. (1999). The modeling of alcohol consumption: a meta-analytic review. *Journal of Studies on Alcohol, 60*, 90–98.

Suls, J. & Green, P. (2003). Pluralistic ignorance and college student perceptions of gender-specific alcohol norms. *Health Psychology, 22*, 479–486.

Urberg, K. A., Değirmencioğlu, S. M., & Pilgrim, C. (1997). Close friend and group influence on adolescent cigarette smoking and alcohol use. *Developmental Psychology, 33*, 834–844.

Urberg, K. A., Luo, Q., Pilgrim, C., & Değirmencioğlu, S. M. (2003). A two-stage model of peer influence in adolescent substance use: Individual and relationship-specific differences in susceptibility to influence. *Addictive Behaviors, 28*, 1243–1256.

Van Baaren, R. B., Holland, R. W., Kawakami, K., & Van Knippenberg, A. (2004). Mimicry and pro-social behavior. *Psychological Science, 15*, 71–74.

Van Zundert, R., Van Der Vorst, H., Vermulst, A. A., & Engels, R. C. M. E. (2006). Pathways to alcohol use among Dutch students in regular education and education for adolescents with behavioral problems: the role of parental alcohol use, general parenting practices, and alcohol-specific parenting practices. *Journal of Family Psychology, 20*, 456–467.

Vink, J. M., Willemsen, G., Engels, R. C. M. E., & Boomsma, D. (2003). Does the smoking behavior of parents, siblings and friends influence smoking behavior in adolescent twins? *Twin Research, 6*, 209–217.

Wang, M. Q., Eddy, J. M., & Fitzhugh, E. C. (2000). Smoking acquisition: Peer influence and selection. *Psychological Reports, 86*, 1241–1246.

CHAPTER 4

The Rocky Road of Adolescent Romantic Experience: Dating and Adjustment

Wyndol Furman, Martin J. Ho, and Sabina M. Low
University of Denver, USA

INTRODUCTION

Adolescent romantic relationships have long been a centerpiece of our media culture. Romeo and Juliet and Dante and Beatrice are classic love stories that have enchanted generations of individuals. Today's movies are full of similar tales, such as that between Jack Dawson and Rose DeWitt Bukater in the movie Titanic. In effect, these relationships are depicted in idealized terms. They are seen as very special and essential in one's life. In fact, many young adolescent girls say that they expect to be in love all the time (Simon, Eder, & Evans, 1972).

Although our own adolescent relationships may not have been as idealized, many of us still reflect on them with fondness. They were important and exciting experiences in our adolescence. In fact, adolescents will commonly neglect their close friends in order to spend time with a romantic partner (Roth & Parker, 2001). Consistent with this depiction, social scientists have found that adolescents have more strong positive emotions about the other sex than about family, same-sex peers, or school (Wilson-Shockley, 1995). Although no direct evidence exists, we believe that homosexual youth may have more strong positive emotions about same-sex relationships than about other key relationships.

Romantic partners also increasingly become sources of support. For example, in an earlier study (Furman & Buhrmester, 1992), we examined age differences in perceptions of support in different relationships. Mean ratings of support for relationships with romantic partners, same-sex friends, mothers, siblings, grandparents and teachers at four different grades are shown in Table 4.1. Not surprisingly, fourth grade children (10–11 years) were unlikely to report having a romantic partner, and those who said they had a romantic

Friends, Lovers and Groups: Key Relationships in Adolescence. Edited by Rutger C.M.E. Engels, Margaret Kerr and Håkan Stattin. Copyright © 2007 John Wiley & Sons, Ltd.

Table 4.1 Mean levels of support for close relationships at four grade levels

	Grade			
	4	7	10	13+
Romantic Partner	$2.77_{4,c}$	$3.08_{2,b,c}$	$3.19_{2,a,b}$	$3.50_{1,a}$
Same-sex friend	$3.41_{3,a,b}$	$3.61_{1,a}$	$3.57_{1,a}$	$3.37_{1,b}$
Mother	$3.90_{1,a}$	$3.51_{1,b}$	$3.32_{2,c}$	$3.42_{1,b,c}$
Father	$3.89_{,,a}$	$3.39_{1,b}$	$2.98_{3,c}$	$3.16_{2,c}$
Sibling	$3.43_{2,3,a}$	$2.99_{2,c}$	$3.11_{3,b,c}$	$3.22_{1,2,b}$
Grandparent	$3.64_{2,a}$	$3.01_{2,b}$	$2.75_{4,6,c}$	$2.68_{3,c}$
Teacher	$2.61_{5,a}$	$1.86_{3,b}$	$1.93_{5,b}$	—

Note. The numbers in subscripts indicate the rank order of the means across relationships within each grade. The letters in subscripts indicate the rank order of means across grade levels within each type of relationship. Means with different letters or numbers are significantly different from each other.

relationship did not see it as particularly supportive. Similarly, seventh grade adolescents (13–14 years old) reported that these relationships were not as supportive as their relationships with parents, although the ratings were similar to those given to relationships with siblings and grandparents. Tenth grade adolescents (15–16 years of age) saw them as more supportive than other significant relationships except their same-sex friendships. College males (19 years of age) reported that romantic relationships were their most supportive relationship, whereas college females said that the romantic relationship was among their most supportive relationships. A similar pattern is emerging in the longitudinal research described subsequently in this chapter. In the tenth grade, same-sex friends are seen as the most supportive, followed by mothers and romantic partners. By the twelfth grade, romantic partners and same-sex friends are perceived as the most supportive people in the network.

Similarly, when asked about the advantages of romantic relationships, high school adolescents most commonly mention support, companionship, and intimacy (Feiring, 1996; Hand & Furman, 2005b). In fact, more adolescents mentioned support and companionship as advantages of romantic relationships than as advantages of same- or other-sex friendships. Not surprisingly, physical intimacy and caretaking were also seen as distinct advantages of romantic relationships.

Not only are romantic relationships perceived quite positively, but they are also thought to contribute to psycho-social development in several important domains (Furman & Shaffer, 2003). They are a primary context for the development of sexuality. The majority of adolescents first have intercourse with someone they are going steady with or know well and like a lot (Abma, Chandra, Mosher, Peterson, & Piccinino, 1997; Rodgers, 1996). Adolescent experiences may also serve as the foundation for subsequent romantic relationships, including marriage (Erikson, 1968; Furman & Flanagan, 1997; Sullivan, 1953). Although theorists have emphasized the effects peers have on romantic relationships (e.g. Brown, 1999; Furman & Wehner, 1992b), it seems likely that romantic relationships will influence peer relationships as well (Furman & Shaffer, 2003). In fact, romantic experience is positively related to peer social competence (Neeman, Hubbard, & Masten, 1995). Romantic experiences may also promote autonomy as adolescents increasingly rely less on parents (Dowdy & Kliewer, 1998; Gray & Steinberg, 1999). Finally, they may contribute to different facets of identity, including sexual orientation, sex-role identity, and romantic self-concept (Furman & Shaffer, 2003).

In contrast to the preceding positive portrayal of romantic relationships and their contributions to development, adolescent romantic relationships have also been associated with adverse consequences. Just as members of the other sex are the most common source of strong positive emotions, they are also the most common source of strong negative emotions (Wilson-Shockley, 1995). In fact, romantic breakups are one of the strongest predictors of depression, suicide attempts and suicide completions (Brent et al., 1993; Joyner & Udry, 2000; Monroe, Rohde, Seeley, & Lewinsohn, 1999). Teen pregnancy and sexually transmitted diseases are also risks that come with romantic experiences, as having a romantic relationship is the strongest predictor of intercourse and its associated risks (Blum, Beuhring, & Rinehart, 2000). Romantic partners are the perpetrators of between one-half to two-thirds of sexual victimization incidents in late adolescence (Flanagan & Furman, 2000). More than 25% of adolescents are victims of dating violence or aggression (see Wolfe & Feiring, 2000), and dating violence precedes serious marital violence in 25% to 50% of cases (Gayford, 1975; Roscoe & Benaske, 1985). Between 10 and 15% of 16 and 17 year girls experience sexual violence (Silverman, Raj, Mucci, & Hathaway, 2001); such physical or sexual violence is associated with significantly greater risk for substance usage, unhealthy weight control, sexual risk behavior, pregnancy, and risk of suicide (Silverman et al., 2001). Those who are dating are more likely to use alcohol and drugs (Aro & Taiple, 1987; Thomas & Hsiu, 1993). Those who are dating are more likely to be in social contexts where substance use occurs, and resisting offers of drugs from a romantic partner is particularly difficult to do (Trost, Langan, & Kellar-Guenteher, 1999).

The long list of risks associated with adolescent dating and romantic relationships raises serious concerns about the consequences of dating and romantic experiences. In fact, one would have to wonder why any parent would permit an adolescent to date if it were this risky? One would even have to ask why an adolescent would want to date if, as some have argued, it leads to depression (Joyner & Udry, 2000). On the other hand, if dating and romantic relationships promote psycho-social development, parents may want to encourage their adolescents to date and have romantic relationships. These different descriptions of the potential impact of adolescent romantic experiences may not only seem confusing to a parent, but present a complex picture for social scientists to interpret. Is one of these characterizations inaccurate or can the different descriptions be reconciled?

Neeman et al. (1995) observed that romantic relationships require some social skills, which may have been learned in other peer relationships. At the same time, romantic relationships often involve a significant amount of time, and may take away from the time needed in other domains of life. Aside from Neeman et al.'s ideas, the seeming discrepancy in the portrayal of romantic relationships has received little attention in the literature. In part, this is because most investigators only examined a limited number of indices of adjustment, and may not have observed such a discrepancy in their own work. In any case, we will argue that descriptions of romantic experiences that only stress their potential benefits or only focus on their risks do not provide a complete picture of the impact of romantic experiences. Dating and romantic relationships may bring both potential benefits and potential risks. In fact, the risks and benefits are likely to occur simultaneously because of the social context in which romantic experiences are embedded. We present results from two large-scale studies of dating and adjustment. These studies illustrate that when one looks at a range of different outcomes simultaneously, dating yields both benefits and risks. Additionally, they demonstrate that the benefits and risks depend upon the timing and nature of dating. Finally, we discuss how other dimensions of romantic experience may be important, and point out several issues to consider in assessing effects of romantic experience.

TWO EMPIRICAL STUDIES OF DATING AND ADJUSTMENT

Currently, we are conducting a longitudinal study of romantic relationships, other close relationships, and adjustment. Participants were 100 females and 100 males who were initially recruited when they were in the tenth grade (14 to 16 years old). By design, the ethnicity of the sample closely approximated that of the United States; specifically, the sample was 70% Euro-American, 12.5% African-American, 12% Hispanic, 2.5% Asian, and 3% Other/Biracial. We recruited the participants from a range of schools and neighborhoods to obtain a diverse community sample. Consistent with our goals, the mean scores on most measures of adjustment, substance use, and sexual activity closely approximate the means of normative samples or large surveys.

The participants also had a range of different dating and sexual experiences. Approximately 85% of the 10th grade participants reported that they had begun dating; 75.5% had had a romantic relationship of one month duration or longer. In the 10th grade, 31% of the participants reported that they had engaged in sexual intercourse. The vast majority of the participants reported that they were heterosexuals, although approximately 6% of the 10th graders reported that they were sexual minorities or questioning their sexual orientation. These participants were included in the analyses, as most of them had dated as well.

In the first year of the study the adolescents participated in either two or three laboratory sessions, depending upon whether they had had a romantic relationship or not. Separate interviews were conducted to assess their experiences and views or representations of their relationships with parents, friends, and past and present romantic partners (if applicable). Additionally, they were observed interacting in a series of structured tasks with their mother, with a close friend, and with a romantic partner (if applicable). Participants used a computer assisted self-interviewing program to answer questions about sensitive topics, such as sexual activity, substance use, and criminal behavior. Other questionnaires were completed between sessions. Parents, friends, and partners also completed questionnaires.

In the second wave of data collection a year later when most were in the 11th grade, the participants were interviewed about their romantic relationships, completed questionnaires, and were observed with a romantic partner (if applicable). Parents and friends completed questionnaires. All 200 adolescents participated in this second wave.

In each wave of data collection, we gathered a number of measures of adjustment and other psycho-social constructs that were thought to be relevant to dating. The key constructs we assessed were: externalizing symptoms, internalizing symptoms, scholastic competence, substance use, genital sexual behavior, non-genital sexual behavior, peer acceptance, friendship competence, romantic competence, peer acceptance, and physical appearance. Externalizing symptoms were assessed by having the participant complete the Youth Self-Report (Achenbach, 1991) and the mother and friend complete the Child Behavior Checklist (Achenbach, 1991). Internalizing symptoms were assessed by having the participant complete the Youth Self Report (Achenbach, 1991), Beck Depression Inventory (Beck, Rush, Shaw, & Emery, 1979), and Spielberger (1983) Trait Anxiety Inventory. Substance use was assessed by participant and friends' reports of the frequency of alcohol use, frequency of drug use, and substance use problems (Eggert, Herting, & Thompson, 1996). Genital sexual activity was assessed by measuring the frequency of intercourse and oral sex, and risky sexual activity, whereas non-genital sexual activity was assessed by measuring the frequency of necking ('making out'), light petting, and heavy petting (Furman & Wehner, 1992b; Metzler, Noell, & Biglan, 1992). Scholastic competence was assessed by self-reported grade point average, and participants', mothers', and friends' reports of scholastic competence using Harter's (1988) Adolescent Self-Perception Profile. We also assessed social acceptance, friendship competence, romantic competence, and physical attractiveness by having the participant, mother, and friend complete the pertinent scales on Harter's Adolescent Self-Perception Profile. As these descriptions illustrate, we included at least three indices of each general domain, using multiple reporters when appropriate. Confirmatory factor analyses revealed that these different indices of each domain loaded on a common latent factor. We standardized the scores on the measures and averaged them to derive the composites discussed here.

Dating and the Timing of Onset of Dating

First, we examined whether those 10th graders who had already begun dating and those who had not differed on the various indices of adjustment and peer-related social behavior. Dating was defined quite broadly as spending time with someone you are seeing or going out with. Whereas dating was once a formal, prearranged occasion, it is typically quite informal among adolescents in the United States now. Accordingly, we included informal, spontaneous instances as well as prearranged dates. We also included both dyadic dating and group dating.

We also examined the timing of the onset of dating as that too has been linked to various adjustment indices. For example, romantic experiences in late childhood or early adolescence are associated with substance use, minor delinquency, disordered eating tendencies, and lower levels of academic achievement (Aro & Taiple, 1987; Cauffman & Steinberg, 1996; Neeman et al., 1995). At the same time, those who are romantically involved at an early age are also more socially accepted (Neeman et al., 1995). We designated those who began dating in the 6th grade or before as early daters (n = 54; 27%), as this yielded a group comparable in size to those who had not begun dating and could ultimately be considered late starters (n = 32, 16%). The remaining participants who had begun dating in the 7th to 10th grade (n = 114, 57%) were designated to be typical onset daters.

Figures 4.1 and 4.2 present the mean scores for the three groups. We found significant differences between daters and nondaters on most of the indices of psycho-social adjustment and competence. Daters had significantly more externalizing symptoms. No differences were found in internalizing symptoms

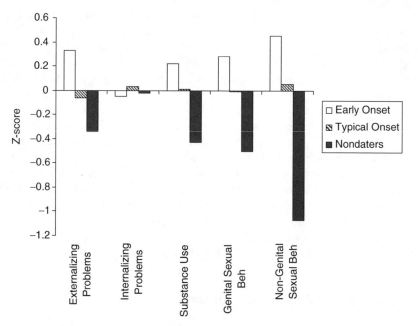

Figure 4.1 Differences among early onset daters, typical onset daters, and nondaters in symptoms and risky behaviors

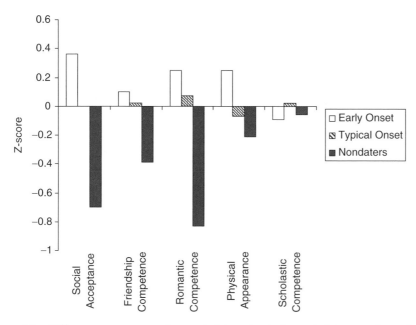

Figure 4.2 Differences among early onset daters, typical onset daters, and nondaters in interpersonal competence

or scholastic competence. Consistent with prior work (Aro & Taiple, 1987), daters engaged in more substance use. Not surprisingly, they also engaged in more non-genital and genital sexual activity. At the same time, daters also were higher in social acceptance, friendship competence, and romantic competence.

Differences were also observed between those who started dating at an early age and those whose timing was more typical. The early onset daters were higher in externalizing problems and nongenital sexual behavior than the typical onset daters. At the same time, the early onset daters were rated as more socially accepted and more physically attractive. Thus, consistent with the literature's general portrayal of dating and the timing of dating, we found links with indices of psycho-social competence as well as risky or problematic behaviors.

Of course, the findings are cross-sectional in nature. It seems at least as plausible that externalizing symptoms may lead to dating as the reverse. Similarly, friendship competence and social competence could as easily lead to dating as the reverse. In fact, one might be tempted to think that the characteristics of the adolescents who date, rather than the experience of dating, may be responsible for the associations as differences were found between the early and typical onset dating groups as well between these two groups and nondaters. For example, youth who engage in delinquent behavior or otherwise act out may be more likely to enter the dating arena earlier, perhaps because of familial conflicts. Similarly, those who are

more socially accepted and attractive may be prominent in the peer group
and thus may be more likely to date earlier (Dunphy, 1963; Franzoi, Davis,
& Vasquez-Suson, 1994). On the other hand, the nature of dating experiences in early adolescence is likely to be qualitatively different from that in
middle adolescence, and those differences in the nature of the dating experience could contribute to the differences in adjustment. For example, females'
early dating partners are commonly older males, who may be more likely to
exploit the young adolescents (Pawlby, Mills, Taylor, & Quinton. 1997). Thus,
we cannot tell whether the differences in adjustment reflect the experiences
of dating or the characteristics of those who start dating early or some third
factor.

In any case, these findings provide an interesting contrast to an earlier study
of a relatively similar sample of 208 adolescents who were in the 12th grade
(ages 16 to 19). In that study, assessment of adjustment was not as extensive as
the current study. Participants completed the Brief Symptoms Inventory,
which assesses nine types of symptoms (Derogatis, 1993). Unlike the other
study where daters reported greater symptomatology, those who had had
only minimal or no experience dating reported greater numbers of symptoms
on three of the nine scales (depression, interpersonal sensitivity, and psycho-
tocism). These findings have led us to hypothesize that beginning dating at the
time when most peers begin is associated with better adjustment than either
an early or late onset of dating. Early onset may be linked with externalizing
problems and substance use, whereas late onset may be associated with
internalizing problems and low interpersonal competence.

Dimensions of Dating

It is also important to recognize that the distinction among early daters, typical
onset daters, and nondaters is a simple division that is inherently limited in
nature. Adolescents who are dating may vary widely in the degree and nature
of their experiences. Some may have dated only one or two times, whereas
others may have had long-term relationships or a number of different
relationships. In the first study of 10th graders, we administered a Dating
History Questionnaire to examine a range of aspects of romantic experience
(Furman & Wehner, 1992a). We asked if they had experienced each of 16
romantically relevant events and what grade they had first experienced them.
The list of 16 ranged from activities that typically occur earlier in adolescence
(e.g. mixed gender parties) to those that typically occur at older ages (e.g.
committed relationships). Emotional experiences, such as crushes or being in
love, were also included. As with our other measures, the questions appear to
be appropriate for both sexual minorities and heterosexual youth. It is,
however, likely that some activities that are more relevant to sexual minorities
may not have been included, for example, internet contacts, participation
in gay lesbian bisexual and transsexual clubs, and passionate friendships
(Diamond, 2000; Diamond, Savin-Williams, & Dubé, 1999).

Table 4.2 Correlations of dating dimensions with adjustment composites

	Romantic Experience	Casual Dating	Serious Romantic
Externalizing Problems	.29**	.36**	−.13
Internalizing Problems	−.01	−.01	.02
Scholastic Competence	−.09	−.19*	−.08
Substance Use	.39**	.24**	−.15+
Genital Sexual Behavior	.44**	.47**	.11
Nongenital Sexual Behavior	.67**	.52**	.20*
Social Acceptance	.36**	.17*	.13
Friendship Competence	.18*	.03	.01
Romantic Competence	.54**	.19*	.48**
Physical Appearance	.17*	.18*	.23**

**p< .01. * p< .05. +p< .10.

Because of the limitations of using a simple dating/nondating dichotomy, we summed the number of different experiences participants had had to derive a continuous index of romantic experience. The pattern of relations with the different adjustment composites are presented in the left hand column of Table 4.2. The results were similar to those obtained with the dating/nondating dichotomy. That is, greater romantic experience was associated with more externalizing problems, substance use, and non-genital and genital sexual activity on the one hand, and greater social acceptance, friendship competence and romantic competence on the other hand. It was also associated with physical attractiveness, a finding that had not appeared with the simple dichotomous measure. In fact, the magnitude of most relations was generally a little stronger with the romantic experience measure rather than the dichotomous dater/nondater measure. Thus, it would seem best to conceptualize and measure romantic experience as a continuous variable.

A more detailed examination of the characteristics of romantic experiences revealed a more differentiated picture. Specifically, we asked a series of questions about the nature of their experiences. These questions were found to load on two factors: (1) a Casual Dating factor, whose specific indices were the number of individuals dated in the last year, the total number of individuals dated, grade of onset of dating, perceptions of oneself as a 'player,' number of people cheated on, and number of people who had cheated on them; and (2) a Serious Romantic factor, whose specific indices were length of relationships, proportion of relationships that were long, and dating satisfaction. The proportion of time dating and overall amount of romantic experience loaded on both, suggesting that these indices reflected the sheer quantity (vs. nature) of dating. Factor scores were derived by standardizing and averaging the scales that uniquely loaded on each factor.

As shown in Table 4.2, the casual dating factor was related to the same indices of externalizing symptoms, substance use, and genital and nongenital sexual activity that overall romantic experience was; additionally, it was associated with poor scholastic competence. These findings are consistent with prior research in which the number of dating partners an adolescent had had in the prior year was correlated with externalizing and internalizing symptoms, poor academic performance, and poor emotional health (Zimmer-Gembeck, Siebenbruner, & Collins, 2001). At the same time, the casual dating factor was also related to social acceptance and romantic competence, although not friendship competence.

On the other hand, the serious romantic dimension was not as strongly related to these various indices of problematic adjustment (see Table 4.2). Only the association with nongenital sexual activity was significant, and, in fact, the serious romantic dimension tended to be negatively related to substance use. Moreover, the serious romantic dimension was strongly related to romantic competence. We also did median splits on the two dimensions and categorized participants into the resulting four groups. Those who were high on casual dating and low on serious romantic experiences were higher in externalizing symptoms, substance use, and genital sexual behavior than those low on casual dating and high on serious romantic experiences. The primary difference in social acceptance was between those who were low on both and the other three groups. Similarly, the primary difference in physical attractiveness was between those who were low on both the casual and serious versus those who were high on both. The overall pattern of results suggest that the dimensions of casual dating and serious romantic experience may either have distinctly different impacts on adolescents, or the characteristics of adolescents who have primarily serious or casual relationships are quite different.

Changes in Romantic Experiences and Adjustment

The analyses that have been presented to this point have been cross-sectional, thus limiting any inferences about directionality of effect. To examine directionality, we analyzed whether the degree of romantic experience was predictive of changes in adjustment indices from the first wave of data collection to the second wave of data collection a year later. Conversely, we examined whether adjustment was predictive of the amount of romantic experience by the second wave after controlling for scores on the romantic experience dimension in the first wave. These analyses were limited to those variables, which covaried with romantic experience at wave 1.

Romantic experience at wave 1 predicted increases from wave 1 to wave 2 in genital and non-genital sexual behavior, and romantic competence (see Table 4.3). Conversely, genital sexual behavior and romantic competence at wave 1 predicted increases in romantic experience, and non-genital sexual activity tended to predict changes in romantic experience over that year as well. Romantic experience at wave 1 predicted increases in substance use, but substance use did not predict changes in romantic experience over the year.

Table 4.3 Prediction of changes at wave 2 from wave 1 romantic experience or adjustment composite

Adjustment Composite	Romantic Experience Predicting Change In Composite	Composite Predicting Change in Romantic Experience
Externalizing Problems	.02	−.01
Substance Use	.20**	.01
Genital Sexual Behavior	.26**	.08
Nongenital Sexual Behavior	.30**	.17**
Social Acceptance	−.01	.19**
Friendship Competence	.00	−.00
Romantic Competence	.22**	.19**
Physical Appearance	.01	.15**

Note. The middle column depicts the standardized betas for romantic experience in a regression equation predicting changes in the outcome variables listed in the right colum. The right column depicts the standardized betas for the outcome variables predicting changes in romantic experience from wave 1 to wave 2.
**$p<.01$.*$p<.05$.+$p<.10$.

On the other hand, social acceptance and physical appearance predicted changes in romantic experience, but romantic experience did not predict increases in either of the two. Finally, externalizing symptoms and friendship competence each covaried with romantic experience at wave 1, but neither predicted increases in romantic experience, nor did romantic experience predict increases in them. The diversity of the pattern of relations illustrates the critical importance of examining the pattern of relations longitudinally before making assertions about the healthy or unhealthy effects of dating or other social experiences.

Substantively, it appears that reciprocal links may occur when the two constructs are closely related to each other. Romantic experience may readily lead to sexual activity, which may in turn lead to increased romantic experience. Similarly, romantic experience may typically promote feelings of romantic competence, which may in turn promote romantic experience. These links between romantic experience and romantic competence are certainly not surprising but do suggest that adolescents may be acquiring skills and knowledge from their experiences that may carryover to subsequent relationships, or at the very least, they are acquiring some sense of confidence.

In other instances, one variable seems to serve as a context for the other one. For example, dating may lead to increased drinking, perhaps because of the social nature of dating life in adolescence. Similarly, peer acceptance and physical attractiveness may provide opportunities for individuals to become romantically involved with others. These findings are consistent with prior work, showing links between friendships and subsequent romantic relationships (Connolly, Furman, & Konarski, 2000).

What might account for the absence of predictive links between romantic experience and the externalizing symptoms and friendship competence variables? Perhaps a third factor is responsible for the covariation. Perhaps any effect of one variable on the other requires more time than a year to occur. Or perhaps the causal action has occurred earlier in development, and the pattern reflects a current state of stasis. For example, antisocial youth may become prematurely involved in romantic activities at an early age as a way of acting out, but such externalizing behavior may not continue to foster further romantic experiences when they have reached high school.

ROMANTIC RELATIONSHIPS AND EXPERIENCE

In the present chapter, we have focused on the links between dating and adjustment. This, however, does not provide a full picture of romantic experiences and their potential links with adjustment. Collins (2003) proposed examining five features: involvement, quality, partner selection, content and cognitive and emotional processes. Our own work has been guided by a similar framework depicted in Table 4.4.

The first additional feature to examine is the quality of the romantic relationship. As has been found with other close relationships (see Adler &

Table 4.4   Dimensions of romantic relationships and experience

Romantic experience
   Dating/NonDating
   Timing of Onset of Dating
   Casual Dating
   Serious Romantic Relationships
Romantic Relationship Qualities
   Support
   Negative Interactions
   (or Control/Dependency)
Behavioral Systems (Interaction Content)
   Affiliation
   Sexuality
   Attachment
   Caretaking
Partner Characteristics
   Gender, Age, and Other Demographic Characteristics
   Prosocial or Antisocial Characteristics
   Similarities/Dissimilarities
Views
   Working Models of Romantic Experiences
   Romantic Styles
   Rejection Sensitivity
   Dating Anxiety
Related Experiences
   Other Sexual Activity
   Friendships (Other-Sex Friendships/Passionate Friendships)
   Specific Events

Furman, 1988; Furman, 1996), support and negative interactions are two key dimensions of romantic relationships. We have also further differentiated negative interactions into participant controlling-partner dependent and partner controlling-participant dependent dimensions (Furman, 2001). We have hypothesized that the importance of relationship quality will change developmentally. In early and middle adolescence, having a romantic relationship may be more important than its actual quality (Brown, 1999). Consistent with this idea, Daniels and Moos (1990) found depressed early adolescents obtained fewer social resources from their friends than non-depressed ones, but no differences were found in the resources obtained from their romantic partners. Yet, at the end of high school, the links between relationship dysfunction and depression have been found to be stronger in romantic relationships than in friendships (Daley & Hammen, 2002). Thus, adjustment and romantic relationship quality should become more closely connected later in development. Consistent with this idea, we found ratings of partner controlling-participant dependent and perceived negative interactions to be associated with greater symptomatology in our prior study of 12th grade adolescents (Furman, 2000), but we find relatively few links with romantic relationship quality in the study of 10th graders (see Laursen's commentary for further elaboration). In fact, we find relationship quality to only be related to romantic competence and not the other indices of competence or risky behavior examined in this chapter. These findings are similar to those reported by Zimmer-Gembeck et al. (2001) who found middle adolescent romantic relationship quality to be associated with romantic competence and social acceptance, but not with indices of emotional health, symptomatology, and scholastic performance.

With regard to the content of romantic relationships, we've proposed that romantic relationships become key contexts for the affiliative, sexual, attachment, and caregiving systems (Furman & Wehner, 1994; Furman, 1998). Early romantic relationships are expected to be characterized primarily by affiliation and sexual activity, but in late adolescence or adulthood partners may begin to serve as key attachment figures, and individuals may provide caregiving for their partners. The links to adjustment are likely to vary substantially as a function of the nature of the relationship.

Additionally, the characteristics of the partner may play a major role in shaping the nature of the relationship and its potential impact on adjustment. For many years, social psychologists have examined the links between interpersonal attraction and similarity in adults (see Berscheid & Reis, 1988). In young adulthood, a partner who is similar may promote continuity in adjustment, whereas a dissimilar one may lead to changes in the course of development and adjustment (Quinton, Pickles, Maughan, & Rutter, 1993). For example, a supportive, prosocial adult can disrupt patterns of childhood conduct disorder, whereas a deviant/antisocial one may promote its continuity. As yet, however, we know relatively little about how the characteristics of partners in adolescence may affect the relationship or adjustment.

One of the key elements of our framework is views or cognitive representations of romantic relationships, the self in that type of relationship, and the partner in that kind of relationship (Furman & Wehner, 1994; Furman & Simon, 1999). These views are conceptualized as expectations regarding intimacy and closeness. Views are expected to influence a person's behavior toward a romantic partner and serve as a basis for predicting and interpreting the partner's behavior. In past research, we have found that adolescents' romantic views are related to their views of friendships and to some degree their views of their relationships with parents (Furman, Simon, Shaffer, & Bouchey, 2002). More recently, we have found that views, especially female's views, are linked to patterns of interactions with romantic partner (Furman & Simon, 2004). To date we know little about the links between adjustment and romantic views. In our study of 12th grade adolescents, however, we found that preoccupied views were associated with greater symptomatology and lower self-esteem, whereas dismissing views were associated with poor school performance.

Several related phenomena also entail examination, most especially sexual behavior. Ironically, the research fields of sexual behavior and romantic relationships have remained largely isolated from each other. We know surprisingly little about how the romantic partner characteristics or romantic relationship qualities influence sexual activity; in fact, we still know much more about how a parent or friend affects sexual behavior than how a partner does. With the emerging interest in romantic relationships, one might have expected this oversight to be corrected, but relationship researchers have primarily focused on other characteristics, such as conflict or intimacy. In effect, romantic relationships are studied as if they are platonic in nature. Clearly, however, sexual behavior and romantic experiences are closely related. As described previously, sexual activity and romantic experience were found to be linked, each predicting changes in the other. Moreover, genital and non-genital sexual behavior and substance use were similarly linked, underscoring the potential impact of sexual behavior on psycho-social adjustment.

It is also important to remember that sexual activity is not constrained to romantic relationships or even short-term dating partners; in our study of 12th grade adolescents, we found that over 90% engaged in light sexual activity with their closest other sex friend, with whom they had never had a romantic relationship; 26% engaged in light petting, and 15% engaged in heavy petting, oral sex, or intercourse (Hand & Furman, 2005a). The developmental significance of this activity remains uncharted.

More generally, work is needed on relationships that share some similarities with romantic relationships. For heterosexual youth, these would be other-sex friendships; for homosexual youth, these would be same-sex friendships, particularly passionate friendships (Diamond, 2000; Diamond, Savin-Williams, & Dubé, 1999). Such individuals may not only become romantic partners in some instances, but also they can be a conduit to other potential romantic partners (Connolly, Furman, & Konarsky, 2000) and an important source of information about romantic relationships (Hand & Furman, 2005b). It will be important to discern what the unique contributions of dating and romantic relationships provide, and what contributions they may provide as part of the peer social arena.

Finally, it is important to differentiate between the general influence of having a romantic relationship, and particular experiences or qualities of a relationship. Physical violence, sexual victimization or breakups may occur in the context of romantic relationships, but these events, rather than having a relationship per se, may underlie certain effects. For example, Joyner and Udry (2000) reported that those who had a romantic relationship were more depressed than those who had not. However, when the effect of having a breakup is controlled for, the difference is substantially attenuated, suggesting break-ups are likely to be the responsible mechanism, not the simple existence of a romantic relationship.

THE ANALYSIS OF EFFECTS

In the present chapter, we have primarily examined the effects of dating on adjustment by conducting a series of regression analyses. As additional waves of data are completed, we will be able to conduct latent growth curve models to identify either the predictors or consequences of both the average level of dating activity and changes in dating activity (i.e. the intercepts and slopes). Such an approach will provide a means for assessing an alternative, yet complementary, model of change (Curran, 2000; Curran & Willoughby, 2003).

One issue that warrants further consideration is the time between assessments. Yearly assessments may not be ideal for some questions. For example, although longitudinal studies have commonly found a link between deviant peer association and substance use, one of the most compelling demonstrations of such is Dishion and Medici Skagg's (2000) finding that substance use in a particular month covaried with exposure to peer problem behavior in that month. Some effects of romantic experience may be short lived and missed if the time-lag between assessments is too long (Collins & Graham, 2002). Some of the effects of dating may be a function of the current status, and not the typical status in a year. Links of these kinds would require alternative strategies of data collection, such as daily diaries or experience sampling methods.

On the other hand, some effects may take longer than a year or may require repeated exposure. For example, one poor relationship may have no effects or at least no long-term effects, but a string of failed relationships might.

It is important to remember that adolescents vary substantially in the timing of their romantic experiences. As shown here, the timing of experiences is associated with various indices of adjustment. On the other hand, having certain experiences may be comparable even if the exact time of the experience is somewhat different. For example, those who have had a serious relationship may be comparable in some respects, even if they vary somewhat in the age of that experience. If we are to understand the influence of romantic experiences, we need to find means of being sensitive to the variability in the timing. Otherwise, similarities (or differences) in the trajectories of experience may be masked.

Finally, inferences about causality from correlational data are inherently limited, whether the data are longitudinal or not. Experimental studies would be ideal, but it is difficult to imagine manipulating romantic experiences or relationships. The pragmatic and ethical considerations would be challenging to say the least. However, intervention programs for preventing partner violence or treatments of dysfunctional relationships may provide experimental opportunities to examine the links among variables (e.g. Wolfe, Wekerle, & Scott, 2003). One could also include assessments of romantic experiences in other interventions with adolescents.

CONCLUSION

In summary, we believe that dating and romantic experiences cannot simply be characterized as simply having positive or negative effects. Some of the variables associated with romantic experience are indices of social competence and others are risky behaviors. Moreover, some of these variables do not appear to be causally affected by romantic experience, but are simply correlated with romantic experience (e.g. friendship competence and externalizing symptoms). In other instances, the causal paths may be in the other direction; for example, it appears that social acceptance and physical attractiveness are more likely to lead to romantic experience than the reverse. Furthermore, the seeming effects of romantic experience are also varied in nature. In some cases, reciprocal relations exist, such as between sexual behavior and romantic experience. In other instances, dating seems to serve as a context for certain events to occur, such as substance use.

Importantly, the links between romantic experiences and adjustment are qualified by the nature of the experience. For example, casual dating experiences and serious romantic involvement were found to be related differently to our adjustment indices. The variation in outcomes is likely to be even greater when we take into account the full range of dimensions of romantic experiences described previously.

Thus, if a parent were to ask us if dating and romantic experiences were fraught with risks or full of potentials for positive growth, we would not answer with a simple yes or no. An answer that both are true would be accurate, but an even better answer would be that the effects depend heavily on the kinds of experiences or relationships their adolescent has.

In effect, we believe that dating and romantic experiences are like learning how to drive an automobile. Driving can be fun and rewarding, and it can lead one to places we want or need to go to. At the same time, it entails some risk whenever we turn the ignition key and start the car. Such risks are particularly likely to occur when we are young and inexperienced. And the degree of risk will depend on the nature of our car and how we drive it. We have learned a lot about how to make automobiles and roads safe. Our challenge as scientists is to identify the factors that lead to healthy and unhealthy romantic experiences, so that we may promote safe drives on the rocky road of adolescent romantic experience.

AUTHORS' NOTE

Preparation of this manuscript was supported by Grant 50106 from the National Institute of Mental Health.

REFERENCES

Abma, J., Chandra, A., Mosher, W., Peterson, L., & Piccinino, L. (1997). Fertility, family planning, and women's health: New data from the 1995 National Survey of Family Growth. National Center for Health Statistics. *Vital Health Statistics, 23 (No. 19)*.

Achenbach, T. M. (1991). *Integrative guide for the 1991 CBCL/4-18, YSR, and TRF Profiles*. Burlington: University of Vermont, Department of Psychiatry.

Adler, T. & Furman, W. (1988). A model for close relationships and relationship dysfunctions. In S.W. Duck (ed.), *Handbook of Personal Relationships: Theory, Research, and Inventions*, (pp. 211–229). London: Wiley.

Aro, H. & Taipale, V. (1987). The impact of timing of puberty on psychosomatic symptoms among fourteen- to sixteen-year-old Finnish girls. *Child Development, 58*, 261–269.

Beck, A.T., Rush, A. J., Shaw, B. F., & Emery, G. (1979). *Cognitive Therapy of Depression*. New York: Guilford.

Berscheid, E. & Reis, H. T. (1998). Attraction and close relationships. In D. T. Gilbert, S. T. Fiske, & G. Lindzey (eds.). *The Handbook of Social Psychology* (vol. 2, pp. 193–281). New York: McGraw-Hill.

Blum, R. W, Beuhring, T., & Rinehart, P. M. (2000). *Protecting Teens: Beyond Race, Income, and Family Structure*. Minneapolis, MN: Center for Adolescent Health, University of Minnesota.

Brent, D. A., Perper, J. A., Moritz, G., Baugher, M., Roth, C., Balach, L. et al. (1993). Stressful life events, psychopathology, and adolescent suicide: A case control study. *Suicide and Life-Threatening Behavior, 23*, 179–187.

Brown, B. B. (1999). 'You're going out with who?!': Peer group influences on adolescent romantic relationships. In W. Furman, B. B. Brown, & C. Feiring (eds.). *The Development of Romantic Relationships in Adolescence* (pp. 291–329). Cambridge, UK: Cambridge University Press.

Cauffman, E. & Steinberg, L. (1996). Interactive effects of menarcheal status and dating on diet and disordered eating among adolescent girls. *Developmental Psychology, 32*, 631–635.

Collins, L. M. & Graham, J. W. (2002). The effect of the timing and spacing of observations in longitudinal studies of tobacco and other drug use: Temporal design considerations. *Drug and Alcohol Dependence, 68*, 585–596.

Collins, A. W. (2003). More than myth: The developmental significance of romantic relationships during adolescence. *Journal of Research in Adolescence, 13*, 1–25.

Connolly, J., Furman, W., & Konarski, R. (2000). The role of peers in the emergence of romantic relationships in adolescence. *Child Development, 71*, 1395–1408.

Curran, P. J. (2000). A latent curve framework for the study of developmental trajectories in adolescent substance use. In J. S. Rose & L. Chassin (eds.) *Multivariate Applications in Substance Use Research: New Methods for New Questions*. Mahwah, NJ: Lawrence Erlbaum Associates, pp. 1–42.

Curran, P. J. & Willoughby, M. T. (2003). Implications of latent trajectory models for the study of developmental psychopathology, *Development and Psychopathology, 15*, 581–612.

Daley, S. E. & Hammen, C. (2002). Depressive symptoms and close relationships during the transition to adulthood: Perspectives from dysphoric women, their best friends, and their romantic partners. *Journal of Consulting & Clinical Psychology, 70 (1)*, 19–24.

Daniels, D. & Moos, R. H. (1990). Assessing life stressors and social resources among resources among adolescents: Applications to depressed youth. *Journal of Adolescent Research, 5(3)*, 268–289.

Derogatis, L. R. (1993). *Brief Symptom Inventory: Administration, Scoring, and Procedures Manual*. Minneapolis, MN: National Computer Systems.

Diamond, L. J. (2000). Passionate friendships among adolescent sexual-minority women. *Journal of Research on Adolescence, 10*, 191–209.

Diamond, L. M., Savin-Williams, R. C., & Dubé, E. M. (1999). Sex, dating, passionate friendships, and romance: Intimate peer relations among lesbian, gay, and bisexual adolescents. In W. Furman, B. B. Brown, & C. Feiring (eds.), *The Development of Romantic Relationships in Adolescence* (pp. 175–210). New York, NY: Cambridge University Press.

Dishion, T. J. & Medici Skaggs, N. (2000). An ecological analysis of monthly 'bursts' in early adolescent substance use. *Applied Developmental Science, 4*, 89–97.

Dowdy, B. B. & Kliewer, W. (1998). Dating, parent-adolescent conflict, and behavioral autonomy. *Journal of Youth and Adolescence, 27*, 473–492.

Dunphy, D. C. (1963). The social structure of urban adolescent peer groups. *Sociometry, 26*, 230–246.

Eggert, L. L., Herting, J. R., & Thompson, E. A. (1996). The drug involvement scale for adolescent (DISA). *Journal of Drug Education, 26*, 101–130.

Erikson, E.H. (1968). *Identity, Youth, and Crisis*. New York: Norton.

Feiring, C. (1996). Concepts of romance in 15-year-old adolescents. *Journal of Research on Adolescence, 6*, 181–200.

Flanagan, A. S. & Furman, W. C. (2000). Sexual victimization and perceptions of close relationships in adolescence. *Child Maltreatment, 5*, 350–359.

Franzoi, S. L., Davis, M. H., & Vasquez-Suson, K. A. (1994). Two social worlds: Social correlates and stability of adolescent status groups. *Journal of Personality and Social Psychology, 67*, 462–473.

Furman, W. (1996). The measurement of children and adolescent's perceptions of friendships: Conceptual and methodological issues. In W. M. Bukowski, A. F. Newcomb, & W. W. Hartup (eds.), *The Company They Keep: Friendships in Childhood and Adolescence*. pp. 41–65. Cambridge, MA: Cambridge University Press.

Furman, W. (1998). Friends and lovers: The role of peer relationships in adolescent romantic relationships. In W. A. Collins & B. Laursen (eds.), *Relationships as Developmental Contexts: The 30th Minnesota Symposia on Child Development*. pp. 133–154. Hillsdale, NJ: Erlbaum.

Furman, W. (2000, March). *Quantity or quality of romantic experience: What matters?* Paper presented at the meeting of the Society for Research in Adolescence, Chicago.

Furman, W. (2001). Working models of friendships. *Journal of Social and Personal Relationships, 18*, 583–602.

Furman, W. & Buhrmester, D. (1992). Age and sex differences in perceptions of networks of personal relationships. *Child Development, 63*, 103–115.

Furman, W. & Flanagan, A. (1997). The influence of earlier relationships on marriage: An attachment perspective. In W. K. Halford & H. J. Markman (eds.), *Clinical Handbook of Marriage and Couples Interventions*, John Wiley & Sons.

Furman, W. & Shaffer, L. (2003). The role of romantic relationships in adolescent development. In P. Florsheim (eds.) *Adolescent Romantic Relations and Sexual Behavior: Theory, Research, and Practical Implications* (pp. 3–22). Mahweh, NJ: Lawrence Erlbaum.

Furman, W. & Simon, V. A. (1999). Cognitive representations of romantic relationships. In W. Furman, B. B. Brown, & C. Feiring (eds.), *The Development of Romantic Relationships in Adolescence* (pp. 75–98). New York: Cambridge University Press.

Furman, W. & Simon, V. A. (2004) *Adolescents' working models, styles, and patterns of interact interactions with romantic partners*. Unpublished manuscript, University of Denver.

Furman, W., Simon, V. A., Shaffer, L., & Bouchey, H. A. (2002). Adolescents' representations of relationships with parents, friends, and romantic partners. *Child Development, 73*, 241–255.

Furman, W. & Wehner, E. A. (1992a). *Dating History Questionnaire.* Unpublished Measure, University of Denver.

Furman, W. & Wehner, E. A. (1992b). *Sexual Attitudes and Behavior Questionnaire.* Unpublished Measure, University of Denver.

Furman, W. & Wehner, E. A. (1994). Romantic views: Toward a theory of adolescent romantic relationships. In R. Montemayor, G. R. Adams, & T. P. Gullota (eds.), *Advances in Adolescent Development: Personal Relationships During Adolescence, vol. 6* (pp. 168–195). Thousand Oaks, CA: Sage.

Gayford, J. J. (1975). Wife battering: A preliminary survey of 100 cases. *British Medical Journal, 1*, 194–197.

Gray, M. R. & Steinberg, L. (1999). Adolescent romance and the parent-child relationship: A contextual perspective. In W. Furman, B. B. Brown, & C. Feiring, (eds.), *The Development of Romantic Relationships in Adolescence* (pp. 235–265). Cambridge, UK: Cambridge University Press.

Hand, L. S. & Furman, W. (2005a). *Other-sex friendships: An unexamined context for adolescent sexual experience.* Manuscript in preparation.

Hand, L. S. & Furman, W. (2005b). *Other-sex friendships in adolescence: Just friends?* Manuscript under review.

Harter, S. (1988). *Manual for the self-perception profile for adolescents.* Unpublished manuscript. University of Denver.

Joyner, K. & Udry, J. R. (2000). You don't bring me anything but down: Adolescent romance and depression. *Journal of Health and Social Behavior, 41*, 369–391.

Metzler, C. W., Noell, J., & Biglan, A. (1992). The validation of a construct of high-risk sexual behaviors in heterosexual adolescents. *Journal of Adolescent Research, 7*, 233–249.

Monroe, S. M., Rohde, P., Seeley, J. R. & Lewinsohn, P. M. (1999). Life events and depression in adolescence: Relationship loss as a prospective risk factor for first onset of major depressive disorder. *Journal of Abnormal Psychology, 108*, 606–614.

Neeman, J., Hubbard, J. & Masten, A. S. (1995). The changing importance of romantic relationship involvement to competence from late childhood to late adolescence. *Development and Psychopathology, 7*, 727–750.

Pawlby, S. J., Mills, A. & Quinton, D. (1997). Vulnerable adolescent girls: Opposite-sex relationships. *Journal of Child Psychology and Psychiatry, 38*, 909–920.

Pawlby, S. J., Mills, A., Taylor, A., & Quinton, D. (1997) Adolescent friendships mediating childhood adversity and adult outcome. *Journal of Adolescence, 20*, 633–644.

Quinton, D., Pickles, A., Maughan, B., & Rutter, M. (1993). Partners, peers, and pathways: Assortative pairing and continuities in conduct disorder, *Development and Psychopathology, 5*, 763–783.

Rodgers, J. L. (1996). Sexual transitions in adolescence. In J. A. Graber, J. Brooks-Gunn, & A. C. Peterson (eds.), *Transitions Through Adolescence: Interpersonal Domains and Context* (pp. 85–110). Mahwah, NJ: Erlbaum.

Roscoe, B. & Benaske, N. (1985). Courtship violence experienced by abused wives: Similarities in patterns of abuse. *Family Relations, 43*, 419–424.

Roth, M. A. & Parker, J. G. (2001). Affective and behavioral responses to friends who neglect their friends for dating partners: influences of gender, jealousy, and perspective. *Journal of Adolescence, 24*, 281–296.

Silverman, Raj, Mucci, L. A., & Hathaway, J. E. (2001). Dating violence against adolescent girls and associated substance usage, unhealthy weight control, sexual risk behavior, pregnancy, and suicidality. *Journal of American Medical Association, 286*, 572–579.

Simon, R. W., Eder, D. & Evans, C. (1972). The development of feeling norms underlying romantic love among adolescent females. *Social Psychological Quarterly, 55*, 29–46.

Spielberger, C. D. (1983). *State-Trait Anxiety Inventory (Form y)*. Redwood City, CA: Mind Garden.

Sullivan, H. S. (1953). *The Interpersonal Theory of Psychiatry*. New York: Horton & Co.

Thomas, B. S. & Hsiu, L. T. (1993). The role of selected risk factors in predicting adolescent drug use and its adverse consequences. *International Journal of the Addictions, 28*, 15–49.

Trost, M., Langan, E. J., & Kellar-Guenteher, Y. (1999). Not everyone listens when you 'just say no': Drug resistance in relational context. *Journal of Applied Communication Research, 27*, 120–138.

Wilson-Shockley, S. (1995). *Gender differences in adolescent depression: The contribution of negative affect.* Unpublished master's thesis. University of Illinois at Urbana-Champaign, Champaign, IL.

Wolfe, D. A. & Feiring, C. (2000). Dating violence through the lens of adolescent romantic relationships. *Child Maltreatment, 5*, 360–363.

Wolfe, D. A., Wekerle, C. & Scott, K. (2003). Dating violence prevention with at-risk youth: A controlled outcome evaluation. *Journal of Consulting & Clinical Psychology, 71*, 279–291.

Zimmer-Gembeck, M. J., Siebenbruner, J. & Collins, W. A. (2001). Diverse aspects of dating: associations with psychosocial functioning from early to middle adolescence. *Journal of Adolescence, 24*, 313–336.

CHAPTER 5

Individual Differences in Adolescent Dating and Adjustment

Brett Laursen
Florida Atlantic University, USA

Karen S. Mooney
University of Illinois, Springfield, USA

INTRODUCTION

Individual well-being is intimately bound to experiences in romantic relationships. For many, there is no greater source of happiness and disappointment than romantic relationships (Berscheid & Reis, 1998). Once considered unworthy of serious study because of their fleeting and inconsequential nature, scholars now recognize that early romantic relationships may make significant contributions to individual well-being (Collins, 2003). Adolescent dating involvement is positively associated with severity of mood swings (Larson & Richards, 1984), increases in externalizing problem behaviors (Zimmer-Gembeck, Siebenbruner, & Collins, 2001), and elevated rates of depression (Joyner & Udry, 2000). Paradoxically, there is also evidence that participation in romantic relationships is associated with feelings of positive self-worth (Connolly & Konarski, 1994) and an improved capacity for intimacy (Shulman, Levy-Schiff, Kedem, & Alon, 1997). Adolescents with romantic partners indicate that romantic relationships are one of their closest (Laursen & Williams, 1997) and most conflict-ridden relationships (Laursen, 1995). In their review of the literature, Furman and colleagues (this volume) conclude that romantic relationships proffer risks and benefits to adolescents: concurrent and over-time adjustment varies as a function of dating involvement and romantic experiences such that more short-term dating and earlier participation in romantic relationships predict increases in behavior problems and improvements in social competence.

Friends, Lovers and Groups: Key Relationships in Adolescence. Edited by Rutger C.M.E. Engels, Margaret Kerr and Håkan Stattin. Copyright © 2007 John Wiley & Sons, Ltd.

Based on this evidence, one might reasonably assume that romantic relation-ships uniquely predict adolescent outcomes, a conclusion we reached in the not-too-distant past (Laursen & Jensen-Campbell, 1999). We revisit this assertion in the present chapter. What is the influence of romantic relation-ships on adolescent adjustment? We argue that the answer to this question depends upon (a) whether romantic relationships are considered in isolation or in conjunction with other close relationships, and (b) whether analyses focus on associations between variables across populations or on patterns of individual differences unique to subgroups within a population. Variable-centered analyses that focus exclusively on romantic relationships are apt to paint a different picture of influence pathways than person-centered analy-ses that describe networks of close relationships that include romantic relation-ships alongside family and friend relationships. The former will inevitably emphasize the unique significance of romantic affiliations and the latter will emphasize outcomes linked to different patterns of close relationships.

The next section will provide a conceptual framework for the chapter. Three research models will be presented that describe the contributions of romantic relationships to adolescent outcomes. Two models focus exclusively on roman-tic relationships and the third places romantic relationships in the larger context of affiliations with friends and parents. Two analytic models will be presented that address the manner in which romantic relationships contribute to indivi-dual adjustment. The first identifies links between relationship variables and outcome variables, whereas the second describes differences between groups of individuals who share similar relationship attributes. In the remainder of the chapter, findings from Project STAR (Study of Teens and Relationships; Fur-man, Ho, & Low, this volume) will be presented that contrast conceptual and analytic models. The results support the view that outcomes previously ascribed to participation in romantic relationships may be better described as the product of a network of relationships that are of similar quality.

CONCEPTUAL AND ANALYTIC MODELS

Several conceptual models have been advanced to explain links between romantic relationships and adolescent outcomes in domains such as self-esteem, mental health, behavior problems, peer and family relations, and academic achievement (Collins, 2003). Our discussion shall focus on three models. The *romantic relationship status model* traces adolescent adjustment to participation in romantic relationships. This view holds that romantic relation-ships independently shape adolescent outcomes through unique provisions of the relationship, such as affiliation, attachment, caregiving, and sex. Experi-ence in romantic relationships is thought to be beneficial because it provides an opportunity to master new forms of socially desirable behavior, but this experience may also be detrimental because it provides an opportunity to master new forms of risk-taking behavior. In this chapter we give special consideration to social acceptance by peers, an outcome where romantic experience ought to be advantageous. Youth who participate in romantic relationships should be better accepted by age mates because this provides them with access to mixed-gender peer groups that are not open to youth without experience in romantic relationships.

The *romantic relationship quality model* emphasizes adolescent perceptions of relationship characteristics. This view holds that adolescent outcomes are not simply a product of participation in romantic relationships but are also related to the quality of romantic relationships. Positive relationships are thought to promote beneficial outcomes and negative relationships are thought to elicit detrimental outcomes. Social acceptance should be linked to romantic relationship quality to the extent that success in this new type of relationship fosters status, competence, and confidence with peers.

The *relationship network quality model* expands the focus beyond romantic relationships to include different types of close relationships. According to this view, adolescent adjustment is a function of the quality of experiences with family members, friends, and romantic relationships. Beneficial outcomes should increase as positive relationships increase; detrimental outcomes should reflect the number of negative relationships. Social acceptance should follow adolescents who participate in a network of supportive relationships because they have access to resources that enable them to overcome adversity and because they have the benefit of a broad array of positive experiences that promote self-worth and increase their attractiveness as interaction partners.

Two complementary analytic models are available to evaluate these research hypotheses: the variable approach and the person approach. These approaches carry fundamentally different assumptions about treatment of and generalizations from data (Magnusson, 2003). The variable approach concerns associations between variables where the focus of interest is on identifying links between constructs that are shared across individuals. Analyses of this sort are designed to identify processes that are found to a similar degree in all members of a group. Correlations, regressions, and structural equation models are typical of this approach. Variable-centered analytic models are appropriate for questions that concern the relative importance of predictor variables in determining outcome variables: how much do different dating experiences contribute to adolescent well-being? Which relationship characteristics best predict adolescent adjustment? In contrast, the person approach concerns individual differences where the focus of interest is on identifying groups of individuals who are similar way to one another on key constructs but different from other groups of individuals on the same constructs. This kind of analysis is designed to identify processes that are unique to individuals who share particular attributes. Profile, class, and cluster analyses are typical of this approach. Person-centered analytic models are appropriate for questions that concern differences in patterns of individual development or adjustment: Do adolescent romantic relationships work in concert with other close relationships? Which adolescents benefit from romantic relationships and which are at risk for adverse consequences?

ILLUSTRATIVE FINDINGS FROM PROJECT STAR

The sample and the method are described in considerable detail in the preceding chapter (Furman et al., this volume). Participants included 100 males and 100 females, ages 14 to 16 years old, who were recruited from public schools in a large metropolitan area in the western United States. Of this total, 170 (85%) reported that they had begun dating and 145 (72.5%) had participated in a long-term (one month or more) romantic relationship. Nearly all of these romantic relationships were heterosexual.

Participants completed a dating history questionnaire that included a measure of romantic experiences. For each of 16 items, adolescents indicated whether their experiences included establishing initial contact (e.g., going to parties and dances), dating (e.g., going out on dates with a group), participating in close relationships (e.g., having a committed relationship), and harboring romantic feelings (e.g., being in love). Items answered in the affirmative were summed to create a *romantic involvement* score. Participants also completed the Behavioral Systems Version of the Network of Relationships Inventory (Furman, 2000) that describes provisions of mother-child, friend, and long-term romantic relationships (prior long-term romantic relationships were described for adolescents who were not involved in long-term romantic relationships at the time of assessment). The present investigation focuses on perceived support in each of these relationships. This measure of perceived support included subscales that describe five facets of attachment and affiliation: (1) companionship; (2) seeks safe haven; (3) provides safe haven; (4) seeks a secure base; and (5) provides a secure base. For each relationship, adolescents rated 21 items on a scale ranging from *little or none* (1) to *the most* (5). Item scores were summed and averaged to create three separate variables: (1) *maternal support*; (2) *friend support*; and (3) *romantic partner support*. Finally, adolescents completed the Self-Perception Profile for Adolescents (Harter, 1988). Mothers and friends also completed the inventory to describe perceptions of the target adolescent's self-worth in several different domains. The present investigation concerns perceived social acceptance (e.g., some teenagers find it hard to make friends BUT for other teenagers it's pretty easy), a five-item subscale with responses that range from low self-worth (1) to high self-worth (4). Item scores were summed and averaged for each respondent. Participant, mother, and friend scores were summed and averaged to create a composite *social acceptance* score.

Romantic Relationship Status and Social Acceptance

Variable and person-centered analytic models were used to identify links between social acceptance and romantic relationship status. With variable-centered analyses, we tested the proposition that romantic involvement would be positively associated with social acceptance. The results of regression analyses in which social acceptance was the outcome variable revealed a

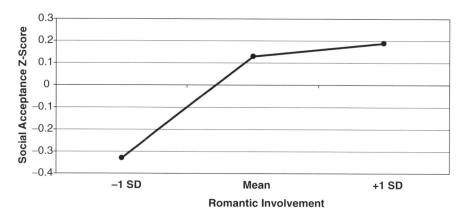

Figure 5.1 Curvilinear Association Between Romantic Involvement and Social Acceptance

linear association between romantic involvement and social acceptance ($\Delta R^2 = 0.13$, $\beta = 0.36$, $p < 0.01$) such that greater participation in romantic relationships was linked to higher levels of social acceptance. A curvilinear association ($\Delta R^2 = 0.13$, $\beta = -0.36$, $p < 0.01$) qualified this finding (see Figure 5.1). Social acceptance increased as romantic involvement increased from one standard deviation below the mean to the mean; increases in romantic involvement beyond the mean were not associated with statistically significant changes in social acceptance.

With person-centered analyses, we tested the proposition that adolescents with experience in a long-term romantic relationship would have higher levels of social acceptance than adolescents without experience in a long-term romantic relationship. Figure 5.2 describes results of a two (gender) by two (romantic relationship status) ANOVA with social acceptance as the

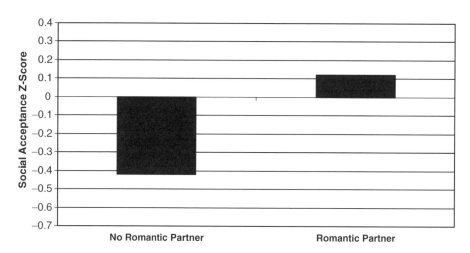

Figure 5.2 Social Acceptance as a Function of Romantic Relationship Status

dependent variable. Social acceptance was higher for those with long-term romantic relationships than for those without long-term romantic relationships, $F(1, 193) = 16.20$, $p < 0.01$.

Both sets of analyses provide support for the romantic relationship status model, which asserts that adolescent outcomes are a function of participation in romantic relationships. Specifically, degree of involvement predicted concurrent social acceptance and levels of social acceptance differed for those with and without experience in long-term romantic relationships.

Romantic Relationship Quality and Social Acceptance

Next, variable and person-centered analyses were used to explore social acceptance outcomes associated with romantic relationship quality. With variable-centered analyses, we tested the hypothesis that romantic partner support would be positively associated with social acceptance. These analyses were limited to the 145 participants with experience in a long-term romantic relationship. Results of regression analyses with social acceptance as the outcome variable failed to reveal statistically significant linear ($\Delta R^2 = 0.02$, $\beta = 0.15$, $p = 0.08$) or curvilinear ($\Delta R^2 = 0.00$, $\beta = 0.00$, $p = .99$) associations between romantic partner support and social acceptance.

With person-centered analyses, we tested the hypothesis that adolescents with high levels of support from romantic partners would have greater social acceptance than both adolescents with low levels of support from romantic partners and adolescents who did not participate in long-term romantic relationships. To this end, median splits were conducted to divide adolescents with experience in long-term romantic relationships into two groups: those with high romantic relationship support and those with low romantic

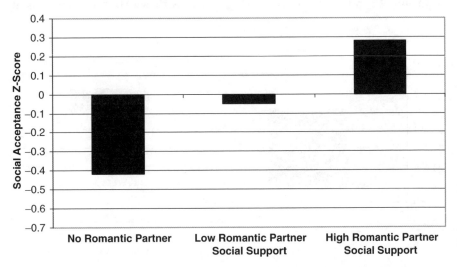

Figure 5.3   Social Acceptance as a Function of Romantic Relationship Quality

relationship support. Figure 5.3 describes results from a two (gender) by three (romantic relationship support groups) ANOVA with social acceptance as the dependent variable. Adolescents with high romantic relationship support were rated higher on social acceptance than adolescents with low romantic relationship support who, in turn, were rated higher on social acceptance than adolescents who had never participated in a long-term romantic relationship, $F(2, 189) = 11.11$, $p < 0.01$.

Thus, variable-centered and person-centered analyses differed in terms of support for the romantic relationship quality model. There were no reliable associations between romantic relationship support and social acceptance in variable-centered analyses. In contrast, results from person-centered analyses indicated that social acceptance varied not only according to participation in a romantic relationship, but also according to whether the relationship was high quality or low quality.

Relationship Network Quality and Social Acceptance

Finally, variable-centered and person-centered analyses were conducted to explore social acceptance outcomes associated with the quality of relationships in an interpersonal network. With variable-centered analyses, we tested the prediction that support from mothers, friends, and romantic partners would be positively associated with social acceptance. These analyses were limited to the 145 adolescents who reported participating in a long-term romantic relationship. Regression analyses were conducted with social acceptance as the outcome variable. No statistically significant associations emerged for gender, which was entered on the first step as a control variable ($\Delta R^2 = 0.00$, $\beta = 0.04$, $p = 0.63$). Statistically significant associations emerged on the second step for friend support such that higher levels of perceived social support from friends predicted greater concurrent social acceptance ($\Delta R^2 = 0.10$, $\beta = 0.31$, $p < 0.01$). On this same step, support from mothers ($\beta = -0.13$, $p = 0.14$) and support from romantic partners ($\beta = 0.11$, $p = 0.20$) were not reliably linked to social acceptance. There were no higher order interactions between gender and relationship support or between support from different relationships.

With person-centered analyses, we tested the prediction that adolescents with high levels of support from mothers, friends, and romantic partners would enjoy greater social acceptance than adolescents without high levels of support in these relationships. As a first step, adolescents were classified into groups on the basis of perceived relationship support. Using a median split procedure, adolescents with experience in long-term romantic relationships were classified as high or low on romantic partner support; the remaining adolescents comprised a group without experience in a long-term romantic relationship. Median split procedures were also applied to relationships with mothers and friends, yielding high and low support groups for each relationship. In the final step, each adolescent was uniquely categorized into one of 12 groups on the basis of perceived support from romantic partners (high, low, or none), mothers (high or low), and friends (high or low).

Latent profile analyses were conducted to identify types, which specify cells in which observed frequencies exceed expected frequencies at levels greater than chance. Three types emerged from these analyses. The first type included adolescents with high support from romantic partners, friends, and mothers; 46% of adolescents who reported high support in romantic relationships also reported high support in relationships with mothers and friends. The second type included adolescents with low support from romantic partners, friends, and mothers; 42% of adolescents who reported low support in romantic relationships also reported low support in relationships with mothers and friends. The third type included adolescents with low support from friends and mothers and no experience in a long-term romantic relationship; 45% of adolescents without romantic relationships reported low support from mothers and friends.

Figure 5.4 describes results from a two (gender) by three (relationship network quality types) ANOVA with perceived social support as the dependent variable. Adolescents with three high support relationships had greater social acceptance than adolescents with three low support relationships and adolescents without romantic relationships with low mother and low friend support, $F(2, 79) = 8.54$, $p < 0.01$.

Thus, findings from variable-centered and person-centered analyses differed in terms of support for the relationship network quality model. In variable-centered analyses, perceived support from friends was positively associated with social acceptance among adolescents with experience in long-term romantic relationships. There were no reliable associations, however, between social acceptance and support from mothers and romantic partners. In

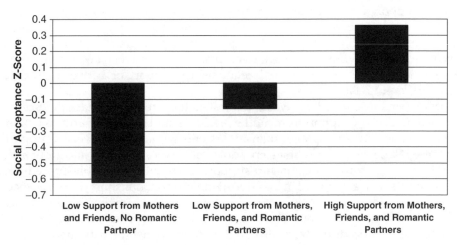

Figure 5.4 Social Acceptance as a Function of Romantic Relationship Network Quality Types

person-centered analyses, social acceptance varied according to the quality of the relationships in the network. Most adolescents with high quality romantic relationships also reported high quality mother and friend relationships, whereas most adolescents with low quality romantic relationships or no long-term romantic relationships also reported low quality relationships with mothers and friends. Social acceptance was greater for adolescents embedded in a network of supportive relationships than for those who lacked a network of support.

CONCLUSIONS

The results illustrate the importance of matching conceptual models with appropriate analytic tools. Most previous research on the significance of adolescent romantic relationships does not include the range of conceptual and analytical models described in this chapter. Typically, romantic relationships are the sole focus of inquiry, with analyses contrasting adolescents with and without romantic partners or analyses exploring whether outcomes vary as a function of the extent or timing of participation in romantic relationships. In those few instances where relationship quality is considered, the focus tends to be on the contributions of romantic relationships. We argue that the limited scope of prior research may give rise to the misleading impression that romantic relationships uniquely shape adolescent adjustment. The analyses presented in this chapter demonstrate that participation in and quality of romantic relationships must be considered in the context of the broader quality of the entire network of close relationships. These findings suggest that for most adolescents, romantic relationships operate in concert with parent and friend relationships to shape individual adjustment.

We have demonstrated that variable-centered analyses link social acceptance to romantic involvement but not to romantic relationship quality. Put simply, greater participation in romantic relationships is associated with higher levels of social acceptance. These results could be interpreted as providing support for the romantic relationship status model, which suggests that beneficial outcomes flow from participation in romantic relationships. But person-centered analyses tell a different story. Differences between adolescents with and without romantic relationships are more accurately described as differences between adolescents with high quality romantic relationships, adolescents with low quality romantic relationships, and adolescents with no experience in long-term romantic relationships. These differences, in turn, are more aptly characterized as differences between adolescents embedded in high and low quality relationship networks. These person-centered analyses provide support for a relationship network model, which suggests that romantic relationships combine with other close relationships to shape adolescent outcomes.

This is not the first study to identify additive relationship effects. Previous findings indicate that optimal adolescent outcomes tend to be associated with high levels of support in family and friend relationships (e.g., Scholte, van Lieshout, & van Aken, 2001; Way & Robinson, 2003), but this is one of the first studies to suggest that romantic relationships should not be excluded from networks of influential relationships. New evidence from Project STAR underscores this point (Laursen, Furman, & Mooney, 2006). Prospective reports indicate that global self-worth, friendship competence, and romantic competence were all highest for adolescents reporting high levels of support from mothers, friends, and romantic partners, and lowest for adolescents without romantic relationships reporting low levels of support from mothers and friends. Conclusions about findings that link romantic relationships to mental health and behavior problems (e.g., Joyner & Udry, 2000; Zimmer-Gembeck et al., 2001) should be carefully qualified because these associations may also be a product of the network of relationships in which romantic affiliations are embedded.

In conclusion, adolescent romantic relationships tend to be similar in quality to those with friends and mothers. For youth with these relationship networks, it does not make sense to attribute an outcome to a particular affiliation. Rather, outcomes are more likely to be the product of a constellation of close relationships. This implies that differences attributed to romantic relationships in past research may be more accurately described as differences between adolescents who share a network of high or low quality relationships. Our analyses suggest that beneficial outcomes tend to prevail among adolescents embedded in networks of supportive relationships and we suspect that future research will reveal that detrimental outcomes are most common among adolescents grounded in networks of negative relationships.

AUTHORS' NOTE

Brett Laursen received support for the preparation of this chapter from the U.S. National Institute of Mental Health (MH58116).

REFERENCES

Berscheid, E. & Reis, H. T. (1998). Attraction and close relationships. In D. T. Gilbert, S. T. Fiske, & G. Lindzey (eds.), *The Handbook of Social Psychology* (4th ed., pp. 193–281). New York: Addison-Wesley.

Collins, W. A. (2003). More than myth: The developmental significance of romantic relationships during adolescence. *Journal of Research on Adolescence, 13,* 1–24.

Connolly, J. A. & Konarski, R. (1994). Peer self-concept in adolescence: Analysis of factor structure and of associations with peer experience. *Journal of Research on Adolescence, 4,* 385–403.

Furman, W. (2000). *Network of Relationships Inventory: Behavioral Systems Version.* Unpublished measure, University of Denver.

Harter, S. (1988). *Manual for the Self-Perception Profile for Adolescents.* Denver: University of Denver.

Joyner, K. & Udry, J. R. (2000). You don't bring me anything but down: Adolescent romance and depression. *Journal of Health and Social Behavior, 41*, 369–391.

Larson, R. & Richards, M. H. (1994). *Divergent Realities: The Emotional Lives of Mothers, and Adolescents.* New York: Basic Books.

Laursen, B. (1995). Conflict and social interaction in adolescent relationships. *Journal of Research on Adolescence, 5*, 55–70.

Laursen, B., Furman, W., & Mooney, K. S. (2006). Predicting interpersonal competence and self-worth from adolescent relationships and relationship networks: Person-centered and variable-centered perspectives. *Merrill-Palmer Quarterly 52*, 572–600.

Laursen, B. & Jensen-Campbell, L. A. (1999). The nature and functions of social exchange in adolescent romantic relationships. In W. Furman, B. B. Brown, & C. Feiring (eds.), *The Development of Romantic Relationships in Adolescence* (pp. 50–74). New York: Cambridge University Press.

Laursen, B. & Williams, V. A. (1997). Perceptions of interdependence and closeness in family and peer relationships among adolescents with and without romantic partners. In S. Shulman & W. A. Collins (eds.), *New Directions for Child Development. Romantic relationships in adolescence: Developmental perspectives* (No. 78, pp. 3–20). San Francisco: Jossey-Bass.

Magnusson, D. (2003). The person approach: Concepts, measurement models, and research strategy. In S. C. Peck & R. W. Roeser (eds.), *New Directions for Child and Adolescent Development. Person-centered approaches to studying development in context* (No. 101, pp. 3-23). San Francisco: Jossey-Bass.

Scholte, R. H. J., van Lieshout, C. F. M., & van Aken, M. A. G. (2001). Perceived relational support in adolescence: Dimensions, configurations, and adolescent adjustment. *Journal of Research on Adolescence, 11*, 71–94.

Shulman, S., Levy-Shiff, R., Kedem, P., & Alon, E. (1997). Intimate relationships among adolescent romantic partners and same-sex friends: Individual and systemic perspectives. In S. Shulman & W. A. Collins (eds.), *New Directions for Child Development. Romantic Relationships in Adolescence: Developmental Perspectives* (No. 78, pp. 37–51). San Francisco: Jossey-Bass.

Way, N. & Robinson, M. G. (2003). A longitudinal study of the effects of family, friends, and school experiences on the psychological adjustment of ethnic minority, low SES adolescents. *Journal of Adolescent Research, 18*, 324–346.

Zimmer-Gembeck, M., Siebenbruner, J., & Collins, W. A. (2001). The divergent influence of romantic involvement on individual and social functioning from early to middle adolescence. *Journal of Adolescence, 24*, 313–336.

CHAPTER 6

Three Perspectives on Gender Differences in Adolescent Sexual Development

Roy F. Baumeister and Ginnette C. Blackhart
Florida State University, USA

INTRODUCTION

Adolescence is a period marked by several important transitions. There is the transition out of the role of economically dependent child and into an adult occupational role, or at least into the commitment to a path designed to lead to such an occupational role. There are transitions in relationships, with the beginnings of romantic attachment. There is also the movement to adopt the role of sexually ready and sexually active member of society.

The purpose of this chapter is to give an overview of three perspectives that provide context for the sexual transitions of adolescence. These three themes are largely irrelevant to preadolescent life but become important as the adolescent begins to explore sexuality, and they eventually become more or less unavoidable facts of life insofar as they characterize adult sexuality. The first author has written more extensively about each of these themes elsewhere, and although the central ideas have been featured in his work, they all emerged from large-scale reviews of previously published studies by other researchers.

The three themes are as follows. First, we will cover gender differences in erotic plasticity, which is to say the degree to which sexual responses are shaped by social, cultural, and situational factors. Second, we will cover gender differences in sex drive, defined as the frequency and intensity of sexual motivation. Third, we will describe a theory of sexual economics, which

Friends, Lovers and Groups: Key Relationships in Adolescence. Edited by Rutger C.M.E. Engels, Margaret Kerr and Håkan Stattin. Copyright © 2007 John Wiley & Sons, Ltd.

is an interpersonal theory of heterosexual interactions based on social exchange theory, and which recognizes that the two genders typically play different and complementary roles in the exchange process.

EROTIC PLASTICITY

Without question, the behavioral and role transitions of adolescence are rooted partly in biology and partly in the sociocultural context. At the broadest level, it is apparent that adolescence has some universal features, probably indicative of biological realities, and it also exhibits significant variation, much of which can be understood as reflecting the historical and cultural context. For example, historians suggest that the view of adolescence as a time of identity crisis, marked by uncertain and fluctuating self-definitions and as a period of awkwardness and vulnerability is a relatively recent historical development peculiar to the modern era. In contrast, the view of adolescence as a time of proneness to trouble-making, mischief, and sporadic rebelliousness is not at all a modern invention and instead appears to have been the norm at most times and places (Kett, 1977; Stone, 1977). The proneness to trouble may be rooted in the hormonal changes associated with adolescence; the identity crisis may reflect how modern culture offers and withholds roles and opportunities to adolescents.

Sexuality is likewise subject to influence by both nature and culture, and indeed the relative importance of natural, biological causes versus social, cultural causes has been the focus of ongoing disputes and periodic paradigm shifts in sexuality theory. There is no simple answer as to whether the sexual transitions of adolescence should be put down to biology or to social influences.

My own contribution to the nature–nurture debate about sexuality has been to present a large amount of evidence indicating that the balance between natural and cultural influences on sexuality differs by gender (Baumeister, 2000). More precisely, female sexuality is less directly tied to natural and biological causes than is male sexuality, whereas the sociocultural factors loom larger in female. I use the term *erotic plasticity* to refer to the degree to which the sex drive is shaped by social, cultural, and biological factors. Women have higher erotic plasticity than men. This is neither inherently good nor bad, but the difference is probably essential to understanding gender differences in sexuality, including adolescent sexuality.

The difference in erotic plasticity can be seen in three broad patterns in the data about sexual responses (Baumeister, 2000). First, higher plasticity entails that as a female moves through her adolescent and adult life and her social circumstances change, her sexuality will exhibit much greater change than would be expected from a male. Many a young man's sexual tastes emerge soon after puberty and remain relatively constant for decades thereafter, whereas a young woman's sexual responses may continue to change and evolve throughout her life. Homosexual versus heterosexual orientation, for example, tends to be fixed and stable in men, whereas women can move back and forth between the two categories and seemingly find it easier to have consecutive partners with different genders (Diamond, 1998, 2003). Men try to keep their total amount of sexual activity rather constant, such as by compensating for a loss of an active sexual partner by increasing their frequency of masturbation, whereas women report far more peaks and valleys, even having periods of no sexual activity whatsoever alternating with periods of frequent, intense, and highly satisfying sex (Kinsey et al., 1953). Even when gender, type, and availability of partners remain the same, females may change their preferences over time regarding various practices such as oral and anal sex, whereas the male's preferences remain more stable.

The second broad pattern indicative of erotic plasticity is that particular social, cultural, and situational variables have greater impact on female sexuality than on male. These include religion and education. Thus, the most educated women have very different sex lives from the least educated, and the same is true of the most versus the least religious women, whereas for men the corresponding differences are much smaller (see especially Laumann et al., 1994). Some sociocultural influences are especially apparent at adolescence. For instance, the sexual activities of adolescent girls seem substantially influenced by their peer groups, to a much greater extent than is true of boys (Mirande, 1968; Sack et al., 1984; Billy & Udry, 1985). Likewise, parental influences and behaviors appear to have a greater and more lasting impact on the sex lives of their daughters than of their sons (Lewis, 1973; Newcomer & Udry, 1987; Thornton & Camburn, 1987). Of course, there are some alternative explanations in both sets of findings, but these do not seem adequate to account for all the evidence. For example, it is possible that parents try harder to influence their daughters than their sons about proper sexual behavior; but even such factors as parental divorce seem to affect the daughter's sexuality more than the son's, and it is implausible to view parental divorce as a deliberate attempt to change the daughter's sexual responses.

The third pattern relevant to plasticity is low consistency between attitudes and behaviors. The theoretical basis for this is that broad attitudes will predict behavior successfully most strongly when the immediate situational context is largely irrelevant (i.e., when the sexual response is the same across many different circumstances). Because female sexual responses depend on the situation, including many very specific issues of meaning and interpretation, these responses will correlate less well with broad measures of attitude. For example, the Laumann et al. (1994) survey asked people whether they found the idea of same-gender sex appealing and whether they had engaged in same-gender sexual activity in the past year. These items were highly correlated for men but relatively uncorrelated among women. A woman may find the idea of lesbian sex unappealing or even distasteful in the abstract, but then she may fall in love with a particular woman and have a sexual relationship with her (see also Diamond, 2003). Conversely, many women may like the idea of same-gender sex in the abstract but never seek out or find an opportunity to engage in it. For men, the wanting and the doing are much more closely linked.

One sign of attitude-behavior inconsistency in adolescence involves engaging in sexual activity of which one disapproves. Multiple studies have found that adolescent girls are more prone than adolescent boys to have sex or to have some form of sexual activity to which they have moral or other objections, and they may continue over some time to engage in that activity while continuing to disapprove (Christensen & Carpenter, 1962; Croake & James, 1973; Antonovsky et al., 1978). Another sphere of possible inconsistency, also relevant to adolescents, involves infidelity, especially engaging in minor sexual activity (short of intercourse) with someone else when one already has a relationship partner. Among adolescent and young adult males, attitudes toward such 'extradyadic' activity predict behavior rather closely, whereas the correlations are substantially weaker for adolescent and young adult females (Hansen, 1987). Again, this is probably because the girl's and woman's responses depend more heavily on the immediate situation and context, and so the broad attitudes are less predictive.

Our conclusion from reviewing an extensive body of research is that the gender difference in erotic plasticity is quite solid and hence very unlikely to be overturned by subsequent findings, though the reasons for it remained less clear. Also less clear is whether there are any reversals or exceptions. The most likely exception was based in a smattering of findings suggesting that male sexuality is actually open to sociocultural influence during childhood. If so, then the transition of puberty is fundamentally different for males as compared to females. Puberty for a female means the start of a long sexual odyssey that may be marked by a series of changes. The ongoing plasticity means that a long and unpredictable series of social and cultural factors will come to play important roles, at unpredictable intervals, in shaping the course of the woman's sex life. In contrast, puberty for males signifies a sharp reduction in openness to influence by social and cultural factors. The male sex drive after puberty is likely to be experienced as strong and largely immutable, and the main long-term change is the gradual reduction in urge that accompanies aging.

The gender difference in erotic plasticity has a variety of further implications for adolescent development. One is that sexual self-knowledge will be much more difficult for girls than for boys (see Vanwesenbeeck et al., 1998). Higher plasticity means that the sexual self is essentially a moving target, and so even if a woman or girl manages to achieve a deep and thorough understanding of her current sexuality, that understanding might be obsolete a year or two later, because her sexuality is capable of extensive change. Another implication is that adapting to changing circumstances may be easier for the girl than for the boy, insofar as plasticity confers the advantage of adaptability.

STRENGTH OF SEX DRIVE

The possibility that there is a gender difference in sex drive has been a perennial theme of both popular culture and researchers' theorizing. Many popular television comedies and other entertainments use jokes and dramatic themes based on the idea that men want sex more than women. Sex theorists have however questioned these popular views, and some experts such as Hyde and DeLamater (1997) have not only rejected the view that the male sex drive is stronger, but even explicitly proposed that in the long run the truth will emerge that the female sex drive is stronger than the male. The latter view was supported in part by feminist ideology, which seemingly feared that having a weaker sex drive would be viewed as a bad thing and which therefore refused to countenance the view that men might want sex more than women.

Given the controversy, Baumeister, Catanese, and Vohs (2001) set out to review the literature on possible gender differences in strength of sex drive. Direct, unambiguous measures of sexual motivation are, of course, not readily available. On self-ratings of strength of sex drive, men score higher than women (Mercer & Kohn, 1979), but it is possible that such differences reflect a priori theories, biased information processing, differing prescriptions for socially desirable responses, or other confounding factors. Hence, Baumeister et al. (2001) approached the question by trying to imagine two women who differed in strength of sex drive and asking what behavioral differences one would predict based on the drive difference. Then they took that list of behavioral differences relevant to sex drive and surveyed published studies for possible evidence of gender differences.

By and large, every type of measure and every study pointed to the conclusion that men desire sex more than women (Baumeister et al., 2001). Men think about sex more often than women (Eysenck, 1971; Laumann et al., 1994) and are sexually aroused more often than women (Eysenck, 1971; Beck et al., 1991). Men have more sexual fantasies, involving more partners and a greater variety of sex acts, than women (Leitenberg & Henning, 1995). Men desire sex more often early in a relationship (McCabe, 1987), in a long-term stable relationship (Ard, 1977), and after many years of a relationship (including old age; Johannes & Avis, 1997; Bergström-Walan & Nielsen, 1990). Men also desire sex more when no relationship is involved (Beck et al., 1991). Men desire more partners than women (Buss & Schmitt, 1993) and desire a greater variety of sex acts (Laumann et al., 1994). Men masturbate more frequently than women (Oliver & Hyde, 1993; Laumann et al., 1994), and non-masturbating men are less likely than non-masturbating women to cite a lack of desire as the reason for abstaining (Arafat & Cotton, 1974). Men initiate sex more often and refuse it less often (Brown & Auerback, 1981). Men make more sacrifices and take more risks to get sex (Laumann et al., 1994). Men have a harder time abstaining from sex (Leiblum & Rosen, 1988) and are less successful at celibacy or abstinence (Murphy, 1992), including in contexts such as a religious commitment in which the single standard of sacred commitment to total abstinence is equally clear and equally accepted by both genders. Boys commence sexual activity sooner after puberty than girls (Lewis, 1973; Asayama, 1975; Leigh et al., 1994). Males have more positive attitudes toward genitals (both their own and their partners') than females

(Reinholtz & Muehlenhard, 1995). No findings indicated that women had more frequent or more intense sexual desires than men.

It is important to distinguish the sex drive from other variables that are sometimes confused with it. The capability for sexual response and performance is not the same as the desire for sex. Women are generally regarded as more capable than men of having multiple orgasms and of being able to continue having sex immediately after an orgasm, but this capability is not the same as desire. Also, enjoyment is not the same as sex drive. The question of which gender enjoys sex more is very difficult to answer in any reliable manner. Our tentative conclusion is that female sexual enjoyment is more variable than male sexual enjoyment, particularly at the low end of the spectrum (i.e., women may have more neutral and bad sexual experiences than men), and it is possible that women also have higher peaks of supreme sexual enjoyment. For present purposes, the fact that women have less desire for sex does not mean that women lack enjoyment of sex.

Feminists and other politically motivated theorists may have been politically correct to deny any gender difference in sex drive or to propose that women's sex drive is stronger than men's, but that view is scientifically untenable. Although on scientific grounds one may be dismayed by a reluctance to look at the facts, the actual sex lives of adolescents are undoubtedly touched by the political climate and its pressures. The same forces that made some portions of the research community refuse to consider that men want sex more than women will quite possibly conspire to make life difficult for adolescents whose feelings indicate a reality that cannot be acknowledged.

The gender difference in sex drive is indisputable but not necessarily constant. The distributions may overlap some, so it is possible that some couples will find themselves coping with the reverse pattern in which the woman wants sex more than the man. Some research has identified a statistically unusual but genuine category of women with very high sex drives (Blumberg, 2003). Also, even given the general pattern of men wanting sex more than women, the size of the discrepancy may vary. While falling in love, when rising intimacy produces a high degree of passion, it is likely that women's desires are close in magnitude to those of men, and many couples are probably misled by this period into expecting that their lives together will be marked by a close matching of sexual desires and wishes. When the bloom of romantic passion subsides, however, the couple may revert to their respective baselines, and they will find that the man wants sex more than the woman (see Baumeister & Bratslavsky, 1999). Another plausible moderating variable is age, and it may well be that during adolescence, or at least during certain parts of it, girls' sexual desires will be comparable to boys'. Such fluctuations in the discrepancy between male and female sex drive are likely to complicate further the adolescent transitions such as the establishment of relationships on foundations and expectations that cannot be sustained over many years.

SEXUAL ECONOMICS

No doubt many adolescents' first sexual awakenings involve private, solitary experiences such as masturbation, but for most people sex becomes a deeply interpersonal endeavor, and satisfaction is generally sought in dyadic inter-actions. Sex between partners often requires some degree of negotiation. Given that men and women have different tastes, preferences, and wishes, some degree of compromise or mutual understanding must often be reached.

The central idea behind the theory of sexual economics (see Baumeister & Vohs, 2004; also Baumeister & Tice, 2000) is that most cultures and societies treat female sexuality as a valued resource and basis for social exchange. Men will or must, therefore, give women other resources in exchange for sex. These may include attention, respect, love, commitment, and money, among others. Male sexuality is typically not treated as having any inherent value. The precise value that a woman gets in return for her sexual favors depends on many factors that reflect the operation of a market community subject to economic principles. At one extreme, which may be exemplified in the example of rock music groupies, a young woman may have sex with a man in return for little more than the attention that he pays to her during the sex act itself. At the other extreme, a man may have to make a lifetime commitment to the woman to forsake all other women and share all his wealth, property, and future earnings with her before they have their first intercourse or even first kiss. It is safe to assume that coming to understand these contingencies in the sexual marketplace is an important aspect of the adolescent transition in most places.

Why a sexual marketplace should exist at all is an interesting question that can, perhaps, be answered from multiple perspectives, including evolutionary and feminist ones, but a simple and proximal answer would invoke the gender difference in sex drive. Social exchange theorists dating back to Waller and Hill (1951) have cited the 'principle of least interest,' which means that whichever person wants something less is in the stronger bargaining position, and the person who wants it more must often sweeten the deal by offering other incentives. Hence women may desire sex, but as long as men desire it more, they may have to give the woman some added inducements.

There is a wide assortment of evidence about how the sexual marketplace operates, and some are of particular relevance to adolescent sexuality. The so-called laws of supply and demand insist that the local price depends on the relative balance between those two factors. In sex, women constitute the supply, men the demand. A classic work by Guttentag and Secord (1983) confirmed that sexual morality fluctuates with the sex ratio. When there is an oversupply of women relative to men, sex is relatively free and easy, and the women cannot expect serious commitment or much else in exchange for sex. In contrast, when there are more men than women, the price of sex rises steeply, and sex tends to be restricted to highly committed relationships. Such factors may be especially important in adolescent life, because many adolescents attend single-gender schools or live in other environments where it is not possible to expect that there are enough partners to go around for everyone of both genders. Learning about dating and sex must be quite different if you are in the majority as opposed to the minority gender, and in sexual economics, the majority does not rule. Rather, in sex as in other marketplaces, scarcity confers an advantage in bargaining.

The economic perspective can illuminate some seemingly paradoxical patterns in teen sexuality. A girl becomes pregnant by having intercourse with a male, and so the fewer males around, the smaller her risk of pregnancy ought to be. Barber (2000) showed however that the reverse is true: the fewer available males, the higher the rate of teen pregnancy. The explanation is that a shortage of male partners forces young women to compete harder for their attention, and this typically includes lowering the price of sex. When there are not enough young men around, the young women consent more readily to risky sex.

The economic analysis also illuminates likely motivations behind sexual curiosity and sexual norms. For a young person entering the sexual market-place, the activities of others are of more than passing interest. Each couple may negotiate its pace of sexual activities between themselves, but their decisions are not entirely divorced from the community norms. In particular, if a particular man gives his girlfriend a higher than normal price for sex, then she is getting a relatively good deal and he a relatively bad one, and the reverse is true if she accepts a lower than typical price. A girl may quickly develop a reputation as 'cheap' (note the economic term) if she grants her sexual favors in return for less than what other girls accept.

Intrasex competition is probably the norm everywhere, but there may be gender differences in such competition, and these will conform to the economic patterns. Sellers seek to increase their price by making themselves more attractive by advertising, such as by wearing sexy outfits.

Furthermore, in economic history, collusion among sellers has been far more common and successful than collusion among buyers. Sellers control the supply, and if they can form a cartel and cooperate, they can restrict the supply artificially and drive up the price. The supply of sex depends in part on the ratio of available women to men, but it also depends on those women's willingness to have sex. It would be economically rational for women to try to influence each other to restrain their sexual activities, just as the member nations of OPEC (the Organization of Petroleum Exporting Countries) seek to restrict each others' oil production so as to keep the world supply somewhat short and therefore keep its price high. Consistent with this view, the available evidence suggests that the cultural suppression of female sexuality is mainly rooted in the female community, and nearly all social pressures on women to restrict their sexual activity come from other women (see Baumeister & Twenge, 2002, for review).

All of this makes the female sexual role and its decision-making process more complicated than the male. A woman's sexual desires, plus any advantage she may gain toward attracting her most desired mate by under-bidding the competition (that is, offering him sex at a lower price than what is typical among her peers) may push her toward offering sex rather readily and easily. However, her long-term self-interest, and the pressure from the female community (in which she has a self-interested stake too), would push her toward sexual restraint. Her actual decisions would be shaped by seeking a balance between those opposing forces. In contrast, for a male, there are no such competing forces, and rational self-interest would simply dictate that he seek the most and best sex he can get for the lowest price.

IMPLICATIONS FOR ADOLESCENT DEVELOPMENT

I have indicated three major gender differences in sexuality. It is reasonable to assume that baby girls and boys are not born with the knowledge of any of them, and that by the time they become adults most people have been affected by them. Adolescence is therefore likely to be marked by the emergence of these forces and a recognition, if not of the patterns themselves, at least of their implications and consequences.

The sexual economics theory asserts that female sexuality has exchange value whereas male sexuality does not. Young people must gradually acquire this knowledge, as well as come to understand how to play their roles in the sexual marketplace. Shifting norms and misleading public ideologies may complicate the matter further. For example, most western cultures are currently awash with talk of gender equality in all spheres, but men are still expected to pay for most of the expenses on dates. (One older single acquaintance recently remarked, 'The women I date are nearly all liberated feminist types, at least until the check comes.') Once the rules of exchange are learned, men and women must gradually learn how to compete successfully in the sexual marketplace, which requires knowing how attractive one is and developing strategies to increase that attractiveness, as well as how to negotiate an outcome that is advantageous to the self (e.g., for a woman, getting the most respect and commitment that she can in exchange for sex). Most girls will also come under conflicting pressures from boys and boyfriends who encourage her to explore more sex, versus the pressures from the female community that sets limits to appropriate behavior and punishes girls who are seen as exceeding those limits.

The differences in plasticity and sex drive probably emerge during adolescence. How much people recognize them is far from clear, and there is much less need for an individual to appreciate those differences accurately than there is need, say, to learn the working rules of the sexual marketplace. At least, those gender differences will make it more difficult for men and women to understand each other using empathy and intuition, because their own experiences will be misleading as to what someone of the other gender is likely to be feeling. It may be difficult for adolescent boys to realize that their girlfriends are not as sexually driven as they are, and by the same token many girls may have trouble appreciating how intense the sexual feelings of their boyfriends are. In addition, if the female sex drive is nearly comparable to that of the male sex drive during adolescence or at the beginning of a relationship, men may have trouble understanding why a woman's sex drive is lower either during young adulthood or later in a long-term relationship, as the female sex drive is likely to decrease. Likewise, plasticity is probably experienced in terms of the importance of situational context and meaning for sex. Boys may find girls' sexuality mysterious, unfathomably complicated, and marked by seemingly unpredictable fluctuations on the basis of minor factors, whereas girls may perceive the boys' as sexually simple, predictable, and insensitive to a wide range of subtleties.

Additionally, how the state of the sexual economy during adolescence affects sexual development and sexual behaviors in the future should be considered. Does the sexual economy of the community during adolescence affect later sexual behavior? Is there an interaction between the sexual economy in adolescence and erotic plasticity on later sexual behavior? For instance, does how a girl learns what her sexual marketplace roles are in adolescence affect her sexual behaviors and how she views sex in adulthood, or does her greater erotic plasticity allow her to adjust accordingly? Does what a boy learns about his role in the sexual marketplace in adolescence affect his sexual behavior, and does this behavior remain stable as men have lower erotic plasticity, not allowing him to adjust to a different sexual economy? If the sexual economy changes, how readily can a man or woman adjust to these changes? These are questions for future research to study.

Adolescence commences when the body is ready for mating and reproduction, but in most cases the mind and self have considerable work to do before the person can successfully form a sexual relationship. This work includes gaining some understanding of oneself and one's body, some understanding of the opposite gender and how to deal with them, and of the community or marketplace in which sexual transactions take place. An appreciation of gender differences in erotic plasticity, in strength of sex drive, and in marketplace roles may help researchers conceptualize and study the processes of adolescence that take a mostly asexual preadolescent and eventually produce a sexually functioning adult.

REFERENCES

Antonovsky, H. F., Shoham, I., Kavenocki, S., Modan, B., & Lancet, M. (1978). Sexual Attitude - behavior discrepancy among Israeli adolescent girls. *Journal of Sex Research, 14*, 260–272.

Arafat, I. S. & Cotton, W. L. (1974). Masturbation practices of males and females. *Journal of Sex Research, 10*, 293–307.

Ard, B. N. (1977). Sex in lasting marriages: A longitudinal study. *Journal of Sex Research, 13*, 274–285.

Asayama, S. (1975). Adolescent sex development and adult sex behavior in Japan. *Journal of Sex Research, 11*, 91–112.

Barber, N. (2000). On the relationship between country sex ratios and teen pregnancy rates: A replication. *Cross-Cultural Research, 34*, 26–37.

Baumeister, R. F. (2000). Gender differences in erotic plasticity: The female sex drive as socially flexible and responsive. *Psychological Bulletin, 126*, 347–374.

Baumeister, R. F. & Bratslavsky, E. (1999). Passion, intimacy, and time: Passionate love as a function of change in intimacy. *Personality and Social Psychology Review, 3*, 49–67.

Baumeister, R. F., Catanese, K. R., & Vohs, K. D. (2001). Is there a gender difference in strength of sex drive? Theoretical views, conceptual distinctions, and a review of relevant evidence. *Personality and Social Psychology Review, 5*, 242–273.

Baumeister, R. F. & Tice, D. M. (2000). *The Social Dimension of Sex*. New York: Allyn & Bacon.

Baumeister, R. F. & Twenge, J. M. (2002). Cultural suppression of female sexuality. *Review of General Psychology, 6*, 166–203.

Baumeister, R. F. & Vohs, K. D. (2004). Sexual economics: Sex as a female resource for social exchange in heterosexual interactions. *Personality and Social Psychology Review, 8*, 339–363.

Beck, J. G., Bozman, A. W., & Qualtrough, T. (1991). The experience of sexual desire: Psychological correlates in a college sample. *Journal of Sex Research, 28*, 443–456.

Bergström-Walan, M. B. & Nielsen, H. H. (1990). Sexual expression among 60 to 80-year-old men and women: A sample from Stockholm, Sweden. *Journal of Sex Research, 27*, 289–295.

Billy, J. O. & Udry, J. R. (1985). The influence of male and female best friends on adolescent sexual behavior. *Adolescence, 20*, 21–32.

Blumberg, E.S. (2003). The lives and voices of highly sexual women. *Journal of Sex Research, 40*, 146–157.

Brown, M. & Auerback, A. (1981). Communication patterns in initiation of marital sex. *Medical Aspects of Human Sexuality, 15*, 105–117.

Buss, D. M., & Schmitt, D. P. (1993). Sexual strategies theory: A contextual evolutionary analysis of human mating. *Psychological Review, 100*, 204–232.

Christensen, H. T. & Carpenter, G. R., (1962). Value–behavior discrepancies regarding premarital coitus in three Western cultures. *American Sociological Review, 27*, 66–74.

Croake, J. W. & James, B. (1973). A four-year comparison of premarital sexual attitudes. *Journal of Sex Research, 9*, 91–96.

Diamond, L. M. (1998). Development of sexual orientation among adolescent and young adult women. *Developmental Psychology, 34*, 1085–1095.

Diamond, L. M. (2003). What does sexual orientation orient? A biobehavioral model distinguishing romantic love and sexual desire. *Psychological Review, 110*, 173–192.

Eysenck, H. J. (1971). Masculinity-femininity, personality and sexual attitudes. *Journal of Sex Research, 7*, 83–88.

Guttentag, M. & Secord, P. F. (1983). *Too many women? The sex ratio question*. Beverly Hills, CA: Sage.

Hansen, G. L. (1987). Extradyadic relations during courtship. *Journal of Sex Research, 23*, 382–390.

Hyde, J. S. & DeLamater, J. (1997). *Understanding human sexuality* (6th ed.). Boston: McGraw-Hill.

Johannes, C. B. & Avis, N. E. (1997). Gender differences in sexual activity among mid-aged adults in Massachusetts. *Maturitas, 26*, 175–184.

Kett, J. F. (1977). *Rites of Passage: Adolescence in America 1790 to the Present*. New York: Basic Books.

Kinsey, A. C., Pomeroy, W. B., Martin, C. E., & Gebhard, P. H. (1953). *Sexual Behavior in the Human Female*. Philadelphia: Saunders.

Laumann, E. O., Gagnon, J. H., Michael, R. T., & Michaels, S. (1994). *The Social Organism of Sexuality: Sexual Practices in the United States*. Chicago: University of Chicago Press.

Leiblum, S. R. & Rosen, R. C. (1988). Changing perspectives on sexual desire. In S. Leiblum & R. Rosen (eds.), *Sexual Desire Disorders* (pp. 1–20). New York: Guilford.

Leigh, B. C., Morrison, D. M., Trocki, K., & Temple, M. T. (1994). Sexual behavior of American adolescents: Results from a U.S. national survey. *Journal of Adolescent Health, 15*, 117–125.

Leitenberg, H. & Henning, K. (1995). Sexual fantasy. *Psychological Bulletin, 117*, 469–496.

Lewis, R. A. (1973). Parents and peers: Socialization agents in the coital behavior of young adults. *Journal of Sex Research, 9*, 156–170.

McCabe, P. (1987). Desired and experienced levels of premarital affection and sexual intercourse during dating. *Journal of Sex Research, 23*, 23–33.

Mercer, G. W. & Kohn, P. M. (1979). Gender difference in the integration of conservatism, sex urge, and sexual behaviors among college students. *Journal of Sex Research, 15*, 129–142.

Mirande, A. M. (1968). Reference group theory and adolescent sexual behavior. *Journal of Marriage and the Family, 30*, 572–577.

Murphy, S. (1992). *A Delicate Dance: Sexuality, Celibacy, and Relationships Among Catholic Clergy and Religious*. New York: Crossroad.

Newcomer, S. & Udry, J. R. (1987). Parental marital status effects on adolescent sexual behavior. *Journal of Marriage and the Family, 49*, 235–240.

Oliver, M. B. & Hyde, J. S. (1993). Gender differences in sexuality: A meta-analysis. *Psychological Bulletin, 114*, 29–51.

Reinholtz, R. K. & Muehlenhard, C. L. (1995). Genital perceptions and sexual activity in a college population. *Journal of Sex Research, 32*, 155–165.

Sack, A. R., Keller, J. F., & Hinkle, D. E. (1984). Premarital sexual intercourse: A test of the effects of peer group, religiosity, and sexual guilt. *Journal of Sex Research, 20*, 168–185.

Stone, L. (1977). *The Family, Sex and Marriage in England 1500-1800*. New York: Harper & Row.

Thornton, A. & Camburn, D. (1987). The influence of the family on premarital attitudes and behavior. *Demography, 24*, 323–340.

Vanwesenbeeck, J., Bekker, M., & van Lenning, A. (1998). Gender attitudes, sexual meanings, and interactional patterns in heterosexual encounters among college students in the Netherlands. *Journal of Sex Research, 35*, 317–327.

Waller, W. & Hill, R. (1951). *The Family: A Dynamic Interpretation*. New York: Dryden (Original work published 1938).

CHAPTER 7

Peers, Parents, and Processes of Adolescent Socialization: A Twin-Study Perspective

Richard J. Rose
Indiana University, USA

CHALLENGES FROM AN EARLY TWIN STUDY

Thirty years ago, results from a landmark twin study, published as *Heredity, Environment, and Personality* (Loehlin & Nichols, 1976), challenged basic assumptions about the nature and nurture of behavior development. The study was of 850 adolescent twin pairs who so identified themselves among nearly 600,000 U.S. high school student participants in an annual national scholarship examination. The twins were neither a random nor representative sample, but comparisons to non-twins revealed no evidence of serious sampling bias, and these 1700 people comprised what was, at the time, one of the largest sample of twins ever studied, a study sufficiently large to permit novel analyses of the effects of heredity and environment on individual differences in adolescent behavior.

The Role of Heredity

The study's findings about the important role of heredity in personality development created no surprise: genes matter, accounting for about half of the variance in major dimensions of self-reported personality. But the study's findings about the role of the environment were more than merely surprising; they were truly puzzling.

Friends, Lovers and Groups: Key Relationships in Adolescence. Edited by Rutger C.M.E. Engels, Margaret Kerr and Håkan Stattin. Copyright © 2007 John Wiley & Sons, Ltd.

The Role of the Environment

To the questions of whether, and how much, similarities and differences in parental treatment and childhood environmental experience influenced the similarities and differences of adolescent twin's personalities, the surprising answer was: 'not much.' Environment 'carries substantial weight in determining personality ... but that environment is one for which twin pairs are correlated close to zero' (Loehlin & Nichols, 1976, p. 92). All correlations between the differences co-twins experienced in childhood and the differences in their adolescent personalities were near zero. Whether twins were dressed the same or differently, whether they played together as children or spent time together as adolescents, whether they were dressed alike or shared the same bedroom or had the same school teachers, whether their parents tried to treat them identically, or individually, seemed not to matter. Neither the frequency of parents' discipline, nor the nature or amount of family interaction systematically related to the behavioral differences found between the twins. Differences in childhood treatment of adolescent twins failed to predict differences in their self-described personalities. And the personality differences observed between genetically identical co-twins, differences that must be due to differences in their environmental experiences, were no better predicted from measures of childhood treatment than the personality differences of fraternal co-twins, who are but half as alike, genetically.

At least for dimensions of self-reported personality, neither parental rearing practices, the home atmosphere parents created, nor differences in family structure and status influenced the relative similarity of adolescent co-twins.

More on the Effects of Environments

Three decades and hundreds of twin-family studies later, the challenges posed in the analyses of these 850 twin pairs remain important, provocative, and controversial. Publications over the last decade have popularized the notion that family and household influences are of limited effect in children's development. In a book provocatively titled *The Limits of Family Influence*, David Rowe (1994) argued that environmental variables often held as influential in children's behavior, variables such as social class and parental warmth, are of no causal influence on child outcomes. Four years later, Harris (1998) argued that parents matter less than do peers and that household environments are less relevant to children's development than the school and neighborhood environments which adolescents experience outside their homes. A cover story in the popular press headlined the blunt question: 'Do parents matter?' (*Newsweek*, September 7, 1998). And a year later, another book's subtitle asked: 'Do Parents Really Shape their Child's Personality, Intelligence, or Character?' arguing not only that parenting has little influence on children's outcomes, but that siblings show little more resemblance to one another beyond that expected between age-matched and cohort-matched genetic strangers (Cohen, 1999).

One version of the 'Do parents matter?' argument is that peers, not parents, are the major source of environmental influence and that, accordingly, the more relevant environment is found in schools and neighborhoods, not in households. The more general, more controversial argument is that environmental effects on behavior are almost entirely environmental effects unique to individuals – that experiences shared by siblings while growing up together have negligible effects on their resemblance. Both arguments are overstated and misleading (Rose, 1995; Rutter, Pickles, Murray & Eaves, 2001).

Are the common experiences shared by siblings irrelevant to their behavioral resemblance? Are differences in family environments of no consequence to children? Is transmission of their genes the only influence parents have on their children's behavioral outcomes? By what processes are adolescents influenced by the peers with whom they associate? How do adolescent select their friends? What explains the behavioral similarities between adolescents and their friends? And what role do parents and parenting behaviors play in an adolescent's behavioral development? These questions form the context for this chapter review of the influence of peers and parents as agents in the social development of adolescents. We selectively review the influence of peers and parents from the perspective of recent twin-family studies, citing data from two ongoing longitudinal twin-family studies conducted in Finland. These *FinnTwin* studies were designed to assess behavioral precursors and consequences of adolescent alcohol use and abuse; featuring multi-occasion, multi-rater assessments and adding the twins' parents, siblings, or classmates to the sampling structure, the studies yield relevant results for evaluating processes of influence from peers and parents.

Because peers must exert their influence on an adolescent within the context of experiences they share with that adolescent, we reconsider effects of shared environmental experience. And because such effects are difficult to demonstrate in traditional twin comparison data, we consider other designs: studies of non-biological siblings who are reared together and an extended twin study design that yokes a gender-and age-matched classmate control to each twin. In so doing, we ask whether effects of shared environments are to be found in schools and neighborhoods as well as within households, in interactions with peers, as well as with parents. We also evaluate evidence that reciprocal sibling interactions modulate an adolescent's genetic dispositions, and we similarly ask whether the influences parents have on their children's development are to be found not in direct effects, but in interactions that modulate their children's dispositional tendencies.

NO EFFECTS OF COMMON ENVIRONMENT?

Begin with the comparisons Loehlin and Nichols made, 30 years ago. It is important to understand that Loehlin and Nichols *did* show effects from common environments in two behavioral domains. One was in the abilities measured by subtests from the National Merit Scholarship Qualifying Test. That common environment is an influential factor in individual differences in adolescent abilities has been demonstrated repeatedly. The second, more interesting dimension of behavior to yield strong effects of common experience was in a series of activities assessed via self-reports of observable behaviors. Included were participation in sports and musical events, religious activities, behaviors stereotypically associated with one gender but not the other, and with conventional attitudes of masculinity and femininity. Included also were adolescent patterns of smoking and drinking: using or abstaining from alcohol or smoking cigarettes, becoming intoxicated. For these activities, correlations for both identical and fraternal twins were significant and substantial, with only modest systematic differences between identical and fraternal twins.

So, to restate the matter: Loehlin & Nichols's 30-year-old twin study found effects of common environment to be a significant source of individual variation in activities and abilities, but not in personality. Many subsequent twin studies have replicated this fundamental finding: substantial genetic variance in adolescent abilities and observable behaviors, but little or none for self-reported personality dispositions. Four caveats should be added. First, the comparative similarity of identical and fraternal twin pairs does not robustly evaluate effects of common environments. Traditional twin studies have limited power to detect influences from familial environments, because such effects are not directly measured; they are modeled as residual variance not fully explained by the twin's differences in genetic resemblance. Such effects are more sensitively detected in other research designs, including studies of non-biological siblings, genetically strangers who are reared together. For example, significant effects of common environmental influence were found for body mass index when same-age unrelated siblings ('virtual twin pairs') were added to a standard twin study design (Segal & Allison, 2002). Second, effects of common environments *are* evident for some dimensions of self-reported personality (Rose, 1988). Third, even for personality dimensions for which conventional twin comparisons show little effect of common environments, comparisons of genetically-identical twins pairs who differ in duration of cohabitation or frequency of social contact after separation, yield such evidence. Such study of MZ twins is instructive. Duration of cohabitation of MZ twins prior to their separation and the frequency of their contact subsequent to their separation correlate with pairwise resemblance for many behaviors: co-twins who cohabit longer and those who maintain more frequent contact are more alike (Rose & Kaprio, 1988; Rose, Kaprio, Williams, Viken, & Obremski, 1990). Fourth, observational assessments of the behavior of children and adolescents, including behaviors that define temperament and personality, reveal sibling similarities too great to be attributed solely to their shared heredity; perhaps that result is not surprising, since observable behaviors are directly available to the reinforcing effects of child-rearing and community expectation. While self-reports by twin children and ratings by their parents often show very modest resemblance among DZ twins and non-twin siblings, substantial sibling resemblance is evident in observable behaviors rated by teachers and classmate peers. In a representative study of children's observable behavior, Lewin, Hops, Davis, & Dishion (1993) found sibling correlations exceeding 0.60 for teacher-rated adjustment. And in *FinnTwin* data, ratings from both classmate peers and classroom teachers yielded correlations significantly greater than zero for both same-sex and opposite-sex DZ co-twins for every one of 11 domains of behavior measured; teacher ratings of SSDZ twin pairs yielded correlations narrowly ranging from 0.50 to 0.60 across the 11 dimensions of rated behavior (Pulkkinen, Kaprio, and Rose, 1999).

Yet, it is true (indeed, it is an oft replicated finding) that social activities and observable behaviors are more heritable than self-reported dispositions. Perhaps the behavior for which effects of common environments are most widely documented is the initiation of drinking and smoking.

ABSTINENCE/INITIATION OF SUBSTANCE USE

Familial but not Heritable

A consistent result from recent analyses of twin and family data is that initiation of substance use is highly familial, but negligibly heritable (Hopfer, Crowley, & Hewitt, 2003; Pagan, Rose, Viken, Pulkkinen, Kaprio, & Dick, 2005; Rose & Dick, 2005). Whether or not an adolescent at a given age has initiated drinking or smoking, or remains abstinent, is dominantly influenced by shared environmental influences. In early and mid-adolescence, concordances for that dichotomous status are equivalent across identical and fraternal twin pairs and equivalent across same-sex and opposite-sex twins, yielding compelling evidence that the environments shared by twin siblings influence their decision to remain abstinent or to initiate drinking. Data from the two *FinnTwin* studies illustrate. At age 14 (Rose, Dick, Viken, Pulkkinen, & Kaprio, 2001), a minority (approximately 36%) of individual twins reported using alcohol. The proportion of concordant twin pairs (pairs in which both co-twins report using alcohol) was equivalent for genetically identical (monozygotic or MZ) and fraternal or dizygotic (DZ) pairs, and equivalent, as well, between DZ twin pairs of same- and opposite-sex. Analyses of these data found that environmental factors shared by co-twins – including both their familial household environment and the non-familial environments of peers, schools, and neighborhoods – accounted for more than 75% of the variance in drinking initiation in both boys and girls. In a parallel study of older adolescent Finnish twins, first assessed at age 16 (Rose, Kaprio, Winter, Koskenvuo, & Viken, 1999), twice as many (approximately 75%) had initiated drinking but, again, concordance did not differ across zygosity or twin type. Figure 7.1 illustrates the equivalent concordance for initiation at the two ages; concordances are a bit higher among sisters than among brothers, but differences between MZ and DZ twins are negligible.

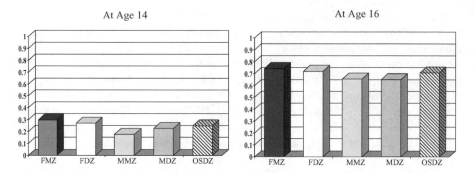

Figure 7.1   Equivalent concordances for alcohol initiation at the two ages

Equivalent concordances, such as those evident in Figure 7.1, have an unambiguous interpretation. Twin studies more readily establish environmental influences than those of heredity. Uncertain assumptions about equal exposure to relevant environments are always necessary to infer genetic variance from classic twin study comparisons. In contrast, results like these, showing equivalent resemblance across large and representative samples of MZ and DZ twins, permit the confident inference that heredity plays little or no role. So it is clear that shared environment is important in sibling similarity for drinking/abstaining. What do we know about the nature of that shared environment?

Sibling Influences

Some influences from shared experiences may be unique to siblings. How do experiences shared by siblings growing up together make them behaviorally alike? One way is via the siblings' direct interactions. Effects of reciprocal sibling interactions were first suggested in sibling similarities for delinquency and substance use (Rowe & Gulley, 1992). Sibling relationships modulated sibling resemblance: same-sex siblings were significantly similar in their self-reported delinquency and substance use; brother-sister sibling pairs were not. And same-sex siblings who reported frequent interactions with mutual friends were much more alike ($r = 0.70$) than those whose peer networks were dissimilar (0.26). Parallel effects have been shown in adoptive siblings who share their environments, but not their heredity; correlations for patterns of alcohol involvement reported by 255 pairs of non-biological siblings were significantly higher in pairs of same sex and similar age, results interpreted as evidence that sibling environmental effects influence alcohol use via 'social modeling or facilitation' (McGue, Sharma, & Benson, 1996). Co-twin dependence importantly modulates genetic effects on their drinking patterns (Penninkilampi-Kerola, Kaprio, Moilanen, & Rose, 2005). Co-twin dependent twins are more alike in several measures of alcohol use both in mid-adolescence and in early adulthood, and shared environmental factors make a more important contribution to their drinking patterns than is true for twins not reporting dependence on their co-twin. Nor are sibling effects limited to substance use. Common environmental effects on initiation of sexual intercourse among adolescent same-sex siblings were highly significant, accounting for more than 40% of the variance among siblings in frequent contact; in contrast, among brother-brother and sister-sister twin pairs whose contact was limited, genetic effects were much stronger and influences from common experience were negligible (Hunt & Rowe, 2003).

If the reciprocal effects of siblings are enhanced among sibs who are age-matched and of the same gender, twin siblings can be expected to exert great effects on one another through direct reciprocal social modeling. A formal model of effects of cooperative sibling interaction was offered by Carey (1986, 1992) and illustrated with data on criminality. In Carey's model, behavior of a twin influences that of the co-twin, and because twins' behavior is correlated, their reciprocal influences on one another result in more extreme behavior in both co-twins. The behavioral variance in twins will be altered according to the magnitude of their reciprocal interactions and the level of covariance between them. For genetically influenced behaviors, MZ co-twins will be more alike (because they are genetically more alike), and, in Carey's model, they will exhibit a greater shift in prevalence for the less common of dichotomous outcomes. If the genetic effects are sex-limited, same-sex pairs will be more alike and will show a greater shift in prevalence than will brother-sister (opposite-sex or OS) pairs. Under usual assumptions, cooperative social interaction effects will increase the prevalence of the more extreme (i.e., the lower base-rate) condition in a dichotomous behavioral outcome.

Specifically, among 16-year-old adolescents for whom drinking is non-modal, sibling interaction will result in a greater prevalence of abstinence in MZ than in DZ twin individuals, and a greater prevalence of abstinence in SSDZ than among OSDZ twin individuals. Results for adolescent abstinence rates from the *FinnTwin* studies illustrate this. At age 16, the prevalence of abstinence among all individual twin males was ordered MZ > SSDZ > OSDZ to yield a chi square of 10.95, $p < 0.01$. In areas of northern Finland, where access to alcohol is more limited and community surveillance is greater, overall abstinence is more prevalent than in urban Helsinki; yet, the ordering remained the same, and again the chi square was highly significant (Rose et al., 1999). And there's more: in Finnish culture, drinking patterns typically include drinking to intoxication; only a minority (approximately 35%) of individual Finnish twins who, at age 16, had initiated drinking reported never having drunk to intoxication. The prevalence of that non-modal drinking pattern was again ordered as predicted by Carey's model of sibling cooperation effects: MZ > SSDZ > OSDZ. Thus, both the initiation of drinking and the initiation of intoxicating show evidence of cooperative sibling interactions.

THE INFLUENCE OF FRIENDS: PEER SELECTION AND PEER SOCIALIZATION

Another way shared experiences influence adolescent behavior is via the social environments shared with peers. Adolescents resemble their friends, the peers with whom they associate. For some adolescent behaviors, including patterns of smoking, drinking, and delinquent misbehavior, friends resemble one another about as much as do brothers and sisters. Because friends are genetic strangers reared in different households, while siblings share half of their genes and their household environment, the important question becomes: what explains such significant resemblance among adolescent friends? In part, it must reflect an active selection process (Rose, 2002) that is described below. We like those who are like ourselves, and MZ twins, who are more alike, select as their best friends, classmates more behaviorally similar to themselves than do DZ co-twins. And, in part, friends resemble one another due to effects of socialization. We come to resemble those with whom we associate, and adolescent peers can be very influential social models. Patterns of substance use in early adolescence appear to be especially sensitive to both processes – active selection, in which an adolescent seeks to befriend those whose behaviors and attitudes are similar, as well as to the effects of socialization, social modeling, and behavioral contagion. Some relevant results from Finnish twins illustrate similarities in patterns of substance use among adolescent friends.

The 2nd wave questionnaire assessment in *FinnTwin12* was made within three months of each twin's 14th birthday. At that age, nearly two-thirds of all twins reported abstinence, 34% reported using alcohol infrequently, and 3% reported weekly drinking. We collapsed the categories of drinking and classified each twin as abstaining or drinking at age 14 to assess the question: *What predicts whether a given adolescent is drinking or abstaining at age 14?* Significant predictors include accelerated pubertal maturation, externalizing behavioral dispositions as rated by classroom teachers, and reduced parental monitoring (Rose, Dick, Viken, Pulkkinen, & Kaprio, 2001). But among the most robust predictors is whether or not the adolescent reported having friends who drink. Or smoke. Or use drugs. Or engage in delinquent acts (Holliday, Pagan, Pulkkinen, Kaprio, Rose, & Dick, 2005).

Behavioral Similarities Among Friends

Adolescents who report having friends who drink are much more likely to drink themselves; having drinking friends is a potent predictor that an adolescent drinks, one that yields nearly a seven-fold greater risk (an odds ratio, OR, approaching 7.0). Having friends who smoke is also highly predictive of whether or not a 14-year-old Finnish twin reports having initiated drinking; that OR approached 5.0. Having friends who use drugs yielded an OR > 4.0 and having friends who engage in delinquent behaviors an odds ratio of nearly 3.0. Perhaps more surprisingly, having some friends of the opposite sex (which characterizes only 30% of both 14-year-old twin boys and girls) yielded a three-fold risk.

Gender Differences

To add interest to this story: the predictive value of each of these effects is magnified among girls. Having friends who drink yields an OR > 8.0 for girls, against one < 6.0 among boys, and similarly for having friends who smoke, use drugs, or engage in delinquent behaviors: each report predicted drinking rather than abstaining better among girls than among boys. Further, the risk ratio for a twin sister who reports having friends of the opposite sex is substantially greater than is that report among age-matched boys. Perhaps a 14-year-old girl with friends of the opposite sex is a girl with accelerated pubertal maturation, and the association is with older male friends who, themselves, are more likely to be engaged in regular substance use.

A provocative result of analyses we earlier reported (Rose et al., 2001) was evidence that girls are more vulnerable to the consequences of reduced parental monitoring (vide infra). We now add evidence that girls are more vulnerable to the effects of associating with peers who smoke and drink (Holliday et al., 2005). Why should it be so? Perhaps reduced parental monitoring and associations with substance-using friends are more risk-enhancing for girls, because they are normatively more deviant. In Finnish data, girls report greater levels of parental monitoring than do boys. And, more interestingly, they do so within the same family (in comparisons of the amount of parental monitoring reported by brother-sister twin pairs). That the effects of reduced parental monitoring on drinking at age 14 are more salient for girls than for boys may be explained because it is more deviant for them. Is the same true for associating with deviant friends?

HOW DO ADOLESCENTS SELECT THEIR FRIENDS?

It has long been known that behavioral similarity plays an important role in friendship formation. And it does so at a very early age. The behavioral sociality of three- and four-year-old nursery school children, a rated index of their cooperative behavior derived from observational study, correlated more highly with friendship associations than measured IQ or other behavioral variables (Challman, 1932). In adolescence, behavioral similarity remains important for friendship formation. In a study of nominated best-school-friends among nearly 1900 high school adolescents, Kandel (1978) found significant similarities for measures of substance use (kappa = 0.40 for marijuana use, 0.34 for smoking, and 0.25 for drinking) consistent with the inference that behavioral similarity is an important factor in adolescent attraction. In a later study of adolescent best-friend dyads, (Kandel, Davies, & Baydar, 1990) similarity for substance use ranged from 0.25 to 0.45 for use of cigarettes, alcohol, sedatives, stimulants, and other substances, and the analyses led to the conclusion that dyads form *because* of behavioral similarity and the dyads then grow to be more similar over time, a conclusion that both selection and socialization contribute to the observed similarities among adolescent friendships.

We focus on selection for several reasons. First, the evidence from studies of large samples using longitudinal designs (e.g., Ennett & Bauman, 1994; Fisher & Bauman, 1988) indicates that substance use similarities among adolescent friends reflect the effects of selection [similarity → attraction] more than effects of socialization [affiliation → similarity]. Second, long-term longitudinal study of a birth cohort (Fergusson & Horwood, 1999) associated peer affiliations with prospectively measured familial, parental, and individual factors; results showed that peer affiliations are influenced by individual behavioral predispositions, as well as by social and familial factors. Given that most behavioral dispositions are moderately hereditary, this longitudinal study suggests that friendship selection will exhibit genetic influences. And finally, we emphasize selection processes because the fact that adolescents form friendships to their liking, seeking out those who are similar to themselves, illustrates an important general result from twin study research: that within constraints of opportunity, people create their own social environments (Scarr & McCartney, 1983).

Twin Studies of Perceived Friendship Similarity

Are an adolescent's friendship selections directly influenced by that adolescent's genetic dispositions? Several studies of friendship selection using genetically-informative designs have focused on similarities that adolescent twins attribute to their friends (Grant, Bucholz, Madden, Slutske, & Heath, 1998; Manke, McGurie, Reiss, Hetehrington, & Plomin, 1995; *FinnTwin* data reported in Rose, 2002). In this kind of study, twins (or non-twin siblings) are assessed on target behaviors and then asked to attribute to their best friends the same behaviors; in an alternate design used with young twins, the twins' parents rate their twins and then attribute the same set of behaviors to their twins' friends. Either design is easy to execute, but both invite systematic bias in the attributions of perceived similarity. But within their limitations, these studies suggest genetic dispositions influence adolescent peer formation. For example, MZ co-twins attribute to their peers greater similarity to their own patterns of smoking and drinking than do DZ co-twins, but it is uncertain whether peers of MZ co-twins are actually more alike or whether the twins only perceive them to be so. An alternate research design provides further insights.

A Twin Study of Actual Friendship Similarity

In a *FinnTwin* study, we (Rose, 2002) explored genetic contributions to the similarities of adolescents and their friends in a design in which the behaviors of twins and their friends were assessed by classmate peers. Because similarities of twins and their nominated friends were derived from assessments from classmate peers, the design avoids the bias of attributed similarity. School-based assessments of 1150 Finnish twin children, ages 11–12, included a 33-item peer nomination procedure. For each of 33 behavioral attributes, each child in the classroom nominated classmates who best fit the described behavior (Pulkkinen, L., J. Kaprio, & R. J. Rose, 1999). That our research focus was on the twin student(s) in the class was not mentioned. The last of the 33 items included in the peer nomination inventory asked each child to nominate two classmates for the item: 'Who are your best friends?' Data from that item permitted us to identify nominated best friends of MZ and DZ twins and consider three research questions:

(1) Do MZ twins, more than DZ twins, tend to nominate one another and/or common classmates as best friends? (2) Do twins identify as their best friends classmates who are behaviorally similar to themselves? (3) Is the peer-rated similarity of dyads formed from best friends of co-twins greater for best friends of MZ twins? The data answer all three questions affirmatively.

And the results inform us how twins choose their classmate friends. Do twins like those who are similar to themselves? We formed all possible dyads of each twin and that twin's nominated best friends. All correlations for all twin-friend dyads were significant, ranging from 0.33 to 0.46 across the three factor scales of the peer-nomination instrument. All were a bit higher for girls than for boys, albeit with these modest samples, not significantly so. Yet, the pattern is suggestive, for it was found not only for the factor scales, but for every one of the individual scales that comprise the factors. Girls at this age are more psychosexually mature than boys, and, as a result are often given more social responsibility. Is assortative pairing (befriending those similar to one's self) more characteristic of 12-year-old girls as a result?

But caution is necessary: these correlations are inflated by the fact that twins could – and did – nominate their co-twin as their best friend. Some 13% of the studied dyads were of co-twins. And that leads to the most interesting question asked of these data: are friends of MZ co-twins behaviorally more alike than those of DZ co-twins? To answer it, we restricted the nominated friends to independent dyads in which each twin nominated a classmate not nominated by the co-twin, to yield a direct test of the influence of shared genes and shared family environments in active friendship selection. Independent classmate friends of co-twins will be alike if selection (assortative pairing; Rose, 2002) characterizes adolescent friendships. And if assortative pairing is influenced by genetic dispositions, friends of MZ co-twins will be more alike than friends of DZs. Figure 7.2 confirms these expectations with results for twin sisters and their best friends for items comprising scales of anxiety and depression (which of your classmates are 'shy,' 'lonesome, without friends,' 'worry a lot,' 'are easily offended/start crying if someone is nasty to them'). Under the usual assumptions, the relative similarity of the twin sisters would parse nearly half of the variance in these behaviors to additive genes; little surprise to that result. More interestingly, the relative similarity classmates attribute to the friends of MZ and DZ twin sisters also suggests genetic

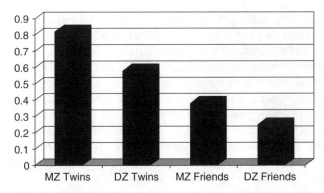

Figure 7.2 Similarities for twin sisters and their best friends for items comprising scales of anxiety and depression

effects – in this case, genetic effects on the friendship selections made by twin sisters at age 12. Similar results were found for items on the peer nomination inventory that load on scales of hyperactivity and aggression among girls. The samples are of modest size and, since this is the first study of its kind, caution is warranted; yet, the data do suggest that adolescent friendship selection is conditioned by genetic dispositions. Interestingly, parallel analyses for twin boys found no significant correlations in their nominated friendship dyads – another bit of suggestive evidence that assortative pairing may be weaker among boys at this age.

NON-FAMILIAL ENVIRONMENTAL EFFECTS

The influence of siblings and peers on an adolescent's behavior makes evident the fact that shared environments are important, *and* that the relevant shared environment extends beyond that experienced within a family household. For adolescents especially, we need to consider the impact of environments which adolescents experience outside their homes – in their neighborhoods, schools, and communities. Neighborhoods affect children's behavior above and beyond the children's genetic liabilities. While genetically vulnerable families do tend to cluster in poorer neighborhoods, informative twin designs clearly suggest that the links between deprived neighborhoods and children's behavior problems are a significant and real environmental effect (Caspi, A., Taylor, A., Moffitt, T.E. & Plomin, R., 2000). And neighborhood effects are found not only in poor neighborhoods, nor is the influence of neighborhoods found only on behavior problems. A novel sampling structure used in *FinnTwin* analyses will illustrate.

We studied 1262 same-sex twins at ages 11–12 and, for each twin, we added a gender- and age-matched classmate control (Rose, Viken, Dick, Bates, Pulkkinen, & Kaprio, 2003). The 631 families of twins resided throughout Finland; all twins and control children attended the public school serving their residential area. In all but a handful of pairs, co-twins attended the same school, so the four children in each double-dyad, composed of a same-sex twin pair and their classmate controls, resided in the same neighborhood and attended the same school. This unusual sample enabled us to distinguish familial environmental effects from the school-based effects that each pair of classmate controls shared with each other and with the twins with whom they were yoked. Because the members of each twin-control dyad attended the same school, we label these extra-familial effects school-based (S), and our analytic model, FASE, distinguishes familial (F) and school-based (S) sources of shared environmental influence. The familial environment (F) is shared by both MZ and DZ co-twins, but it is not shared with unrelated classmates from the same neighborhood or school; in contrast, school-based neighborhood effects (S) are fully shared by all members of each double-dyad, each set of co-twins and their two school classmate controls. Thus, the effects of common experience latently assessed in ordinary twin comparisons are here differentiated into those experiences shared within families (F) and those shared in school-based environments (S) outside the family. The FASE model also includes additive (A) genetic effects and influences from each individual's experiences (E) that are not shared with parents and siblings, as in conventional twin analyses.

The outcome variables we modeled with these data were a set of behavioral experiences scored dichotomously. Figure 7.3 illustrates results of our FASE model fit to two measures of smoking: 'Have you ever smoked cigarettes?' and 'Do you have friends who smoke cigarettes?' School-based shared environments (S) significantly contribute to individual differences in responses to both items, accounting for about a quarter of the total variance. Contrasting the model fits for the two items, familial environments are of more influence in determining one's own smoking initiation, while genetic effects account for

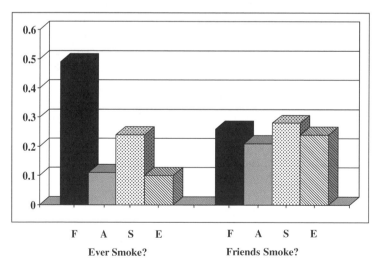

Figure 7.3   Results of the F A S E model for two smoking measures

more (more than 20%) of the variance in having friends who smoke – more evidence that friendship formation in early adolescence is influenced, in part, by genetic dispositions. At ages 11–12, smoking is more prevalent among boys than girls; we added sex of each double dyad to the FASE model to differentiate sex effects from estimates of S, and for one's own smoking, 7% of the variance was attributed to gender differences.

These results document significant non-familial environmental effects on children's behavior. The source of these non-familial effects must be variations across communities, neighborhoods, and schools that have direct influence on children's behavioral development – differences in neighborhood cohesion and community monitoring, access to alcohol and tobacco, regional differences in religious attitudes, and many other unidentified factors (Rose et al., 2003). It is likely that the large neighborhood effects evident in these data may be both behaviorally- and age-specific: substance use measures in early adolescence may be behaviors particularly influenced by peers who share experiences in school and neighborhood environments.

PARENTING EFFECTS ON ADOLESCENT BEHAVIOR DEVELOPMENT

Do parents matter? Traditional research on parenting assumed, incorrectly, direct and deterministic models of parenting effects. Such models assumed uniform effects from patterns of parenting across all children. That assumption is untenable. Children's genetic dispositions influence their response to parenting directives (Collins, Maccoby, Steinberg, Hetherington, & Bornstein, 2000). Children with different temperaments will differentially respond to specific parenting practices, and effects of parenting behaviors will be modulated by the temporal and contextual environments within which they are experienced. Accordingly, we cannot pool parenting effects across families, neighborhoods, and communities. Further, as made evident above, it is important to distinguish familial effects that are experienced within households from non-familial influences experienced outside parent-child dyads. Important aspects of extra-familial environments correlate with parenting practices; e.g., selection of a neighborhood within which to reside is one critical way parents influence their children's peer experiences. Some of the most significant contributions parents make to their children's behavior development are indirect, and the influences parents have on their adolescent interact with influences of their adolescent's peers.

Parents' Influences on their Children

Consider again factors that predict whether a 14-year-old adolescent has initiated drinking or remains abstinent. In addition to individual factors of pubertal maturation and behavioral dispositions and social interactions with

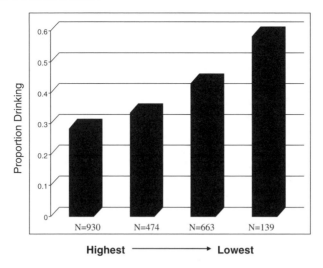

Figure 7.4 Proportion of Finnish twins at age 14 who reported using alcohol, made at age 12 and ranked in order of parental monitoring

peers and friends, differences in parenting practices and household environments are influential. In *FinnTwin* data obtained when the twins were age 14, the twins' reports of parental monitoring, obtained two years earlier at age 12, were added into a logistic regression model with behavior ratings made by the twins' teachers, pubertal development scores, and sex (as, at this age, more girls than boys have initiated drinking and sex differences interact with other predictive factors, including variation in parental monitoring). Figure 7.4 shows the proportion of Finnish twins at age 14 who reported using alcohol ordered by their ratings, made at age 12, of parental monitoring. Compared to the highest level of parental monitoring, the lowest levels of monitoring (caution: perhaps differences in monitoring are better construed as differences in child-disclosure; Stattin & Kerr, 2000) at age 12 are associated with a two-fold risk of drinking at age 14, Further, variation in parental monitoring interacts with dispositional differences and differences in pubertal maturation at age 14, and low parental monitoring is a greater risk factor for early-onset drinking among girls than among boys. For example, accelerated pubertal development in the context of the lowest level of parental monitoring is a potent risk factor for both boys and girls, such that more than 70% of these twins report drinking. But intermediate levels of parental monitoring seem to confer greater risk on girls than boys among those at or above the median in their pubertal development (Rose et al., 2001).

Parenting Measures and Adolescent Substance Use

Thus, Finnish data replicate reports by others that differences in level of parental monitoring reported by adolescent twins (or, reports independently obtained from their parents) are significantly associated with abstinence/ drinking in mid-adolescence. Reduced parental monitoring (caveat: again, perhaps it is reduced child-disclosure; Stattin & Keer, 2000) reported at age 12 is a risk factor for initiated substance use at age 14. But we find, as have others, that when assessed as direct effects, measures of parenting and household environment have but modest effect on adolescent behavioral outcomes. In an analysis of smoking initiation among 1642 same-sex Finnish twin pairs, the latent measure of common environment accounted for 70% of the variance, and when added into the analytic model, measured reports of parental monitoring accounted for but 2% of that total. But when parental monitoring was studied not as a direct effect, but as a moderating one (Dick, Purcell, Viken, Kaprio, Pulkkinen, & Rose, 2005) results revealed a much larger, albeit indirect, role for parenting; details follow.

Parental Effects as Moderators of Children's Dispositions

If peers exert their influence on an adolescent by moderating the adolescent's genetic dispositions, might not the influence of parents be similar? With *FinnTwin* data, we studied the role of several dimensions of parenting and household environment: monitoring, assessed by twins' reports made at age 12; time spent with parents, from reports of twins at age 12; and two factors of parenting style, restrictiveness and nurturance, from a questionnaire completed by a parent in the baseline family questionnaire. The sample included 1642 pairs of same-sex twins, 812 MZ and 830 DZ. We used a G x E interaction model in which the values assumed by a measured moderator can alter the importance of genetic and environmental influences.

Results for parental monitoring illustrate (Dick et al., 2005). Across all same-sex twin pairs, the correlation of reported monitoring scores, derived from individual responses to three questions, was 0.53 – substantial agreement, but also substantial within-pair variation, in perceived monitoring by same-sex twin siblings. Accordingly, each twin's monitoring measure was entered separately into the model: the value assumed by the moderator measure is allowed to change from one twin subject to another, reflecting the value of monitoring attributed by each individual. With this model, we first tested direct parenting effects and then asked whether monitoring has more complex effects on substance use, interacting with and moderating the importance of genetic and other environmental risk factors.

As expected, parenting effects were very modest; e.g., parental monitoring accounted for but 2% of the total variance. But monitoring had a very significant moderating influence on adolescent smoking in that, as monitoring increased, genetic effects linearly decreased and influences from common environment increased. The effect was dramatic: genetic effects accounted for 70% of the variance at the extreme of lowest monitoring, but only 15% of the variance at the highest level of monitoring. Conversely, common environmental effects accounted for less than 10% of the variance at the lowest level of monitoring, but more than 80% at the highest level. Uncertainties over the meaning of parental monitoring as here measured (Stattin & Kerr, 2000) mandate a cautious interpretation of these results; it may be the quality of the parent–adolescent relationship, and not the nature of parenting practices, per se, that is critical. But the results do suggest that aspects of parenting can significantly moderate the expression of an adolescent's genetic dispositions, and aspects of parenting can play a significant role in adolescent substance use. Parents' behaviors offer models for their children, as well, and the effect of parental models on adolescent substance use may be greater for some children than others (e.g., Barman, Pulkkinen, Kaprio, & Rose, 2004).

Gene-Environment Correlations and Interactions

Analyses of *FinnTwin* data on adolescent drinking and its risk factors document gene-environment interplay. Friendship selection appears to represent important gene-environment correlations, as adolescents befriend those who share similar dispositional tendencies, creating social environments in which they are encouraged to express their behavioral dispositions and obtain their social reinforcement. The initiation and the establishment of patterns of smoking and drinking are influenced by genetic differences evident years earlier in children's behavioral dispositions, as well as in environmental factors that influence exposure and access to alcohol and to models of drinking behavior. Although our overall results indicate that drinking initiation is primarily determined by environmental influences, while the establishment of drinking patterns is determined mostly by genetic differences, the latter are themselves subject to moderation by the environment. We have shown that a traditional risk factor such as pubertal maturation is influenced in exquisite environmental interactions. The within-family replication of the association of accelerated pubertal maturation with earlier onset drinking is found *only* in twin sisters residing in more urban environments within Finland. There are no differences in within-family comparisons in more rural environments where exposure is less likely, access is more limited, and peer models less prevalent. Gene-environment interactions and correlations are central to understanding patterns of substance use and abuse (Rose & Dick, 2005).

SUMMARY

This review is a selective one, both in its emphasis on substance use behaviors and in its focus on twin studies conducted in Finland. But results from the *FinnTwin* studies generalize to parallel epidemiological data from non-twins and to results from adolescent twin studies conducted in other cultures. Jointly, these studies provide evidence that shared experiences significantly contribute to individual differences in patterns of adolescent substance use. Both peers and parents exert influence on adolescent development, but such influence is neither general, nor is it direct or uniform. The socializing effects of parents and peers are much more evident in some behavioral domains than others and at some ages than others. Influences of peers and parents are not uniform across different families, different neighborhoods, and different adolescents. Importantly, socialization effects of peers and parents are evident, not so much as main effects, but as processes that modulate the dispositional tendencies of adolescents. Some shared environmental effects are unique to the reciprocal interactions of siblings growing up together. Adolescent choose as their friends peers who are behaviorally similar to themselves, and such active selection processes are evident in the best-friend selections made by young adolescent twins. Selection may be more influential among girls than boys, and, in early adolescence, girls may be more vulnerable than boys to influences from both peers and parents.

We emphasize that some of the environmental effects we have described are behavior- and age-specific, and that substance use may be more sensitive to influences of peers, parents, and extra-familial environments than many other behaviors. But those cautions and caveats do not deny the major inference that at least for some years of adolescent development, and at least for some socially important behaviors, peers and parents exert significant influence on behavioral outcomes. Genetically informative research, including that with twins, their parents, and their peers, will offer new insights into the processes by which such influence is mediated.

ACKNOWLEDGEMENTS

The *FinnTwin* studies, which provide data reported in this chapter, have been supported by the National Institute on Alcohol Abuse and Alcoholism (grants AA 09203, AA 00145, AA 08315, and AA 12502), with supplementary funding from the Academy of Finland, the Finnish Centre of Excellence Programme, and the Yrjö Jahnsson Foundation; the studies are made possible through the collaboration of Professors Lea Pulkkinen, University of Jyväskylä, and Jaakko Kaprio, University of Helsinki.

REFERENCES

Barman, S. K., Pulkkinen, L., Kaprio, J., & Rose, R. J. (2004). Inattentiveness, parental smoking, and early smoking initiation. *Addiction*, 99, 1049–1061.
Carey, G. (1986). Sibling imitation and contrast effects. *Behavior Genetics*, 16, 319–341.
Carey, G. (1992). Twin imitation for antisocial behavior: Implications for genetic and family environment research. *Journal of Abnormal Psychology*, 101, 18–25.
Caspi, A., Taylor, A., Moffitt, T. E., & Plomin, R. (2000). Neighborhood deprivation affects children's mental health: Environmental risks identified in a genetic design. *Psychological Science*, 11, 338–342.
Challman, R.C. (1932). Factors influencing friendships among preschool children. *Child Development*, 3, 146–158.

Cohen, D. B. (1999). *Stranger in the Nest: Do Parents Really Shape Their Children's Personality, Intelligence, or Character?* New York: Wiley.

Collins, W. A., Maccoby, E. E., Steinberg, L., Hetherington, E. M., & Bornstein, M. H. (2000). Contemporary research on parenting, the case for nature and nurture. *American Psychologist*, 55, 218–232.

Dick, D. M., Purcell, S., Viken, R., Kaprio, J., Pulkkinen, L., & Rose, R. J. (2005). Evidence for gene environment interaction associated with parenting practices and adolescent substance use. *Journal of Abnormal Psychology*, in press.

Ennett, S. T. & Baumann, K. E. (1994). The contribution of influence and selection to adolescent peer group homogeneity: findings from studies of adolescent smoking and drinking. *Journal of Personality and Social Psychology*, 67, 653–663.

Fergusson, D. M. & Horwood, L. J. (1999). Prospective childhood predictors of deviant peer affiliations in adolescence. *Journal of Child Psychology and Psychiatry*, 40, 581–592.

Fisher, L. A. & Bauman, K. E. (1988). Influence and selection in the friend-adolescent relationship: Findings from studies of adolescent smoking ad drinking. *Journal of Applied Social Psychology*, 18, 289–314.

Harris, J. R. (1998). *The Nurture Assumption: Why Children Turn Out the Way They Do*. New York: The Free Press.

Holliday, C., Pagan, J., Pulkkinen, L., Kaprio, J., Rose, R. J. & Dick, D. M. (2005). The influence of peers and extracurricular activities on adolescent alcohol initiation. In preparation.

Hopfer, C. J., Crowley, T. J., & Hewitt, J.K. (2003). Review of twin and adoption studies of adolescent substance use. *Journal of the American Academy of Child and Adolescent Psychiatry*, 42, 710–719.

Hunt, C. B. & Rowe, D. C. (2003). Genetic and shared environmental influences on adolescents' timing of first sexual intercourse: The moderating effect of time spent with a sibling. In J. L. Rodgers & H.-P Kohler, eds. *The Biodemography of Human Reproduction and Fertility*. Boston: Kluwer, pp. 161–185.

Kandel, D. B. (1978). Homophily, selection, and socialization in adolescent friendships. *American Journal of Sociology*, 84, 427–436.

Kandel, D. B., Davies, M., & Baydar, N. (1990). The creation of interpersonal contexts: homophily in dyadic relationships in adolescence and young adulthood. In L. Robins and Rutter, M. (eds.), *Straight and Devious Pathways from Childhood to Adulthood*. Cambridge: Cambridge University Press, pp. 221–241.

Kaprio, J., Pulkkinen, L. & Rose, R. J. (2002). Genetic and environmental factors in health-related behaviors: Studies of Finnish twins and twin families. *Twin Research*, 5, 366–371.

Lewin, L. M., Hops, H., Davis, B. & Dishion, T. J. (1993). Multimethod comparison of similarity in school adjustment of siblings and unrelated children. *Developmental Psychology*, 29, 963–96.

Lloyd, J. J. & Anthony, J. C. (2003). Hanging out with the wrong crowd: How much difference can parents make in an urban environment? *Journal of Urban Health*, 80, 383–399.

Loehlin, J. C. & Nichols, R. C. (1976). *Heredity, Environment, and Personality: A Study of 850 Sets of Twins*. Austin: University of Texas Press.

Manke, B., McGuire, S., Reiss, D., Hetherington, E. M., & Plomin, R. (1995). Genetic contributions to adolescents' extrafamilial social interactions: teachers, best friends, and peers. *Social Development*, 4, 238–256.

McGue, M., Sharma, A., & Benson, P. (1996). Parent and sibling influences on adolescent alcohol use and misuse: Evidence from a U.S. adoption cohort. *Journal of Studies on Alcohol*, 57, 8–18.

Pagan, J. L., Rose, R. J., Viken, R. J., Pulkkinen, L., Kaprio, J., & Dick, D.M. (2006). Genetic and environmental influences on stages of alcohol use across adolescence and into young adulthood. *Behavior Genetics*, 36, 483–497.

Penninkilampi-Kerola, V., Kaprio, J., Moilanen, I. K. & Rose, R. J. (2005). Co-twin dependence modifies heritability of abstinence and alcohol use: A population-based study of Finnish twins. *Twin Research*, 8, 232–244.

Pulkkinen, L., Kaprio, J., & Rose, R. J. (1999). Peers, teachers and parents as assessors of the behavioral and emotional problems of twins and their adjustment: The Multidimensional Peer Nomination Inventory. *Twin Research*, 2, 274–285.

Rose, R. J. (1988). Genetic and environmental variance in content dimensions of the MMPI. *Journal of Personality & Social Psychology*, 54,161–171.

Rose, R. J. (1995). Genes and human behavior. *Annual Review of Psychology*, 46, 625–654.

Rose, R. J. (2002). How do adolescents select their friends? A behavior-genetic perspective. In L. Pulkkinen & A. Caspi (eds.), *Paths to Successful Development. Personality in the Life Course* (pp. 106–125). Cambridge, UK: Cambridge University Press.

Rose, R. J. & Dick, D. M. (2004/2005). Gene-environment interplay in adolescent drinking behavior. *Alcohol Research & Health*, 28, 222–229.

Rose, R. J., Dick, D. M., Viken, R. J., Pulkkinen, L., & Kaprio, J. (2001). Drinking or abstaining at age 14: A genetic epidemiological study. *Alcoholism: Clinical and Experimental Research*, 25, 1594–1604.

Rose, R. J. & Kaprio, J. (1988). Frequency of social contact and intrapair resemblance of adult monozygotic cotwins. *Behavior Genetics*, 18, 309–328.

Rose, R. J., Kaprio, J., Williams, C. J., Viken, R., & Obremski, K. (1990). Social contact and sibling similarity: Facts, issues, and red herrings. *Behavior Genetics*, 20, 763–778.

Rose, R. J., Kaprio, J., Winter, T., Koskenvuo, M. & Viken, R. J. (1999) Familial and socioregional environmental effects on abstinence from alcohol at age sixteen. *Journal of Studies on Alcohol*, Supplement No. 13, 63–74.

Rose, R. J., Viken, R. J., Dick, D. M., Bates, J., Pulkkinen, L., & Kaprio, J. (2003). It does take a village: Nonfamilial environments and children's behavior. *Psychological Science*, 14, 273–277.

Rowe, D. C. (1994). *The Limits of Family Influence: Genes, Experience, and Behavior*. New York: The Guilford Press.

Rowe, D. C. & Gulley, B. (1992). Sibling effects on substance use and delinquency. *Criminology*, 30, 217–233.

Rutter, M., Pickels, A., Murray, R., & Eaves, L. (2001). Testing hypotheses on specific environmental causal effects on behavior. *Psychological Bulletin*, 127, 291–324.

Scarr, S. & McCartney, K. (1983). Theory of genotype – environmental effects. *Child Development*, 54, 424–435.

Segal, N. L. & Allison, D. B. (2002). Twins and virtual twins: bases of relative body weight revisited. *International Journal Obstetrics Relat Metab Disorders*, 26, 437–441.

Silberg, J., Rutter, M., D'Onofrio, B., & Eaves, L. (2003). Genetic and environmental risk factors in adolescent substance use. *Journal of Child Psychology and Psychiatry*, 44, 664–676.

Stattin, H. & Kerr, M. (2000). Parental monitoring: A reinterpretation. *Child Development*, 71, 1072–1085.

CHAPTER 8

Peers and Problem Behavior: Have We Missed Something?

Margaret Kerr, Håkan Stattin, and Jeff Kiesner
Örebro University, Sweden and Università di Padova, Italy

INTRODUCTION

Parents of teenagers often worry that their teenager will fall in with the wrong crowd and be drawn into risky or illegal activities. These concerns may be well founded. There is a large literature dating back to the 1970s showing that youths tend to be similar to their peers on problem behaviors such as smoking, drug use, and delinquency (Kandel, 1978; Kiesner, Maass, Cadinu, & Vallese, 2003; Poulin et al., 1997; Rubin, Lynch, Coplan, Rose-Krasnor, & Booth, 1994; Urberg, Degirmencioglu, & Tolson, 1998). Studies also show that when youths have antisocial or disruptive friends, they tend to become more antisocial over time, thus suggesting that antisocial friends actually influence youths (Dishion, Spracklen, Andrews, & Patterson, 1996; Kiesner, Cadinu, Poulin, & Bucci, 2002; Mounts & Steinberg, 1995; Urberg, Degirmencioglu, & Pilgrim 1997; Vitaro, Brendgen, & Tremblay, 2000; Vitaro, Tremblay, Kerr, Pagani, & Bukowski, 1997). A considerable body of work, then, suggests that peer relationships play important roles in the development of adolescent problem behavior.

Despite the importance of these studies, many of them share a possible limitation. Most studies in the peer literature have been conducted in school classrooms, with friends defined as the friends that youths have in the classroom. There are obvious advantages to doing this. Classmates tend to be good informants of each others' behavior, and it is convenient and easy to include all classmates in a study. What is more, most youths nominate as friends those who attend the same school, even when their nominations are not restricted to the school context (Ennett & Bauman, 1994), thus suggesting that classroom-based studies capture the majority of friendships. In fact, early in the history of peer research investigators showed that most friendships could be predicted by gender, age, school grade, and neighborhood (Blyth,

Friends, Lovers and Groups: Key Relationships in Adolescence. Edited by Rutger C.M.E. Engels, Margaret Kerr and Håkan Stattin. Copyright © 2007 John Wiley & Sons, Ltd.

Hill, & Thiel, 1982; Coleman, 1961; Duck, 1975; Dunphy, 1963; Hartup, 1976; Kandel, 1978; Kandel & Lesser, 1972), and these findings justified and legitimized a peer literature based on classroom studies. Coleman (1961), for instance, concluded about pairs of friends, 'the one item that the two members had in common far more often than any other – including religion, father's occupation, father's education, common leisure interests, grades in school, and others – was class in school' (p. 76). A decade later, Kandel and Lesser (1972) drew a similar conclusion about friendship groups, 'since all but a small minority of friendships among both American and Danish adolescents are with schoolmates, a description of friendships and peer influences within the school serves adequately as a description of all adolescent friendship groups' (p. 171). Thus, researchers concluded early on that because most friends or friendship groups are in the school or classroom, school or classroom based studies of peer influences are sufficient to capture what researchers need to know about peer influences.

But even though there is solid evidence that classroom-based studies capture the majority of adolescents' friendships, the minority that they do not capture might be important for understanding the development and maintenance of problem behaviors such as alcohol use, delinquency, bullying or violence, and other forms of norm breaking. Out-of-school friends are more heterogeneous than in-school friends on age and gender (c.f. Allen, 1989; George & Hartmann, 1996; Smith & Inder, 1990), and this raises the possibility that they might introduce youths to a greater variety of behaviors. There might be subgroups of youths for whom out-of-school friends might be important in the development of problem behavior. For instance, compared with average and popular children, unpopular pre-adolescents have more friends outside of school and more who are not their same age (George & Hartmann, 1996). Similarly, for early developing girls, the most influential peers can be those who are older, who are in other classes, or who have quit school (Stattin & Magnusson, 1990). In the only study we know of that has compared in-school with out-of-school peer groups, problem behavior outside of school was more correlated with the out-of-school group's behavior and problem behavior in school was more correlated with the in-school group's behavior (Kiesner, Poulin, & Nicotra, 2003). Since most delinquent acts occur outside of school, this group of peers might be important.

Recent research also suggests that out-of-school peer *contexts* can be important for understanding peer influences on delinquency. For example, youths who start attending unstructured neighborhood youth recreation centers show increases in antisocial behavior, and this cannot be explained by their backgrounds or prior behavioral characteristics (Mahoney & Stattin, 2000; Mahoney, Stattin, & Magnusson, 2001; Persson et al., 2004; Stattin et al., 2005). For girls, the more often a female friend attended a neighborhood youth center, the more antisocial acts the girl reported doing with that friend (Stattin et al., 2003). In other research, when youths could nominate a friend from any context, antisocial youths were more likely than non-antisocial youths to nominate a friend who lived in the same neighborhood and whom they had met in an unstructured, unsupervised setting (Dishion et al., 1995). In short, peers outside of school might be important for subgroups of youths, for behaviors performed outside of school, and in certain out-of-school contexts. Classroom-based studies exclude these peers and peer contexts. Therefore, the question remains open whether we have missed something by focusing peer studies on friends in the classroom.

In addition, however, there are other ways in which studies of friends in the school classroom give limited knowledge about peer influences. The literature on peer influences is largely based on studies of best friends, but peer is a broader construct than friend. Friends are one type of peer, but there are other types of peers that might influence youths, and, to the extent that they do, a peer literature based on friends gives a limited picture of *peer* influences.

One class of non-friend peers that might be important for problem behavior is siblings. Siblings, especially older siblings, might introduce youths to smoking, drinking, or other problem behaviors. It is also possible that older siblings have an influence during a window of time in late childhood or early adolescence, when the older sibling has entered into a desired, more mature stage of life while the younger sibling has not. In recent studies, mixed results appear concerning whether siblings are important antisocial influences relative to other types of peers (cf., Bullock & Dishion, 2002; Shortt, Capaldi, Dishion, Bank, & Owen, 2003). These studies leave open the possibility that siblings might be important peers in adolescence when it comes to understanding the entry into adolescent problem behavior. However, because siblings are not usually in the same classroom, and because they are not usually defined as friends, peer studies that focus on friends in the classroom will miss siblings.

Another class of non-friend peers that might be important for problem behavior is romantic partners. More than a decade ago, investigators postulated that older boyfriends could draw girls into more advanced social networks where problem behaviors were more common, and this could explain the link between early pubertal development and problem behavior in girls (Stattin & Magnusson, 1990). This 'advanced social behavior hypothesis' can be extended to a more general theory about girls' romantic involvement and problem behavior. Boys are, on average, more involved than girls are in problem behaviors; therefore, if a girl enters into a boyfriend's group of male friends, almost by definition she enters into a peer group that is more problematic than her previous group, assuming that her previous peer group was mainly girls. Recently published work supports this idea. Romantic and sexual involvement has been linked to girls' delinquency, particularly for girls who spent time in settings where delinquent boys tended to congregate (Persson et al., 2004; Stattin et al., 2005), and girls have reported doing more delinquent acts with boyfriends than with girlfriends (Stattin et al., 2005). Furthermore, a recent study showed that having an older boyfriend predicted girls' problem behavior over and above preexisting risk factors (Young & d'Arcy, 2005). Thus, there are clear theoretical reasons to believe, and growing evidence to suggest, that girls' romantic involvement with boys is linked to problem behavior.

Other recent evidence, however, suggests that an elaborated theoretical explanation is needed, because boys' romantic involvement with girls has been linked to problem behavior, and this would not follow from the advanced social behavior hypothesis, unless the girlfriends were older and in a higher-norm breaking stage of adolescence. In one study, boys' (as well as girls') over involvement in dating was linked to problem behaviors (Zimmer-Gembeck, Siebenbruner, & Collins, 2001), and boys' antisocial talk with romantic partners was linked to deviant peer involvement (Shortt et al., 2003). Whatever the explanation, there is mounting evidence that romantic partners are important peers when it comes to adolescent delinquency. However, like siblings, romantic partners often are not in the same classroom, and they are not usually defined as friends. Thus, romantic partners and siblings are two types of peers that seem to be important for understanding adolescent delinquency, but, because they are not included in studies of friends in the classroom, a peer literature based on classroom studies gives a limited picture of *peer* influences.

The limitations of research on individual peers also apply to research on peer groups. Studies of peer groups typically involve groups in school, particularly in the classroom (e.g., Urberg et al., 1997), and methodologies have been developed to map the peer groups, or social networks, in the school or classroom (Cairns, Cairns, Neckerman, Gest, & Gariépy, 1988; Richards & Rice, 1981). There have been some studies of peer groups outside of school, and they have provided insight into: how peer groups naturally evolve over time (Dunphy, 1963); how deviant peer groups and gangs are formed and maintained (Goldstein, 1994); group processes and behavior stability (Sarnecki, 2001); and the link between leisure settings and transition behaviors (Silbereisen & Noack, 1988). Seldom, however, have any studies been done comparing peers in school with peers outside of school. One exception was a study of 6th through 8th graders in a neighborhood of Milan, Italy (Kiesner et al., 2003). Participants' out-of-school delinquency and in-school problem behavior were compared with those of their in-school and out-of-school peer groups. The in-school group had the strongest unique relation with the individuals' in-school problem behavior, whereas the after-school group had the strongest unique relation with the individuals' after-school delinquency. This study suggests that if researchers want to understand the role of peers in the development of delinquency, they might be missing something by focusing only on peers in the classroom.

Kiesner and colleagues' (2003) study provides important information about in-school versus out-of-school peer groups. Nevertheless, it raises some additional questions. First, the authors interpreted these findings as suggesting that youths select peers in different settings for the behavioral opportunities they offer. However, an alternative interpretation is also possible – that youths influence each other, and they adjust their behavior to match that of the peers they meet in different settings. Longitudinal data are needed to test the two explanations. Also, although some of the group members belonged to both the in-school and after-school groups, they were not considered separately from those who were specific to each setting. Thus, the common variance in the behavior scores of the two groups, created by overlapping members, was controlled statistically. It is possible, however, that these overlapping members play a unique role in the individual's development. In terms of similarity in delinquency, the peers that youths spend the most time with, or whom they see both in school and in free time might be the most behaviorally similar to them, either because constant companions have the greatest chance to influence one's behavior or because they have been selected into both groups because of similarity. Thus, the youths who appear in both the school and free-time groups could be the most interesting of all.

Taken as a whole, then, the literature on peers and delinquency has revealed much about what *can* happen or what sometimes happens. Youths can select peers who are similar to them, and their peers can influence them. Focusing peer studies on friends in the classroom is not a limitation for showing what *can* happen or sometimes happens. However, to extend this knowledge to what *does* happen, research designs are needed that strive for more ecological validity, or that take into account the complexity of adolescent peer relationships, including different types of peer relationships in different contexts at different ages. In this chapter, we report data from one such study.

'10 TO 18': A WHOLE-CITY STUDY

The study is a longitudinal study of the development of criminality in adolescence. We designed it to build upon the most recent advances in the largely separate literatures on family, peers, and individual characteristics – assessing these factors simultaneously and testing an integrative theory about their combined effects on movements into and out of criminality in adolescence. Thus, the study looks at peer influences on delinquency in the context of other possible influences.

In order to use this study to advance the literature on peers, we wanted information on all potentially influential peers – regardless of relationship (friend, sibling, boy- or girlfriend, etc.), regardless of age, regardless of gender, and regardless of where they met and spent time together. Just as important, we wanted information on these peers that was independent of the youths' own perceptions and biases, which have been shown to yield inaccurate information about peers (e.g. Iannotti, Bush, & Weinfurt, 1996). Finally, we wanted to examine both dyadic relationships and peer group relationships. This meant that all peers who might be influential for a particular youth should be included in the study: classmates, siblings, romantic partners, older friends, younger friends, friends that youths meet in school, and friends that they meet in their free time. Because our broader goals included understanding movements into criminality in early adolescence, we wanted to include pre-adolescents in the study, as well as the older peers who might influence them.

The only design that would provide these data was one that began with preadolescents, included all youths who might be influential peers, and followed them all over time. Here, we drew inspiration from Kiesner et al.'s (2003) study of in- and out-of-school friendship groups among middle-schoolers in a geographically defined neighborhood of a major Italian city. We extended the logic of including all 6th through 8th graders in an isolated neighborhood to all youths from preadolescence through the end of high school in a reasonably self-contained community. Thus, we looked for a community that: (1) had its own high school, so that youths would remain in the city school system over the entire adolescent period, (2) did not offer easy access to neighboring cities, so most youths would have their leisure time peer associations inside the community, and (3) had a population of the appropriate size so that all potentially influential peers could be included in the study. We settled on a small city in central Sweden with a population of about 25,000. With this whole-city design, we ask youths about their peers – not limited to friends and not limited to the classroom – and many or most of those peers have participated in the study. Thus, we have reports of peers' behavior from the peers themselves, so what we know about them is not filtered through the eyes of the adolescent who nominated them.

The design of the study is charted in Figure 8.1. As shown in the chart, each year of the study we are targeting nine cohorts (grades 4 – 12, or roughly ages 10 to 18). Each year, one new cohort comes into the study (those entering the 4th grade) and one cohort leaves the study (those who graduated from high school the year before). As shown in the shaded areas of the chart, this means that we are following three of these cohorts over a range of ages that will allow us to track movements into and out of criminality ($n \approx 1100$, all shaded cells), and every year we are assessing all other youths in the community from about 10 to about 18 years of age ($n \approx 2000$, all unshaded cells). The schools, and the current participants in each grade, are shown in Table 8.1. Youths in the 4th through 6th grades are in the elementary school system, and they attend ten different small schools (some smaller than others) located throughout the city and outlying neighborhoods. The 7th through 9th grades make up the middle-school level, and there are three schools in the city that serve these grades. For high school, or grades 10 through 12, all youths in the city are gathered in one school. We are collecting data each year for all 4th through 12th grade students in these schools.

'Very Important Persons'

'Very Important Persons' is an important construct in the '10 to 18' study. Instead of asking youths about their friends, we ask whom they define as important peers in their lives. A 'Very Important Person' (VIP), we tell them, 'is someone you talk with, hang out with, and do things with. It *cannot* be your parents or another adult. It could, for example, be a friend, a sibling, or a

School year	Grade (approximate age) of Cohorts in the Study								
2001 – 02	4 (10 y)	5 (11 y)	6 (12 y)	7 (13 y)	8 (14 y)	9 (15 y)	10 (16 y)	11 (17 y)	12 (18 y)
2002 – 03	4 (10 y)	5 (11 y)	6 (12 y)	7 (13 y)	8 (14 y)	9 (15 y)	10 (16 y)	11 (17 y)	12 (18 y)
2003 – 04	4 (10 y)	5 (11 y)	6 (12 y)	7 (13 y)	8 (14 y)	9 (15 y)	10 (16 y)	11 (17 y)	12 (18 y)
2004 – 05	4 (10 y)	5 (11 y)	6 (12 y)	7 (13 y)	8 (14 y)	9 (15 y)	10 (16 y)	11 (17 y)	12 (18 y)
2005 – 06	4 (10 y)	5 (11 y)	6 (12 y)	7 (13 y)	8 (14 y)	9 (15 y)	10 (16 y)	11 (17 y)	12 (18 y)
2006 – 07	4 (10 y)	5 (11 y)	6 (12 y)	7 (13 y)	8 (14 y)	9 (15 y)	10 (16 y)	11 (17 y)	12 (18 y)
2007 – 08	4 (10 y)	5 (11 y)	6 (12 y)	7 (13 y)	8 (14 y)	9 (15 y)	10 (16 y)	11 (17 y)	12 (18 y)

Shaded and unshaded cells in each row show cohorts participating in each data-collection wave. Shaded cells show three cohorts that will participate throughout the entire study.

Figure 8.1 Design of '10 to 18' study

Table 8.1 Numbers of youths in the study at one time point by grade and school

Grade	School													n
	1	2	3	4	5	6	7	8	9	10	11	12	13	
4	X		X	X	X	X	X		X	X				319
5	X	X		X	X	X	X		X	X				343
6	X			X		X	X	X		X	X			346
7										X	X	X		339
8										X	X	X		353
9										X	X	X		286
10													X	379
11													X	302
12													X	212
n	172	10	16	116	72	102	83	34	125	387	399	490	893	2899

Dashed lines delineate elementary, middle, and high school grade levels

boyfriend or girlfriend. Your VIPs can live anywhere, they don't have to be the same age as you, and they can be both boys and girls.' Thus, we have allowed for a range of possibilities for the types of relationships they have with the peers who are important to them. A youth's most important peer might be a friend in the school classroom or elsewhere, it might be a sibling at home, or it might be a romantic partner who is two years older and going to another school.

Initial Findings

In a recent study, we examined the relations between antisocial behavior on one hand and the types of important peers that youths reported, the contexts in which they had met, and where they spent time (e.g., school, neighborhood, club) on the other (Kiesner, Kerr, & Stattin, 2004). Youths who nominated romantic partners as their first-mentioned, or *most*, important peers were more antisocial than those who nominated friends or siblings. Surprisingly, this was true for both boys and girls. In addition, youths who had met and spent time with their first-mentioned, or most, important peers in the neighborhood were also the most antisocial, and important peers whom youths had met in the neighborhood were more antisocial than important peers met in other contexts. One of the primary purposes of that study was to test an 'additive homophily' hypothesis, or the idea that youths would show unique simila- rities to multiple important peers. The results confirmed this. Delinquency measures for second- and third-mentioned important peers explained signifi- cantly more variance in individual delinquency than was explained by the delinquency of the first important peer alone. Thus, initial results suggest that research has, indeed, missed something about peers and delinquency by focusing mainly on single friendships in the school classroom.

THE PRESENT STUDY

In this study, we elaborate on that initial investigation. First, we ask whom youths name when they are asked about their most important peers. Do they name a best friend in the school classroom? In other words, how can youths' important peers be described? We also ask whether there are age trends in the types of important peers that youths name. Next, we look at in-school and out-of-school peer *groups*. As discussed earlier, there may be differences between group members who belong only to the school group, those who belong only to the after-school group, and members belonging to both the in-school and after-school groups. Thus, we examine the possibility that the overlapping group might be the most important. Finally, using longitudinal analyses, we test several specific hypotheses about the roles of important peers and in- and out-of-school groups in the development of different problem behaviors: (a) that having older, male important peers is linked to problem behaviors for both boys and girls, (b) that violence in and outside of school might be linked to having the same problematic peers in both contexts, and (c) that for early-maturing girls, problematic peer associations might be concentrated to the peers girls only spend time with outside of school, because in-school peer associations are quite age graded. Support for these hypotheses would suggest that peers outside of the school and classroom can be important for understanding peer influences on problem behavior.

Adolescents' Important Peers

We look first at youths' reports of their important peers, described earlier. Youths could name up to four important peers, in order of importance to them. In these analyses, we focus on the first-mentioned, or most, important peer, as a parallel or alternative to the best friend, which is often the focus of peer research. In addition to naming the important peer, youths reported the sex and age of the person, what their relationship was with the person (friend, sibling, or romantic partner), where they first met, and where they typically spent time together. Of all participants who answered any of the questions we asked about important peers, school and free time friends, classmates youths preferred to be friends with, and peers they wanted to become friends with ($n = 2,815$), only 23 failed to mention an important person and give some information about the person. Thus, nearly everyone had some important person in his or her life.

The numbers of participants included in the analyses vary according to whether we use the adolescents' reports of their peers or the peers' own reports. There were originally 2899 adolescents who responded to our questionnaires. Of them, 2776 subjects reported on important peers. When we use the participants' reports about the gender of important peers, whether they were friends, siblings, or romantic partners, we have marginal attrition. However, when we use independent information given by the friends, siblings, and romantic partners themselves, we have fewer reports because were not able to identify all of the peers. Of the 2776 peers whom the participants named as important peers, we were able to identify 76.1% (2112 of 2776 important peers). We identified about the same proportion of peers mentioned as belonging to the school peer group and free-time peer group.

Who Are Youths' Most Important Peers?

When youths are free to name their most important peers without being restricted to friends in the school classroom, whom do they name? As the most general approach to this question, we looked first at whether the first important peers that youths named tended to be the same sex and age as themselves. The results, by grade, appear in Table 8.2. Concerning sex, these findings show that, in general, the majority of youths' most important peers are of the same sex, but this is less true for high school youths than for younger youths. In fact, for 12th graders, particularly girls, the most important peer is about as likely to be opposite sex as same sex. Before high school, the percentage of youths naming opposite-sex peers as most important is low. Still, around 10% or more do so, and boys are as likely to name girls as girls are to name boys. Concerning age, again, a vast majority of youths name most important peers who are within a year, more or less, of their own age. Nonetheless, approximately 15% to 30% name older or younger youths as their most important peers, and this is somewhat more likely in the youngest and oldest cohorts in the sample. Although same-sex, same-age important peers are normative, then, sizable minorities in each cohort violate those norms.

The consistent proportions of youths naming cross-sex, older, or younger important peers, particularly in the older cohorts, suggest that some important

Table 8.2 Percentages of first-named important peers who are of the same age and sex as the individuals by grade

	Same sex		Same age (± 1 year)	
Grade	Boys	Girls	Boys	Girls
4	86.1% (132/165)	89.9% (134/149)	72.7% (131/165)	64.5% (95/148)
5	87.3% (151/173)	87.8% (144/164)	71.2% (124/174)	75.9% (123/162)
6	89.6% (172/193)	92.4% (158/171)	82.8% (159/192)	75.3% (128/170)
7	88.8% (166/187)	92.7% (139/150)	85.4% (152/178)	83.9% (125/149)
8	90.2% (157/174)	84.0% (147/175)	82.0% (141/172)	81.0% (141/174)
9	79.4% (112/141)	79.6% (109/137)	83.5% (117/140)	73.0% (100/137)
10	80.2% (134/167)	62.0% (98/158)	85.5% (131/153)	64.8% (81/125)
11	71.9% (97/135)	57.6% (76/132)	75.9% (91/120)	65.7% (67/102)
12	59.3% (51/86)	50.6% (43/85)	75.1% (66/88)	70.2% (59/84)

Dashed lines delineate elementary, middle, and high school grade levels

Table 8.3 Percentages of first-named important peers reported to be friends, siblings, or romantic partners across age

	Friend	Sibling	Romantic Partner	Other	n
4	75.6	17.9	2.9^A	3.5	312
5	70.9	21.7^T	4.5^A	3.0	337
6	78.8^T	14.3	2.8^A	4.1	363
7	81.6^T	12.2	2.4^A	3.9	337
8	78.0	10.4	7.8	3.8	346
9	71.8	10.4	13.2	4.6	280
10	65.0^A	8.3	23.6^T	3.1	326
11	57.7^A	12.0	27.0^T	3.4	267
12	58.9^A	4.2^A	36.3^T	0.6	168
Total	72.1	12.9	11.5	3.5	2736

EXACON analysis: ^{T}typical, meaning that the combination occurs more often than expected by chance; ^{A}atypical, meaning that the combination occurs less often than expected by chance. Dashed lines delineate elementary, middle, and high school grade levels.

peers might be siblings or romantic partners. To examine who is nominated as an important peer, we looked, next, at the proportions of most important peers who fell into the different relationship categories (friend, sibling, romantic partner, or other). Overall, about three-quarters were friends and the rest were approximately evenly divided between siblings and romantic partners (72.1% friends, 12.9% siblings, 11.5% romantic partners, 3.5% other). However, as shown in Table 8.3, these figures mask some interesting age trends.

The table shows these results broken down by grade. A visual inspection of the table reveals certain apparent age trends. For testing these trends, we used the program EXACON (Bergman & El-Khouri, 1987). EXACON calculates an exact chi-square and probability for each cell in a contingency table, thus indicating, for each cell, whether there are more or fewer people than expected by chance. In this case, we used the one-tailed probabilities of observed cell frequencies according to the fixed margins model, using the hypergeometric distribution. This is similar to Fisher's exact test. In the table, a combination is labeled T (typical) if it occurs more often than expected by chance after Bonferroni correction. A combination is labeled A (atypical) if it occurs less often than expected by chance. Within each type of relationship, there is an obvious age trend. For instance, naming a friend as one's most important peer was, in general, less common with age; by high school, it was atypical. However, the trend does not seem to be linear. Although naming a friend appears to have been more common among youths in all the earlier grades, it was typical and most frequent among 6th and 7th graders rather than 4th and 5th graders. The same trend appears for naming a sibling as one's most important peer. By visual inspection, this was more common for the younger than the older youths in the sample, and for 5th graders, it was typical, whereas for 12th graders it was atypical. The clearest age trend, however, was for naming a romantic partner as one's most important peer. For youths in the 4th through 7th grades, only around 3% named romantic partners, and it was atypical in each grade. In contrast, it was typical in 10th grade and above. Roughly a quarter to a third of high-school students considered a romantic partner their most important peer. Thus, even though friends are named most often at every age as the most important peer, they seem to be relatively less important and romantic partners seem to be more important as youths approach young adulthood.

We looked at these proportions for boys and girls separately, and the patterns of results are similar for the sexes. For both, the peak for naming a friend is around the 6th through 8th grades, but the drop-off with age is more extreme for girls than boys. This can be explained by the high proportions of girls who named boyfriends as their most important peers in the later grades. Thus, although there might be some differences in degree, the trends are the same for boys and girls.

Are the Most Important Peers in the School Classroom?

Before answering the question whether most important peers are friends in the same classroom, we start more generally by looking at what proportion of first-named, or most, important peers are in the same school. As shown in Table 8.4, the answer depends to some extent on age. As shown in the first column of the table, for youths in grades 4 through 9, about 60% to 70% of the most important peers were in the same school, but for high school students it was only about half. These proportions are somewhat reduced when we narrow the scope to the same grade in school, as shown in the second column of the table. When we

Table 8.4 Percentages of important peers who are in the same school, same grade, and same class

	Same School	Same Grade	Same Class	n
4	61.9	54.0	50.8	315
5	61.2	56.5	45.0	338
6	68.6	60.9	54.8	363
7	70.6	63.2	50.1	337
8	67.9	62.5	47.9	349
9	66.1	63.6	50.7	280
10	50.0	38.4	18.5	336
11	50.6	38.7	17.5	269
12	40.2	28.9	18.6	194
Total	60.9	53.2	40.8	2781

Dashed lines delineate elementary, middle, and high school grade levels consider the classroom (third column), we miss about half of all most important peers mentioned by the 4th through 9th graders and more than 80% of those mentioned by the high school students. In summary, although previous research has shown that most *friendships* are in the school classroom, when the definition of an important peer is not limited to friendships, neither the classroom nor the school captures most of the important peers.

We also looked at whether youths in our study, as in previous studies, primarily named friends in the classroom when they named friends as their most important peers. We selected the important peers that youths defined as friends and looked at the percentages that were in the same class at each of three grade levels (elementary, middle, and high school). For elementary and middle-school youths, the majority were in the same class, 62.9% and 60.2% for elementary- and middle-school youths, respectively. For high-school students, however, only 26.5% of the important peers defined as friends were in the same class at school. Thus, our results for early- and middle-adolescent youths are similar to those reported previously in that the majority named someone in their class when they named a best friend, but the majority in our study was not as large as the vast majorities reported earlier. Perhaps this is because youths in our study were specifically primed to consider friends outside of school by the instructions that told them that their friends could live anywhere.

What Peer Research Has Missed: Older and Opposite-Sex Peers

Previous research has missed some peers that youths define as important, but does that mean that those peers are important for problem behavior? We answer this question by examining one theoretical issue: age and sex of peers. Two well-established phenomena are that: (a) the prevalence of problem behaviors such as alcohol drinking, shoplifting, and vandalism rises sharply in middle adolescence, and (b) boys do these things more than girls do. Accordingly, young adolescent girls who associate with boys, particularly older boys are likely to be drawn into these behaviors (Persson et al., 2004; Stattin & Magnusson, 1988; Stattin et al., 2005). However, perhaps this is not only true for girls. Following the same reasoning, any young adolescent who associates with older peers, particularly older boys, should be at risk for being drawn into the types of problem behaviors that are most common among older adolescents, particularly boys. If this were so, then young adolescents (boys or girls) who name older boys as their most important peers should be at risk for delinquency, and girls who name boys, whether they are older or not, should be at risk for delinquency.

To test this idea, we looked at young adolescents' behavior in relation to characteristics of their important peers. We selected 7th through 9th graders and divided the sample according to two characteristics of most important peers: sex (girl versus boy) and age (younger and same versus older). As criterion variables, we looked at serious and less serious forms of delinquency.

Serious and Less Serious Delinquency

Youths self-reported about various delinquent behaviors. For these analyses, we used two scales that we have extracted through factor analyses. The scales represent serious and less serious delinquent acts. The *serious* acts included breaking and entering with the intention of stealing, car theft, motorcycle theft, and stealing something out of a car. The *less serious* acts included shoplifting, vandalizing public property, taking money from home, painting graffiti, stealing a bicycle, and avoiding paying at a movie, café, or on the bus. Youths were asked whether they had done these things during the past year, and the possible answers ranged from 'No it has not happened' (1) to 'More than 10 times' (5). Because these behaviors become more prevalent over these ages and are more prevalent for boys than for girls, we standardized the serious and less serious delinquency scales within grade and gender. The Chronbach's alphas were 0.91 and 0.81 for serious and less serious delinquency, respectively. The correlation between them was, r (1,711) = 0.51.

Older Male Peers and Problem Behavior

To test the idea that having boys (for girls) or older boys (for boys) as most important peers is a risk factor for problem behavior, we conducted contrast tests on serious and less series delinquency and alcohol drinking. For girls, we contrasted those who named boys (older or same age) with those who named girls. For boys, we contrasted those who named older boys with those who named same-age boys or girls. The results appear in Table 8.6. Concerning girls, the results provide a fair amount of support for the hypothesis. Girls who named boys as their most important peers were higher than the other girls on both less serious and serious delinquency, and girls who named *older* boys were higher on alcohol drinking. It is noteworthy to mention that we are not considering anything about the *behavior* of these peers – just their age and gender. These results show that by knowing only the age and gender of the most important peers that girls named, we know something about those girls' delinquency and alcohol drinking levels relative to others their age.

For boys, however, the results show a mixed picture. For serious delinquency, the results support the hypothesis that having an older male as one's most important peer is a risk factor. However, older male peers were not a risk factor for less serious delinquency and alcohol drinking. On the contrary, visual inspection suggests that having a girl as a most important peer is more associated with these problems. Thus, our hypothesis was only partly supported in the data on boys. In one sense, though, the conclusion is the same for boys and girls. Youths whose most important peers are older or opposite sex tend to be more problematic on several indicators. Older peers and opposite-sex peers would not be defined as friends in the classroom; therefore, they would have been missed by some of the most commonly used peer methodologies.

Table 8.5 Means (standard deviations) by gender for groups representing all combinations of sex and age of the most important peer mentioned

	First-named important peer						Contrast test[a]	
	Girl		Boy				t (df)	p
	Same Age	Older	Same Age	Older				
Girls	$n = 295$	$n = 99$	$n = 22$	$n = 44$				
Less Serious Delinquency	−0.02 (0.98)	−0.08 (0.87)	0.29 (1.60)	0.16 (0.99)			1.92 (451)	*
Serious Delinquency	−0.05 (0.88)	−0.01 (0.87)	0.31 (2.20)	0.20 (1.09)			1.97 (451)	*
Alcohol Drinking	−0.09 (0.89)	−0.01 (1.10)	0.07 (1.42)	0.53 (1.02)			2.46 (450)	*
Boys	$n = 38$	$n = 27$	$n = 319$	$n = 106$				
Less Serious Delinquency	0.25 (1.15)	0.12 (1.29)	−0.09 (0.80)	0.10 (1.25)			−.07 (477)	ns
Serious Delinquency	−0.05 (.74)	−0.02 (0.85)	−0.11 (0.65)	0.26 (1.56)			2.56 (476)	**
Alcohol Drinking	0.44 (1.19)	0.29 (1.49)	−0.11 (0.84)	0.05 (1.18)			−1.20 (480)	ns

*$p < 0.05$; **$p < 0.01$; ***$p < 0.001$. [a]For girls, the contrast was same-age and older boys against girls; for boys the contrast was older boys against same-age boys and girls.

Peer Groups

The above results suggest that to focus on friends in the classroom is to miss some potentially important peer influences, and the same could be said about focusing on *peer groups* in school. As mentioned before, recent findings show that out-of-school peer groups are behaviorally similar to individuals on problem behaviors that are done outside school, and in-school groups are more similar on problem behaviors done in school (Kiesner et al., 2003). In this study, we extend those findings by (1) delineating, in addition to in- and out-of-school groups, the group that is common to both contexts (i.e., for want of a better term, the 'conjoint' group); (2) examining different age groups from preadolescence into high school; and (3) comparing school, free-time, and conjoint peer groups in their influences on problem behavior over time.

Measure of peer groups

We asked youths about their peer groups in school and outside of school, using a method devised by Cairns and colleagues (Cairns et al., 1988). First, the definition of a group was given: 'In all schools there are *groups* of kids (at least three people) who hang out together (groups of friends or several people who are usually together).' Then, students were asked to list the groups that they knew about *in school*. They were told to start with their own group, if they had one, and to reinforce that, the section where they were to list the first group was labeled, 'Your group,' and the first line of the section was labeled, 'Your name.' Later in the questionnaire, a similar question appeared asking about groups *outside of school*. For this study, we focus on the in-school and free-time groups of which the youths reported themselves members.

Peer Group Membership Across Age and Context

As shown in Table 8.6, substantial proportions of youths reported in-school groups and free-time groups. Groups seem to be more important for girls than boys, and they seem to peak in importance for both sexes around grade 9. However, as shown in the table, only a small minority of groups that youths named contained opposite-sex members, and this did not vary dramatically with age. At most, only about a quarter of groups contained opposite-sex members, and this was most consistent for girls' free time groups in 7th grade and above.

We consider, next, the extent of overlap between the two groups, starting with the typical patterns of school, free-time, and overlapping friendship groups. We created three mutually exclusive measures (a) number of peers uniquely in the school group (b) number of peers in both school and free-time

Table 8.6 Percentages of youths reporting groups (percentages of those reporting opposite-sex group members) across age and context

	School group		Free-time group	
	Boys	Girls	Boys	Girls
4	66 (10)	79 (14)	37 (11)	50 (8)
5	69 (6)	76 (9)	43 (8)	50 (20)
6	81 (5)	89 (13)	53 (10)	56 (17)
7	81 (7)	87 (10)	53 (10)	68 (25)
8	81 (6)	89 (5)	50 (13)	66 (21)
9	93 (14)	90 (19)	72 (21)	80 (24)
10	61 (11)	73 (26)	42 (16)	57 (24)
11	53 (19)	76 (16)	41 (13)	63 (26)
12	59 (14)	81 (6)	40 (14)	64 (21)
Total	72 (9)	82 (13)	48 (13)	61 (20)

All percentages are rounded to the nearest whole number. Dashed lines delineate elementary, middle, and high school grade levels.

groups, and (c) number of peers uniquely in the free-time group. These three mutually exclusive variables were subjected to a cluster analysis. We used a hierarchical cluster analysis, with Ward's method and squared Euclidian distances being the similarity measure among individuals. We extracted ten clusters because of a sudden increase in the agglomeration coefficient. The cluster solution accounted for 82.6% of the error sums of squares (this is more than the lower bound of 70%, as suggested by Bergman, Magnusson, and El-Khouri (2003)). These clusters are described in Table 8.7.

Table 8.7 Cluster analysis of school peers, conjoint peers, and free time peers ($n = 2814$)

Cluster	School peers	Conjoint peers	Free time peers	N	Description
1	0.3 (0.6)	5.3 (1.2)	0.6 (0.7)	104	Many conjoint peers
2	0.1 (0.3)	0.1 (0.3)	0.0 (0.2)	582	No peers
3	2.5 (0.5)	0.1 (0.3)	0.5 (0.8)	560	School peers
4	0.1 (0.2)	0.0 (0.2)	3.5 (1.5)	153	Free time peers
5	3.9 (1.3)	.4 (.6)	3.2 (1.0)	402	School & free time peers
6	0.3 (0.5)	2.6 (0.7)	0.2 (0.4)	275	Conjoint peers
7	4.8 (1.1)	0.0 (0.2)	0.0 (0.2)	399	Many school peers
8	2.8 (1.0)	2.2 (0.8)	0.4 (0.6)	156	School & conjoint peers
9	1.3 (1.1)	2.4 (1.0)	3.0 (1.1)	109	All peer types
10	4.6 (1.5)	0.4 (0.7)	6.2 (1.0)	74	Many school & many free time peers

Many = 4 or more peers

As many as 21% of the subjects belonged to the cluster 'No peers.' As to those who belonged to peer groups, four of the clusters (clusters 1, 6, 8, and 9) contained conjoint peers in various types of peer group constellations. The subjects in these clusters accounted for 29% of the subjects who had some constellation of peers who belonged both to peer groups at school and in free time. Also, a substantial amount of the participants solely engaged in peer groups at school (clusters 3 and 7). They amounted to 959 individuals or 43% of the subjects who belonged to a peer group at school or in free time (959 of 2232 pupils). Generally, if we would adopt a school based design, we would have complete information about peer interactions for the majority, 67%, of all subjects (clusters 1, 3, 6, 7, 8; 1494 of 2232 participants). But one of three would have peers outside school that might also be important for their behavior.

We examined which of the peer group constellations obtained in the cluster analysis differed between boys and girls, and between participants at different ages. The results are reported in Table 8.8. As shown in the table, there were few gender differences. An EXACON analysis showed that to have no peers (cluster 2) was more common for boys, whereas to have only conjoint peers (cluster 6), and to have both school, free-time and conjoint peers (cluster 9) was more common for girls.

The situation was different when we compared the peer group clusters over grades. Then, considerably more differences were found. In the younger ages, in elementary school, it was more common than in older ages that the pupils engaged solely with school peers, and/or had peers who were their peer group both at school and in free-time (clusters 3 and 6). In these ages, it seems as if peer group activity much was an issue of being together with other peers at school, of which some the participants also interacted with in free-time. Much seemed to change in middle school. First, the peer groups become

Table 8.8 Percentage of boys and girls, and of participants at different grades, with peer groups of different character

| Cluster | Gender | | Grade | | |
	Boys	Girls	Elementary School	Middle School	High School
1. Many conjoint peers	3.0	4.4	1.9[a]	6.8[t]	2.3
2. No peers	24.4[t]	15.0[a]	21.3	11.6[a]	27.9[t]
3. School peers	20.6	20.8	28.5[t]	18.7	13.4[a]
4. Free time peers	5.5	5.4	5.1	3.8[a]	7.8[t]
5. School & free time peers	14.0	14.6	10.6[a]	14.9	18.1[t]
6. Conjoint peers	7.6[a]	12.1[t]	12.3[t]	11.3	4.7[a]
7. Many school peers	15.3	13.0	13.8	15.2	13.5
8. School & conjoint peers	4.6	6.6	4.5	8.5[t]	3.4[a]
9. All peer types	2.5[a]	5.4[t]	1.7[a]	5.6[t]	4.6
10. Many school & free time p.	2.5	2.7	0.4[a]	3.6	4.3[t]

bigger (cluster 1) and fewer of the pupils lacked a peer group (cluster 2). Second, a stronger mix of peers met in different contexts appear (clusters 8 and 9). In high school, engaging with free-time peers becomes more common than at earlier grades (see clusters 4, 5, and 10). At the same time, there is a substantial minority of subjects (see cluster 2) who do not seem to have stable peer groups. Overall, peer group activity seems to be located at school in the earlier of these grades. It becomes more diversified over time, and free-time peers play more central roles in the older grades.

What Peer Research Has Missed: Group Influences on Violence, Bullying, and Delinquency

We have suggested that the conjoint group, or the peers that one associates with both in and out of school, should have the greatest chance to influence one's behavior. Here, we test this idea by looking at the influences of school, conjoint, and free-time peers on serious and less serious delinquency. In addition, we consider two other problem behaviors: bullying in school and violence on the streets. Previous research suggests that it is largely the same youths who bully others in school and are violent on the streets (Andershed, Stattin, & Kerr, 2001). Although the personal characteristics of the youths could be driving this cross-situational consistency, it might also be peers who are present in both settings reinforcing the behavior. Thus, in this study we test whether the conjoint friends' characteristics seem to influence these behaviors.

Bullying in School

Here, we used a measure of bullying involving physically or verbally attacking others or excluding others that has been used previously (Alsaker & Brunner, 1999). Rather than grouping youths according to whether they had done or repeated these behaviors, however, we used the measure as a continuous bullying variable. Participants used a four-point response scale that ranged from 'No, it has not happened this semester' to 'Yes, it has happened several times a week.' The items dealt with: (1) saying nasty things, mocking or teasing in unpleasant way; (2) hitting, kicking, or attacking; and (3) excluding someone.

Violence on the Streets

Youths were asked about a number of violent acts that they might have done. They were asked to report about the current semester. (The data collection took place at near the end of the semester.) The four-point response scale went from 'No, it has not happened this semester' to 'Yes, it has happened four or more times.' The questions dealt with: (1) attacking others while out at night without them having threatened or attacked oneself or one's friends first;

(2) kicking someone who was lying down or kicking someone in the head; (3) threatening or forcing someone to hand over their money, cell phone, cigarettes or anything else; or (4) carrying a weapon while out at night.

Peer Influences

In these analyses, we look at peer influences by using data from two points in time. We predict problem behavior at the second time point from peers' earlier behavior, controlling for the youth's own earlier behavior. All variables were entered simultaneously in the multiple regression models. All participants were used in these analyses. If they reported a particular type of group, the mean values on problem behaviors (violence, bullying, etc.) for the group members were used. If they did not report any members in a particular type of group, we assigned the value that indicated no problem behaviors for that group. The results of these analyses appear in Table 8.9. For every measure, the best predictor of Time 2 behavior was the youth's own behavior at Time 1. Apart from that, however, the table shows very clearly that the strongest peer influence on boys is the conjoint group. For all problem behavior measures, the conjoint group's, and no other group's, behavior at Time 1 predicts boys' behavior at Time 2 controlling for their earlier behavior. For girls, however, the effects are more scattered. In girls, most of these problem behaviors are substantially stable over time; therefore, group behavior is less influential. Nonetheless, conjoint peers are somewhat influential for violence on the streets and bullying in school. They are the only peers who are

Table 8.9 Multiple regression models predicting violence on the streets, bullying, and delinquency at T2 from the same behaviors among different peers at T1 controlling for youths' own T1 behavior

		Problem behavior (T1)			
Problem behavior (T2)	Individual	School peers	Conjoint peers	Free time peers	R^2
Boys					
Violence on the streets	0.43 ***	0.06	0.36 ***	−0.01	0.40^1
Bullying in school	0.30 ***	0.05	0.14 *	0.01	0.36^2
Serious delinquency	0.41 ***	−0.01	0.25 ***	−0.05	0.24^3
Less serious delinquency	0.49 ***	−0.05	0.19 ***	−0.05	0.32^4
Girls					
Violence on the streets	0.62 ***	−0.05	0.12 *	0.05	0.37^5
Bullying in school	0.45 ***	0.00	0.12 *	−0.03	0.22^6
Serious delinquency	0.37 ***	0.23 ***	0.17 ***	0.12 *	0.34^7
Less serious delinquency	0.65 ***	0.06	−0.04	0.03	0.45^8

Note: beta values are presented
* $p<0.05$; ** $p<0.01$; *** $p<0.001$; those not marked are $p>0.05$
[1.] $F_{(4,243)} = 40.47$, $p<0.001$; [2.] $F_{(4,224)} = 8.22$, $p<0.001$; [3.] $F_{(4,274)} = 21.80$, $p<0.001$;
[4.] $F_{(4,274)} = 32.24$, $p<0.001$; [5.] $F_{(4,244)} = 37.28$, $p<0.001$; [6.] $F_{(4,225)} = 16.12$, $p<0.001$; [7.] $F_{(4,268)} = 33.73$, $p<0.001$;
[8.] $F_{(4,268)} = 55.26$, $p<0.001$

important for those behaviors. Conjoint peers are also important for serious delinquency, but so are school peers and free-time peers. Together, however, the results for boys and girls across these different problem behaviors lend a fair amount of support to the idea that the peers whom youths engage with both in and outside of school have the greatest chance to influence their behavior.

What Peer Research Has Missed: Peer Groups of Early Developing Girls

As a final example, we take an issue for which we expect the free-time peer group to be important. A number of studies in different countries have shown that for girls, early pubertal maturation is associated with problem behavior. One explanation for this is that early developing girls seek out older peers who match their biological age rather than their chronological age. Then, just by virtue of the fact that norm breaking increases from early to middle adolescence, when they make friends with older adolescents they enter peer groups that are higher in norm breaking. Because most of the activities in school are age-stratified, early developing girls have little opportunity to develop friendships with older peers who match their biological maturity. Thus, their in-school groups should be roughly similar to the in-school groups of on-time and later developing girls. In other words, there should be no correlation between age of puberty and the ages of the members of girls' in-school groups. Outside of school, however, early developing girls have more freedom to make friends with older youths who are closer to their physical maturity status. This suggests that the free-time peers of early developing girls should be older than those of the on-time and late maturers. If so, then they should also be more norm breaking, since norm breaking increases from early to middle adolescence. In other words, for girls, the age of puberty should be correlated with both age and problem behavior in free-time peer groups but not in-school peer groups.

   To test this idea, we correlated the age of first menstruation for 7th and 8th grade girls with characteristics of their peer groups: age, gender, and delinquency. In addition, we looked at activities that girls reported doing with their free-time groups, expecting age of puberty to be linked to doing more norm breaking activities with the free-time group.

Activities with the free-time group

Youths were asked which of several activities they had done with their free-time groups during the past month, and how often they had done them. We were interested in several antisocial activities: playing hooky, shoplifting, getting drunk, keeping secrets from parents, talking about illegal things, and doing things other than shoplifting for which one could get caught by the police. The others were filler items that can be characterized as social activities:

Table 8.10 Correlations between the age of menarche and characteristics of school-unique, conjoint, and free-time-unique peer groups.

Peer group characteristics	Girls' pubertal timing and characteristics of three peer groups		
	School Unique	Conjoint	Free time Unique
Age	−0.05	−0.05	−0.37 ***
Gender	0.04	−0.07	−0.10 +
Delinquency	−0.04	0.01	−0.29 **
Activities with free-time group			
Social			−0.02
Antisocial			−0.21 ***

+ p <0.10; **p < 0.01; ***p < 0.001; [b]those not marked are p > 0.05

going out looking for boys (or girls), using the internet or playing video games, chatting on the phone, and watching TV or videos.

The results of these analyses appear in Table 8.10. The age of puberty correlated significantly with age of, delinquency of, and antisocial activities undertaken with free-time-unique peers. There was also a marginally significant relation between free-time peers' gender and pubertal timing, such that early developing girls were somewhat more likely to have boys in their free-time groups. In contrast, but as predicted, pubertal timing was unrelated to the age, gender, or delinquency of school-unique and conjoint peer groups, and it was unrelated to the social activities performed with the free-time group. Thus, these results show that looking at the peer groups that early developing girls have in school, where they are not free to choose older peers, will reveal little about the role of peers in the often-found link between early development and norm breaking. It is uniquely free-time peers who are important in this case.

DISCUSSION

The bulk of the literature on peer influences in adolescence is based on studies of friends in the school classroom. Although a number of studies have gone beyond this, almost none have compared different types of relationships across different contexts. In this study, we showed that many of the peers that adolescents themselves define as most important are not in their school classrooms. Some of those peers are older, including older romantic partners. Some are parts of the peer groups that adolescents see outside of school rather than in school. In still other instances, the most important peers are those that youths interact with both in school and outside of school. Each of these types of peers is important for different subgroups of adolescents when considering different types of behaviors.

Using data from a study of all youths from ages 10 to 18 in an entire city, we were able to chart the age-related trends concerning which peers are important. We have shown, probably for the first time, how much less frequently friends are named as the most important peer as adolescents move through adolescence, and that by the end of high school nearly half of all youths name romantic partners as the most important peers in their lives. We have also shown for the first time that the friendship groups with whom youths engage across contexts – in and outside of school – have the greatest chance to influence their behavior, and that they do influence their behavior when it comes to certain serious problem behaviors. However, we have shown that the peers that girls meet only in school and only in their free-time can also be influential for problem behavior. These phenomena only become apparent when peers in different contexts are included in the same study.

An innovation in this study was to identify and test the influence of the peers whom youths associate with across settings – what we call the conjoint peers. Although school peers and free-time peers have been the focus of past research, the issue of time spent with peers across settings has not come up as a possible determinant of influence. What is more, it is not clear what one should expect, a priori. On one hand, the peers that youths spend the most time with across settings might have the greatest chance to influence their behavior, as we have argued. However, one could also argue that youths habituate to familiar, constant companions, and are little influenced by them, but that they dishabituate to occasional, setting specific acquaintances, and try out any new behaviors that they introduce. Although we did not specifically set out to test these opposing ideas, our results suggest that constant companions, or conjoint peers, are more influential. We have not, however, tested a wide range of problem behaviors, and there might be others for which setting specific peers are more influential. This is a question for future research.

In this chapter, we have talked much about what peer research has missed by using methodologies that focus on peers in the school classroom. Of course, there are a number of lines of research in the peer literature that are not open to that criticism. There is a long history in criminology, psychology, and sociology, of observing and systematically record influence of group processes in naturalistic settings (Dunphy, 1963; Fine & Glassner, 1979; Glueck & Glueck, 1950; Sherif, Harvey, White, Hood, & Sherif, 1961; Trasher, 1927). A number of studies have focused on going into different activities and encountering different types of peers (Brook, Nomura, & Cohen, 1989; Brown, 1990; Fine, 1980; Stattin et al., 2005). Other studies have looked at the settings in which behaviors such as alcohol drinking and delinquency emerge (Cochran & Bo, 1987; Engels & Knibbe, 2000; Engels, Knibbe, & Drop, 1999) or have described peer groups in natural settings, or adolescent behavior in context (Goldstein, 1994; Silbereisen & Noack, 1988; Silbereisen, Noack, & von Eye, 1992). Developmental-contextualist models on social network analysis have shed light on the structure and development of different peer configurations (e.g., best friends, cliques, crowds/social networks) and have addressed central questions through the developmental of new technologies and long-itudinal research (Cairns & Cairns, 1994). These studies are not classroom based. Still, they have not compared peers in more natural settings *with* peers in the school classroom. What we have done in the design of the '10 to 18' study is to try to map the entire territory of peers, peer groups, and settings – to look at the school friends and peer groups and the peers in self-chosen settings simultaneously, and to compare them.

The longitudinal study from which these data come has several methodo-logical strengths. First, it extends a recent methodological advance in studying peers in and outside of the school context (Kiesner et al., 2003). Kiesner and colleagues tried to capture all middle-school peer group members in and outside the classroom by focusing on an isolated neighborhood of a large city with little access to the rest of the city. In this study, we extended that methodology: (1) by expanding the age range to all youths from preadoles-cence through the end of high school in an entire small city; (2) by following the sample over time; and (3) by including measures for important individual peers as well as peer groups. An important methodological aspect of this study is that our measures of the behavior of an individual's peers are from peers' own self-reports rather than from the individual's reports. Thus, our measures of peer behavior are more reliable than they would have been if they had come from friends. These strengths increase the likelihood that we have captured the important peer influences and that we have valid information about their behavior.

There are, however, several limitations of this study, or avenues that we did not pursue. First, we concentrated on youths' most important peers, but did not consider second-, third-, or fourth-mentioned important peers. These peers add uniquely to the prediction of problem behavior, as shown by a recent study (Keisner et al., 2004). Second, we have not considered important peers together with peer groups – looked at how many important peers appear in the in- and out-of-school peer groups or how they compare with each other in each of our empirical examples. These are avenues for future research.

In addition, the larger study offers many possibilities to investigate different issues concerning peers. At present, we have finished the first two waves of this longitudinal study over six years. This study is one of the first reports of findings from this project. Here we have dealt with which peers adolescents at different ages report to be central for them and the friendship groups that youth engage with in and outside of school. There are numerous issues not discussed here but which will be important in future studies in the project. For example: the essential properties of friendships or peer groups; the basis of friendship selection, maintenance, stability and dissolution; gender and age-related differences in friendships and peer group configurations; positive or negative influence of friends and groups; processes of influence; and the influence of context on friendships and peer groups.

One expectation in the present study that was not completely confirmed was that naming an older boy as an important peer would be linked to higher levels of problem behavior in boys as well as girls. This was confirmed for girls, and for boys' serious delinquency. But for less serious delinquency and alcohol drinking, boys who named *girls* as their most important peers, rather than older boys, were more problematic. We have no ready explanation for this finding, and the literature does not help much to clarify our findings. There is research on dating and problem behavior, and although we are not sure that the girls these boys named were all romantic partners (rather than sisters or friends), we can assume that many were and look at whether that research gives any hints for interpreting our findings. In one line of inquiry, over involvement in dating, defined as having a large number of dating partners (up to 35/year), was linked to a range of adjustment problems, including externalizing problems (Zimmer-Gembeck et al., 2001). The over involvement measure seems to indicate instability in relationships; therefore, it is not surprising that boys with many unstable relationships would be poorly adjusted or even delinquent. In fact, one of the indicators used in the assessment of psychopathy, which characterizes the most serious adult criminals, is having had many unstable, short-term relationships. Naming a girl as a most important peer, however, suggests a stable relationship, and thus a very different phenomenon. In the Zimmer-Gembeck et al. (2001) study, relationship quality was not related to adjustment. If naming a girl as one's most important peer indicates relationship quality, it is surprising that boys who did that were more problematic. In other research, including one of the other chapters in this volume, early dating has been linked to problems such as substance use and externalizing problems (Furman, Ho, & Lo, this volume). These results might be seen as parallel to ours if we could consider our 7th through 9th graders as early daters. In Furman and colleagues' study, however, early was defined as younger than 8th grade. Youths in 8th through 10th grades were considered on-time daters. If the same criteria would apply in our study, most of the 7th through 9th graders involved in our findings would be considered on time. Then, given that children start school a year later in Sweden than in the United States, our 7th graders would be roughly the same age as Furman and colleagues' 8th graders. Thus, defining these boys as early daters does not seem to be a way to understand these findings, either. These findings remain a puzzle.

   We expected to see evidence in these data of a shift with age from same-sex cliques to mixed-sex groups to heterosexual couples (Dunphy, 1963), and that was not entirely confirmed. Considering groups, the data did not show an obvious shift from same- to mixed-sex groups over ages. At no age did a majority of youths report mixed-sex groups; most of the time only small minorities did. Thus, any evidence of a shift from cliques to crowds is missing in these data. One possible explanation is that crowds did, indeed, exist, but when asked, youths defined their same-sex peers within the crowds as their groups. The possibility remains, however, that only a minority of youths actually felt that they belonged to mixed-sex groups. On the other hand, in the results concerning important peers, the emergence of heterosexual couples was clearly evident among the oldest cohorts in the sample. A more accurate test of this age shift in peer relationships awaits longer-term longitudinal data so that the same individuals can be followed over time, but the present cross-sectional data provide only mixed support.

There is no doubt that the school classroom is an important developmental context for children and adolescents. Nor is there any doubt that the classroom is the primary setting where children make friends and enemies, and learn to negotiate peer and peer-group relationships. Nonetheless, as children move into adolescence and their social horizons expand, classmates occupy less central roles. Clearly, some school friends are important for understanding problem behavior in some youths; clearly, peers outside of school are important for understanding problem behavior in some youths. Someone once remarked about longitudinal research, 'You can't study development without studying *development*.' Perhaps the same can be said about peers. It seems that the microcosm of peer relationships in any one setting does not represent the macrocosm of relationships across settings, and to understand peer influences, we need to include as many peers as possible.

REFERENCES

Allen, J. P. (1989). Social impact of age mixing and age segregation in school: A context-sensitive investigation. *Journal of Educational Psychology, 81*, 408–416.

Alsaker, F. D. & Brunner, A. (1999). Switzerland. In P. K. Smith, Y. Morita, J. Junder-Tas, D. Olweus, R. Catalano, & P. T. Slee (eds.), *The Nature of School Bullying: A Cross-national Perspective*. London: Routledge.

Andershed, H., Stattin, H., & Kerr, M. (2001). Bullying in school and violence on the streets: Are the same people involved? *Scandinavian Journal of Criminality and Crime Prevention, 2*, 31–49.

Bergman, L. & El-Khouri, B. (1987). EXACON: A FORTRAN 77 program for the exact analysis of single cells in a contingency table. *Educational and Psychological Measurement, 47*, 155–161.

Bergman, L. R., Magnusson, D., & El-Khouri, B. M. (2003). *Studying Individual Development in an Interindividual Context. A Person-oriented Approach*. Mahwah, NJ: Lawrence Erlbaum Associates.

Blyth, D. A., Hill, J. P., & Thiel, K. S. (1982). Early adolescents' significant others: Grade and gender differences in perceived relationships with familial and nonfamilial adults and young people. *Journal of Youth and Adolescence, 11*, 425–450.

Brook, J. S., Nomura, C., & Cohen, P. (1989). A network of influences on adolescent drug involvement: Neighborhood, school, peer, and family. *Genetic, Social, and General Psychology Monographs, 115*, 125–145.

Brown, B. B. (1990). Peer groups and peer cultures. In S. S. Feldman & G. R. Elliott (eds.), *At the Threshold: The Developing Adolescent* (pp. 171–196). Cambridge, MA: Harvard University Press.

Bullock, B. M. & Dishion, T. J. (2002). Sibling collusion and problem behavior in early adolescence: Toward a process model for family mutuality. *Journal of Abnormal Child Psychology, 30*, 143–153.

Cairns, R. B. & Cairns, B. D. (1994). *Lifelines and Risks: Pathways of Youth in Our Time*. New York: Cambridge University Press.

Cairns, R. B., Cairns, B. D., Neckerman, H. J., Gest, S., & Gariépy, J. L. (1988). Social networks and aggressive behavior: Peer support or peer rejection? *Developmental Psychology, 24*, 815–823.

Cochran, M. M. & Bo, I. (1987). Connections between the social networks, family involvement and behavior of adolescent males in Norway. University of Rogaland, No. 75.

Coleman, J. S. (1961). *The Adolescent Society*. New York: The Free Press.

Dishion, T. J., Spracklen, K. M., Andrews, D. W., & Patterson, G. R. (1996). Deviancy training in male adolescent friendships. *Behavior Therapy, 27*, 373–390.

Duck, S. W. (1975). Personality similarity and friendship choices by adolescents. *European Journal of Social Psychology, 5*, 351–365.

Dunphy, D. C. (1963). The social structure of urban adolescent peer groups. *Sociometry, 26*, 230–246.

Engels, R. C. M. E. & Knibbe, R. A. (2000). Alcohol use and intimate relationships in adolescence: When love comes to town. *Addictive Behaviors, 25*, 435–439.

Engels, R. C. M. E., Knibbe, R. A., & Drop, M. J. (1999). Visiting public drinking places: An exploratory study into the functions of pub-going for late adolescents. *Substance Use and Misuse, 34*, 1061–1080.

Ennett, S. T. & Bauman, K. E. (1994). The contribution of influence and selection to adolescent peer group homogeneity: The case of adolescent cigarette smoking. *Journal of Personality and Social Psychology, 67*, 653–663.

Fine, G. A. (1980). The natural history of preadolescent male friendship groups. In H. C. Foot, A. J. Chapman, & J. R. Smith (eds.), *Friendship and social relations in children* (pp. 293–320). New York: Wiley.

Fine, G. A. & Glassner, B. (1979). The promise and problems of participant observation with children. *Urban Life, 8*, 153–174.

Furman, W., Ho, M. H., & Low, S. S. L., (this volume). The rocky road of adolescent romantic experience: Dating and adjustment. From a paper originally presented at a conference in Nijmegan, The Netherlands.

George, T. P. & Hartmann, D. P. (1996). Friendship networks of unpopular average, and popular children. *Child Development, 67*, 2301–2316.

Glueck, S. & Glueck, E. (1950). *Unraveling Juvenile Delinquency*. Cambridge, MA: Harvard University Press.

Goldstein, A. P. (1994). Delinquent gangs. In L. R. Huesmann (ed.), *Aggressive Behavior: Current Perspectives* (pp. 255–273). New York: Plenum Press.

Hartup, W. W. (1976). Cross-age versus same-age peer interaction: Ethological and cross-cultural perspectives. In V. L. Allen (ed.), *Children as Teachers: Theory and Research on Tutoring*. New York: Academic Press.

Iannotti, R. J., Bush, P. J., & Weinfurt, K.P. (1996). Perceptions of friends' use of alcohol, cigarettes, and marijuana among urban schoolchildren: A longitudinal analysis. *Addictive Behaviors, 21*, 615–632.

Kandel, D. B. (1978). Similarity in real-life adolescent friendship pairs. *Journal of Personality and Social Psychology, 36*, 306–312.

Kandel, D. B. & Lesser, G. S. (1972). *Youth in Two worlds. United States and Denmark*. San Francisco: Josey-Bass.

Kiesner, J., Cadinu, M., Poulin, F., & Bucci, M. (2002). Group identification in early adolescence: its relation with peer adjustment and its moderator effect on peer influence. *Child Development, 73*, 200–212.

Kiesner, J., Kerr, M., & Stattin, H. (2004). 'Very important persons' in adolescence: going beyond in-school, single friendships in the study of peer homophily. *Journal of Adolescence, 27*, 545–560.

Kiesner, J., Poulin, F., & Nicotra, E. (2003). Peer relations across contexts: Individual-network homophily and network inclusion in and after school. *Child Development, 74*, 1328–1343.

Kiesner, J., Maass, A., Cadinu, M., & Vallesse, I. (2003). Risk factors for ethnic prejudice during early adolescence. *Social Development, 12*, 288–308.

Mahoney, J. L., Stattin, H., & Magnusson, D. (2001). Youth leisure activity participation and individual adjustment: The Swedish youth recreation center. *International Journal of Behavioral Development*, 25, 509–520.

Mahoney, J. L. & Stattin, H. (2000) Leisure activities and adolescent antisocial behavior. The role of structure and social context. *Journal of Adolescence*, 23, 113–127.

Mounts, N. S. & Steinberg, L. (1995). An ecological analysis of peer influence on adolescent grade point average and drug use. *Developmental Psychology*, 31, 915–922.

Persson, A., Kerr, M., & Stattin, H. (2004). Why a leisure context is linked to normbreaking for some girls and not others: personality characteristics and parent-child relations as explanations. *Journal of Adolescence*, 27, 583–598.

Poulin, F., Cillessen, A. H. N., Hubbard, J. A., Coie, J. D., Dodge, K. A., & Schwartz, D. (1997). Children's friends and behavioral similarity in two social contexts. *Social Development*, 6, 224–236.

Richards, W. & Rice, R. (1981). The NEGOPY network analysis program. *Social Networks*, 3, 215–223.

Rubin, K. H., Lynch, D., Coplan, R., Rose-Krasnor, L., & Booth, C. L. (1994). 'Birds of a feather. . .': Behavioral concordances and preferential personal attraction in children. *Child Development*, 65, 1778–1785.

Sarnecki, J. (2001) *Delinquent Networks: Youth Co-offending Youth Networks in Stockholm*. Cambridge: Cambridge Criminology Series.

Sherif, M., Harvey, O. J., White, B. J., Hood, W. R., & Sherif, C. W. (1961). *Intergroup Conflict and Cooperation: The Robber's Cave Experiment*. Norman: University of Oklahoma Book Exchange.

Shortt, J. W., Capaldi, D. M., Dishion, T. J., Bank, L., & Owen, L. D. (2003). The role of adolescent friends, romantic partners, and siblings in the emergence of the adult antisocial lifestyle. *Journal of Family Psychology*, 17, 521–533.

Silbereisen, R. K. & Noack, P. (1988). On the constructive role of problem behavior in adolescence. In N. Bolger, A. Caspi, G. Downey, & M. Moorehouse (eds.), *Persons in Context: Developmental Processes* (pp. 152–180). Cambridge, MA: Cambridge University Press.

Silbereisen, R. K., Noack, P., & von Eye, A. (1992). Adolescents' development of romantic friendship and change in favorite leisure contexts. *Journal of Adolescent Research*, 7, 80–93.

Smith, A. B. & Inder, P. M. (1990). The relationship of classroom organisation to cross-age and cross-sex friendships. *Educational Psychology*, 10, 127–140.

Stattin, H., Kerr, M., Mahoney, J., Persson, A. & Magnusson, D. (2005). Explaining why a leisure context is bad for some girls and not for others. In J. L. Mahoney, R. W. Larson, & J. S. Eccles (eds.), *Organized Activities as Contexts of Development: Extracurricular Activities, After-school and Community Programs*. Mahwah, NJ: Erlbaum.

Stattin, H. & Magnusson, D. (1990). *Pubertal Maturation in Female Development*. Hillsdale, NJ: Lawrence Erlbaum.

Thrasher, F. M. (1927). *The Gang*. Chicago: University of Chicago Press.

Urberg, K. A., Degirmencioglu, S. M., & Tolson, J. M. (1998). Adolescent friendship selection and termination: The role of similarity. *Journal of Social and Personal Relationships*, 15, 703–710.

Urberg, K. A., Degirmencioglu, S. M., & Pilgrim, C. (1997). Close friend and group influence on adolescent cigarette smoking and alcohol use. *Developmental Psychology*, 33, 834–844.

Vitaro, F., Brendgen, M., & Tremblay, R. E. (2000). Influence of deviant friends on delinquency: Searching for moderator variables. *Journal of Abnormal Child Psychology*, 28, 313–325.

Vitaro, F., Tremblay, R. E., Kerr, M., Pagani, L., & Bukowski, W. M. (1997). Disruptiveness, friends' characteristics, and delinquency in early adolescence: A test of two competing models of development. *Child Development*, 68, 676–689.

Young, A. M. & d'Arcy, H. (2005). Older boyfriends of adolescent girls: the cause or a sign of the problem? *Journal of Adolescent Health, 36*, 410–419.

Zimmer-Gembeck, M. J., Siebenbruner, J., & Collins, A. J. (2001). Diverse aspects of dating: Associations with psychosocial functioning from early to middle adolescence. *Journal of Adolescence, 24*, 313–336.

CHAPTER 9

Peers Among Immigrants – Some Comments on 'Have We Missed Something?'

Rainer K. Silbereisen and Peter F. Titzmann
University of Jena, Germany

INTRODUCTION

That peers represent important influences on young peoples' lives and development is a common place insight, and yet at close scrutiny one realizes that the empirical evidence is based on quite different strands of research. Concerning the role of peers in the development of problem behaviour as studied in research on adolescence, the term 'peers' either refers to friends or best friends in school, or to other young people whom the adolescents meet during their free time in the neighbourhood. Given the fact that there are varying degrees of membership overlap between the groups in and out of school, the peer relationships an adolescent entertains are actually more complex than dealt with in the bulk of previous studies. The variability of peer relationships is further increased by the nature of the people involved, such as friends, romantic partners, or siblings, and one also has to consider trends in the composition of adolescents' peer networks by age and gender.

What we have just described summarizes the outset of Kerr, Stattin and Kiesner's (this volume) provocative search of what has been missed by known research on peers. Our comments on their work begin with a short overview of the main insights provided. Taken together they show the role of adolescents' choices of peers in predicting consequences for adjustment and development. Drawing on our own research on peers among immigrants, we will then report on differences in the concentration of immigrants in school and neighbourhood, and their relationship to the selection of peers. The results further illuminate the choices and constraints adolescents pursue in associating

Friends, Lovers and Groups: Key Relationships in Adolescence. Edited by Rutger C.M.E. Engels, Margaret Kerr and Håkan Stattin. Copyright © 2007 John Wiley & Sons, Ltd.

with peers. We will close with a plea for a more systematic research on the ecological constraints adolescents face when forming their peer network.

In turning to the chapter on what past research has missed, the first important contribution of Kerr et al. (this volume) is the careful analysis of the concept we have just described, i.e., that the world of peers actually involves multiple contexts, and relying on peer research in only one context, such as either schools or neighbourhoods, is likely to be misleading. Their conclusion is to follow a more ecologically valid strategy and to try to catch all peers of a target adolescent, irrespective of their specific location. This is a remarkable undertaking – by choosing a relatively closed ecology of a small isolated town in Sweden with little inward and outward migration, the authors attempt to gather information on peers of various categories in a sample of about 3000 10–18-year-olds. As the participants represent the entire student population in the town, and thanks to a high participation rate, the information gathered on peers was provided by the peers themselves, not by the target adolescents, and thus there was no risk of inflated statistical associations due to the same source of reporting.

Three cohorts of students, originally attending grades 4, 5, and 6, will be observed longitudinally for seven annual waves, up to grades 10, 11, and 12. In addition, at any one wave all other students attending grades 4 to 12 will be included. Consequently, all peers of the three target cohorts can be identified in that age or grade range (see Kerr et al., this volume, Figure 8.1). There is, however, an age asymmetry inherent to the design. For instance, in wave 1 this means that, in principle, information on same-aged and older peers up to grade 12 can be included, whereas at wave 7 only same-aged and younger peers can be analyzed. Given the fact that adolescents in the older grade/age brackets will in all likelihood also have peers beyond grade 12, this is a limitation of an otherwise amazing design.

The second important innovation of the research is the concept of 'VIP', very important person. Adolescents were not asked to nominate, for instance, their best friend, but rather should name up to four VIPs (not including parents or other adults), defined as 'someone you talk with, hang out with, and do things with...' (Kerr, et al., this volume). Information on the type of peer (friend, romantic partner, sibling, or other) was provided by the adolescents themselves, and they also reported whether the context was school or neighbourhood. This new approach allows other relevant peers apart from friends to be investigated.

Based on earlier research on the relationship between peer affiliations and problem behaviour (it should be clear that the ultimate aspirations of the authors go far beyond this particular topic), a few framing hypotheses were formulated and investigated, thereby utilizing data from the first two waves. One hypothesis was that peer influence is context specific. Peers in school are particularly relevant for school-related activities and as such these contacts tend to promote positive adaptation. On the other hand peers in the neighbourhood are particularly relevant for problem behaviours, rooted in the greater opportunities for selecting peers in line with one's own norm-breaking orientations. The other framing hypothesis was that 'conjoint peers' i.e., peers named by the adolescents as VIPs in both school and neighbourhood, are more influential than context-specific peers. If both share norm-breaking orientations, the potentially protective influence of peers concerned with school-related activities will be weakened.

The results reported are manifold, and we can only touch on the most important ones in the present context. Generally speaking, the first VIPs mentioned were of the same sex and the same age, as one would have expected for adolescents in the age range studied. At closer scrutiny, however, among the younger cohort VIPs were friends, typically in the same school, whereas in the older cohort (high school) they were romantic partners. As far as peer groups are concerned, the younger cohort engaged particularly with in-school groups, whereas the older cohort entertained more out-of-school groups. This difference is likely to be a reflection of the developmental shift from same-sex friends to other-sex romantic partners (and the relevant peer groups). In addition, the fact that the one high school in the town drew students from various neighbourhoods (in contrast to the schools for lower grades that are located in the respective neighbourhood) may play a role.

Concerning delinquency, the role of conjoint peer groups indeed stood out. In contrast to peers with whom one engages only in-school or only out-of-school, the delinquent behaviour of conjoint peers was a predictor of the target adolescents' increase in delinquency across the two waves of assessment. This result basically applies to both genders, but the group effect is less pronounced among females. Thus, peers that represent the social network in both contexts (school, neighbourhood) had the strongest effect.

A final result concerning early maturing girls shows that peers or peer groups actively chosen by an adolescent are more relevant than those he/she is constrained by a given context to adopt. As is well-known, early maturation in girls is associated with problem behaviour (see Weichold, Silbereisen & Schmitt-Rodermund, 2003, for an overview). The mechanisms claimed for this association are related to the fact that these girls are interested in (and are approached by) older male adolescents. As we (Silbereisen, Noack & von Eye, 1992) put it, engaging with older males can be a means to overcome the conflict between the early maturing female's actual social status and others' reactions to her more mature physical appearance. Thus, behaviours such as earlier and greater substance use do not necessarily indicate problem behaviour per se, but may actually represent girls' deliberate attempts to match their older peers' behaviour and appearance, regardless of their younger chronological age.

Against such a theoretical backdrop, Kerr et al. (this volume) expected and found that the age of the average target girls' in-school groups was similar to their own age, whereas early maturing girls nominated older peers among out-of-school groups, and that these peers, in turn, showed higher levels of delinquency. The interpretation of this variation rests on the different opportunities for deliberate choice concerning the peers and groups in these two contexts.

In a nutshell, to our mind the most remarkable results reported by Kerr et al. (this volume) point to the role played by actively selected peers, depending on age, in various facets of juvenile delinquency. Among the younger adolescents it is friends, and among the older adolescents it is romantic partners who exert the strongest influence (within the constraints of a correlational design).

This role of individual action in adolescent development was at the core of our own earlier research on the everyday ecology of adolescent leisure behaviours. Silbereisen, Noack and von Eye (1992) found that beyond status variables such as age or gender this choice is a function of the individuals' goals pertaining to their own development. Adolescents who felt a discrepancy between their wish to have a romantic partner and the current state of affairs, for instance, undertook relevant activities in the future, such as going to public locations that offer matchmaking opportunities, like discotheques. Once they had accomplished their goal the choice of activities changed again, this time in favour of more intimate, private locales such as homes.

An implicit presumption in Kerr et al.'s (this volume) design is that the adolescents are free to choose their VIPs, within the constraints of variables such as age and gender, and it is differences and trends with regard to these variables that are of interest to the researchers. Given this background, it makes sense to assume that the nature and potential differences between in-school and out-of-school friends of a target adolescent are indicative of his/her orientations and liabilities with regard to problem behaviours. The choice of a relatively isolated and static community (not offering easy access to neighbouring cities) was an advantage in this regard. As a matter of fact, when we investigated the leisure activities and leisure locales of adolescents, we were interested in 'development as action in context' (Silbereisen, Eyferth & Rudinger, 1986) that is, in their choices among a plenitude of opportunities (as provided in a metropolitan city), thereby expressing preferences that shed light on themselves and their personality.

In reality, of course, people may vary in the degree of choice, and not all such variations may point to the person, but rather reflect constraints of the context. Immigration offers a particular opportunity for the study of the formation of peer networks. Relocating to a new country requires new efforts in approaching peers – not only those sharing one's own immigrant status, but also peers from the local population. Possible ecological constraints operating in such a situation among adolescents refer to the school and the neighbourhood. Both may vary in the share of immigrants, thus reflecting differential opportunities for networking (and perhaps also reflecting discrimination and residential segregation). Probably there were also immigrants in the Swedish sample, but irrespective of that, this observation leads us to our own recent study on acculturation in an immigration context.

In the process of acculturation, one can distinguish various steps that may ultimately lead to full integration into a host society's way of life. According to Esser (1980), a major step toward this is 'social assimilation', meaning the nature of the social network, particularly indexed by its relative composition in terms of immigrants and people from the local population. Among many groups of immigrants, a trend towards a growing representation of members from the host society in the groups' social networks was seen across time of residence in the new country or across generations (Eshel, Sharabany & Bar-sade, 2003; Fong & Isajiw, 2000; Haug, 2003), and this is seen as providing the 'social capital' required for success in the next steps of acculturation.

In actuality, because various modes of acculturation exist, and assimilation is just one among four, the situation is more complicated. According to Berry et al. (2002), two issues have to be combined – does the immigrant group want to maintain their own cultural roots or not, and does the immigrant group want to develop new contacts with the host culture or not? Assimilation means emphasizing new contacts, whereas separation means relying solely on one's cultural roots, and marginalization represents a distraction from both issues, whereas integration captures a mode where both forms of contact are similarly upheld. For immigrant adolescents this model suggests that groups may differ in the degree to which they seek contacts to intra-ethnic friends and/or from the local population.

We have been studying particular groups of first generation young immigrants from the former Soviet Union – ethnic Germans ('Aussiedler') who immigrated to Germany, and ethnic Jews who immigrated in Israel.[1] Both groups are privileged compared to other immigrants because they are entitled to immediate citizenship (they are legally included) in spite of the fact that their cultural affinity ('return'-migration) is often a mere illusion, based on the fact that their ancestors had either left the home country a long time ago, or had lived ever since in a diaspora situation. Among such immigrants, assimilation modes of acculturation (or separation, if a self-containing ethnic network exists in the country of destiny) are quite prevalent.

The age groups we studied are comparable to the Kerr et al. (this volume) sample, and we also gathered data on peers, although much less differentiated. Moreover, we are also able to study the association between peer relationships and delinquency, including a differentiation as to the opportunity structure for intra-ethnic peer contacts.

The German sample (to which we will refer only) comprised 489 male and 570 female adolescents, mainly from Russia and Kazakhstan, who were residing in various regions of Germany. They were on average about 16 years old, and their mean length of residence in Germany was about eight years. By virtue of a particular design already successfully applied in a previous research project on immigration (Schmitt-Rodermund & Silbereisen, 1999), age and length of residence were independent of each other. The correlation of the relative share of intra-ethnic friends among all friends with a measure of delinquency (a count based on a large number of property, violence and status offences) was not significant, whereas the correlation with the absolute number of intra-ethnic friends was positive and significant, in the order of 0.20. This difference in the results is interesting in its own right – the risk of delinquency seems to rest in the number of intra-ethnic participants in the network, not in its composition.

[1] Project: 'The impact of social and cultural adaptation of juvenile immigrants from the former Soviet Union in Israel and Germany on delinquency and deviant behaviour'; Principal investigators: Germany: Rainer K. Silbereisen & Eva Schmitt-Rodermund; Israel: Gideon Fishman, Gustavo Mesch, Zvi Eisikovitz; Funding: German-Israeli-Project Cooperation (DIP), Ministry for Education and Research (BMBF).

One could assume that the above distinction between size and composition of a network applies to a wide range of problem behaviours, but it may also be the case that delinquency and, for instance, depressive mood are different in this regard. Exactly the latter turned up when we conducted the same analysis with a measure of depressive mood – there was a small negative but significant correlation with the share of ethnic Germans among friends, but no relationship with their number in the intra-ethnic network. The number of friends from the local German population, however, was protective: the more friends, the lower the level of depressive mood.

Guided by our wish to demonstrate the relevance of external constraints on the choice of peer networks, we looked first at the association between the share of intra-ethnic friends and the concentration of such immigrants in the respective school, broken down by two age groups, 11–15-year-olds and 16–19-year-olds. The concentration of ethnic Germans in the 53 schools attended by the participants of our study varied between 0% and 40%. As can be seen in Figure 9.1, the share of immigrant friends was generally higher (between 40% and 80%) in the older than in the younger age group (seemingly indicating a problem concerning adaptation to the new context in Germany). Further, the correlation with the concentration variable was positive and significant in the order of 0.25 – the higher the concentration of like immigrants in the school (not necessarily in the same classroom, as we do not have such data), the higher the share of intra-ethnic friends in the network. The graphs depicted in

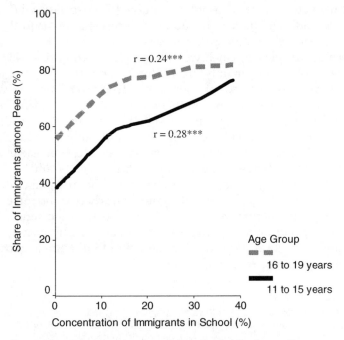

Figure 9.1 Share of immigrant friends among all friends depending on concentration of immigrants at school in two different age groups

Figure 9.1 represent 'LoWeSS' (locally weighted scatterplot smoother) fit lines, i.e., a non-parametric fit of the relation between two variables that follows the trend of the data instead of superimposing a straight regression line or any other mathematical curve (Cohen et al., 2003).

The results are in line with the broader idea of friendship homophily, that is, that adolescents have the tendency to choose peers who share prominent attributes with themselves. Ethnicity represents such an attribute and is deemed as 'the biggest divide in social networks today' (McPherson, Smith-Lovin & Cook, 2001, p. 420). The reason is that ethnicity points to a number of social-psychological differences to the majority population. Examples are dimensions, such as social status, language, attitudes, values or socialization experiences (Maharaj & Connolly, 1994). Most of these attributes also differentiate between ethnic German and local adolescents in Germany, at least during the earlier phases of the acculturation process.

The length of residence in the country of destiny is often taken as a proxy for the latent processes that result in the adaptation to the new context. Consequently, we were further interested in how the share of intra-ethnic friends would associate with the length of residence, thereby proffering the hypothesis that this share declines across time spent in the new country. This was true in a sense, but with a remarkable differentiation when broken down by the concentration of ethnic Germans in the school. As shown in the LoWeSS curves of Figure 9.2, the share declined steeply across length of residence

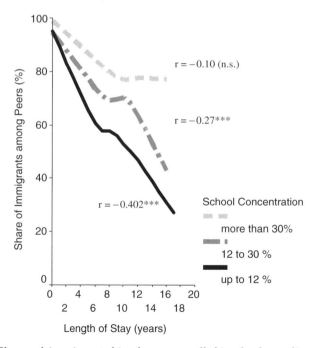

Figure 9.2 Share of immigrant friends among all friends depending on length of residence in three groups differing in concentration of immigrants at school

among adolescents in schools with the lowest concentration of immigrant youth ($r = -0.40$, $p < 0.001$), was also negative but less pronounced in schools with 12% to 30% of immigrants ($r = -0.27$, $p < 0.001$), and was non-significant among students who attended schools with a high-concentration ($> 0.30\%$). More specifically, in the latter case the share of immigrants in the network stayed at a high level even after a longer period of time in the country of destiny.

Given the fact that the homophily of the peer network varies by length of residence, one could assume that the overall association with delinquency and depression already reported would also reveal differences by length of residence. However, as in the total sample, there was no significant correlation between the share of intra-ethnic friends and delinquency even when broken down by the level of concentration (although the correlation with the absolute number was again significant in two out of three coefficients). At closer scrutiny, however, the correlation between the share of intra-ethnic friends among all friends and depressive mood held only among adolescents attending schools with low concentration of ethnic Germans. This result probably indicates consequences of social exclusion – not to have local friends in a school characterized by a low concentration of ethnic Germans is different from the same state of affairs in a high concentration setting.

In order to bring all the variables covered thus far into a joint analytical framework, we regressed the share of ethnic German friends on age, length of residence, concentration of ethnic German immigrants, plus all simple interactions between these variables (centred before analyzing). As shown in Table 9.1 (left-hand columns), age and ethnic concentration in school revealed positive beta coefficients, length of residence negative coefficients – older adolescents in high concentration schools who resided shorter periods of time

Table 9.1 Predicting friendship homophily among ethnic German adolescents

	Share of immigrant friends among all friends		Best friend is immigrant	
	Step 1	Step 2	Step 1	Step 2
	Beta	Beta	EXP(B)	EXP(B)
Age	0.251***	0.237***	1.383***	1.458***
Length of residence	−0.298***	−0.290***	0.838***	0.831***
Concentration in school	0.311***	0.300***	1.065***	1.065***
Age × length of residence		−0.067*		0.955***
Age × concentration in school		−0.008		1.005
Length of residence × concentration in school		0.111***		1.002
R squared	0.207***	0.224***	0.265***[a]	0.289***[a]
Delta R squared (step2)		0.018***		0.024**

[a]For the logistic regression Nagelkerkes R squared is reported – an adjusted value of Cox & Snell's goodness of fit measure – that can also attain a value of 1.00 (Cohen et al., 2003)

maintained higher shares of ethnic Germans among their friends. The variance explained was about 20%, and another 2% was added by the interaction terms. The interaction between length of residence and concentration was most important, as already given in Figure 9.2.

Inspired by Kerr et al.'s (this volume) distinction between types of persons in the VIP network, we also used logistic regression to analyze the role of the same variables in predicting whether the best friend was an ethnic German. As shown in Table 9.1 (right-hand columns), the results are substantively the same – older adolescents who attended schools with higher concentration of immigrants and who had resided in Germany for shorter periods of time revealed a higher likelihood of having an ethnic German as best friend. Concerning the statistical interactions, another 2% on top of the 26% by the main effects was explained, primarily related to the interaction of age and length of residence. The lowest level and least decline with length of residence in the likelihood of having an ethnic German as best friend referred to the youngest age group. Among this group, more of the best friends than otherwise were local Germans, and this did not change much across time, whereas change was much more pronounced among older adolescents.

We also had data on the ethnic composition of 'cliques' that come close to peer groups as studied by Kerr et al. (this volume). Again using logistic regression, the results were basically the same as those on the best friends. The criterion was whether the clique consisted of ethnic Germans only, or whether local German adolescents were also involved (the variance explained by the interaction was about 3%, on top of about 18% for the main effects.

Taken together, whether we used ethnicity of the best friend, friends in more general terms, or cliques of young people the target adolescent belonged to, it was always age, length of residence, and concentration of ethnic Germans in school that played a role in the expected direction. Moreover, with longer residence in the country, adaptation in the sense of declining homophily in ethnic German adolescents' peers was the rule, except where there were really high concentrations of ethnic Germans in school. In this situation the adaptation levelled off after a few years of residence.

The data are clearly in line with what one would have expected in an immigration context, but Kerr et al.'s (this volume) research obviously provides additional insights for acculturation research as well as for research on adolescents' peer relationships. When comparing the results of the studies, we want to make the presumption that most probably a high share among the friends from the local German population were in-school friends, and likewise most probably a high share among the ethnic German friends are out-of-school friends, at least on average across the age-span studied. This differential is likely because the concentration of ethnic German immigrants in the same classrooms is rather low. Assuming this presumption to be true, the trends by age, length of residence, and concentration of ethnic German immigrants can be interpreted in an interesting way, to which we now turn.

First, the share of intra-ethnic German friends in the network increased alike with higher concentration, but this increase happened at a higher level initially among the older adolescents. In light of Kerr et al.'s (this volume) results, this does not necessarily reflect a lower degree of social integration among the older adolescents, but rather mirrors the general trend of having fewer in-school friends with increasing age.

The length of residence in our study was independent of age by design. Consequently, changes in the composition of the peer network across time spent in Germany cannot be attributed to age-related trends, such as the growing preference for out-of-school friends reported by Kerr et al. (this volume). Against this backdrop, and bearing in mind the immigration situation, it is alarming that a decline in the share of intra-ethnic friends with longer residence in Germany levelled off among those attending schools with high concentrations of ethnic German immigrants. For these adolescents there is a risk of separation from the majority society.

A potential criticism of our interpretation arises immediately – what if the concentration of ethnic Germans in school only represents the situation in schools but is not representative of the neighbourhood? Although it is unlikely that in this regard schools represent an enclave atypical for the environment, we repeated the analyses using additional data on the concentration of ethnic Germans in the neighbourhood. The reports were coded so that we could distinguish whether virtually all neighbours were local Germans, whether there was a 50/50 split of locals and ethnic Germans, or whether most were ethnic German immigrants. As shown in Figure 9.3, the

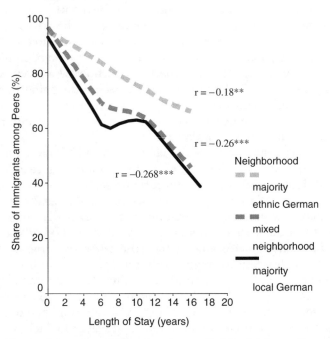

Figure 9.3 Share of immigrant friends among all friends depending on length of residence in three groups differing in concentration of immigrants in the neighbourhood

decline across length of residence in the share of ethnic Germans among friends is similar to the data using concentration in school. The decline shown for neighbourhoods dominated by ethnic German immigrants, however, is less pronounced although it does not totally level off. A regression analysis of the data gave basically the same results as with school concentration, although the effect of neighbourhood concentration was smaller than that of school concentration.

Our results obviously have relevance for research on immigration. The composition and size of the peer network were associated with indices of adjustment, although in a more complex manner than one may have expected. The concentration of intra-ethnic peers in the school and, to a lesser degree, in the neighbourhood, played a moderating role. The distinction between in-school and out-of-school friends, which we borrowed from Kerr et al. (this volume) is likely to be of particular importance for a better understanding of risks for maladjustment. Probably those adolescent immigrants who are able to find friends from the local population both in and out of school have better chances to thrive psychosocially, and to be protected against maladjustment. The conjoint network that Kerr et al. (this volume) found to be especially relevant in their study represents a particular challenge for immigrant adolescents – a closer look at establishing its 'bi-cultural' composition (local adolescents in and out of school as members) is what the process of social assimilation (Esser, 1980) is all about.

In more general terms and beyond the immigration context, our data reveal the role of external constraints in the formation of peer networks. In this regard, the chapter by Kerr et al. (this volume) was relatively mute. But certainly the authors have information on variables such as social class that may serve as a proxy for the differential opportunities adolescents have to choose peers freely. How they handle peer networks under conditions of scarce economic means or insecurity of movement also gives an insight into their determination in pursuing goals and aspirations.

Immigration, similar to other ecological transitions during the life-course, such as changes related to school and education, represents an especially fruitful testing ground for models of human development that stress the active role of the individual. This is so because existing immigration means peer networks will be interrupted and new associations have to be developed. Kerr et al. (this volume) have provided thought provoking conceptual distinctions and fresh empirical insights into peer relationships – if there is anything missing in the current state of their analysis, it is a better understanding of the ecological constraints that shape adolescents' choices of peers – something that is sure to be overcome in due course.

REFERENCES

Berry, J. W., Poortinga, Y. H., Segall, M. H. & Dasen, P. R. (2002). *Cross-cultural Psychology. Research and Applications.* Cambridge: Cambridge University Press.

Cohen, J., Cohen, P., West, S. G. & Aiken, L. S. (2003). *Applied Multiple Regression/correlation Analysis for the Behavioral Sciences.* Mahwah, New Jersey: Lawrence Erlbaum.

Eshel, Y., Sharabany, R. & Bar-sade, E. (2003). Reciprocated and unreciprocated dyadic peer preferences and academic achievement of Israeli and Immigrant students: A longitudinal study. *Journal of Social Psychology, 6,* 746–762.

Esser, H. (1980). *Aspekte der Wanderungssoziologie. Assimilation und Integration von Wanderern, ethnischen Gruppen und Minderheiten. Eine handlungstheoretische Analyse* [Aspects of migration sociology. Assimilation and integration of migrants, ethnic groups, and minorities. An action-theoretical analysis]. Darmstadt, Neuwied: Luchterhand.

Fong, E., & Isajiw, W. W. (2000). Determinants of friendship choices in a multiethnic society. *Sociological Forum, 15,* 249–271.

Haug, S. (2003). Interethnische Freundschaftsbeziehungen und soziale Integration. Unterschiede in der Ausstattung mit sozialem Kapital bei jungen Deutschen und Immigranten [*Inter-ethnic friendship relationships and social integration. Differences in social capital between young Germans and immigrants*]. *Kölner Zeitschrift für Soziologie und Sozialpsychologie, 55,* 716–736.

Maharaj, S. I. & Connolly, J. A. (1994). Peer network composition of acculturated and ethnoculturally-affiliated adolescents in a multicultural setting. *Journal of Adolescent Research, 9,* 218–240.

McPherson, M., Smith-Lovin, L. & Cook, J. M. (2001). Birds of a Feather: Homophily in social networks. *Annual Review of Sociology, 27,* 415–444.

Schmitt-Rodermund, E. & Silbereisen, R. K. (1999).Determinants of differential acculturation of developmental timetables among adolescent immigrants to Germany. *International Journal of Psychology, 34,* 219–233.

Schmitt-Rodermund, E. & Silbereisen, R. K. (2004). 'Ich war gezwungen, alles mit der Faust zu regeln' – Delinquenz unter jugendlichen Aussiedlern aus der Perspektive der Entwicklungspsychologie. ['I needed to resolve everything by force' – delinquency among young ethnic German immigrants in the perspective of developmental psychology]. *Neue Kriminalsoziologie. Sonderheft der Kölner Zeitschrift für Soziologie und Sozialpsychologie, 43,* 240–263.

Silbereisen, R. K., Eyferth, K. & Rudinger, G. (Eds.) (1985). *Development as Action in Context: Problem Behavior and Normal Youth Development.* Heidelberg, New York: Springer.

Silbereisen, R. K., Noack, P. & von Eye, A. (1992). Adolescents' development of romantic friendship and change in favorite leisure contexts. *Journal of Adolescent Research, 7,* 80–93.

Weichold, K., Silbereisen, R. K. & Schmitt-Rodermund, E. (2003). Short-term and long-term consequences of early versus late physical maturation in adolescents. In: C. Hayward (ed.). *Gender differences at puberty* (pp. 241–276). New York, NY: Cambridge University Press.

CHAPTER 10

Understanding the Place of Place in Developmental Psychology

William Bukowski and Carolina Lisboa
Concordia University, Montreal, Quebec, Canada and Universidade Federal do Rio Grande do Sul-UFRGS Porto Alegre, Brazil

INTRODUCTION

Place is one of the lesser angels that watch over the racing hand of developmental psychology, perhaps the one that has gazed benignly enough from off to one side, while others, like theory, constructs, design, and the never ending chase after effect sizes, are doing a good deal of wing beating about her chair. These loftier angels seem to soar most highly and tend to relegate place into the shade. Nevertheless, it is this lowlier angel that concerns us here. There have been signs that she has been rather neglected of late; maybe she could do with a little petitioning.

We wish we could say that we wrote the words in the previous paragraph. But, alas, we did not. We stole them from the first paragraph of Eudora Welty's essay titled 'Place in Fiction' (Welty, 1957). We adapted her words to fit the challenge that we have, specifically to say a few words about the place of place in development. The point that Welty makes in her essay is that when novelists set out to construct a story about human lives the places where these lives occur and intersect are matters of great importance. Place ascribes significance to habits, motives, and temperaments of characters; it creates feelings of security or danger, satisfactions or longings, richness or poverty. Places make characters real and they help us make sense of the characters' concerns, motives, actions, and outcomes. Without place, our sense of a person's feelings is subdued, sensibilities are blunted, and meanings are ambiguous.

Friends, Lovers and Groups: Key Relationships in Adolescence. Edited by Rutger C.M.E. Engels, Margaret Kerr and Håkan Stattin. Copyright © 2007 John Wiley & Sons, Ltd.

In literature place plays a practical role as well. In literature, as in 'real' life, places are affordances for events or important moments. A picnic in a park is used to bring a group of characters together so that an issue can be raised or resolved. A trip is used to explore another dimension of a character's personality. A dinner shared by a couple provides opportunities to make expressions of love, to reveal important secrets, to discuss an important issue, or to break up. Places give events a chance to happen. Without them, fiction would have no meaningful action.

Place appears to be critical for development also, perhaps for many of these same reasons. Ever since Kurt Lewin (1939), place has been given an explicit role in some theories of development and an implicit role in many others. Nearly every developmental psychologist is familiar with the claim that, at the least, development needs to be understood according to the context in which it occurs. Other perspectives are bolder, claiming that context shapes and directs development. Certainly there is probably no developmental psychologist who does not believe that the outcome of development derives from an interaction between the person and the environment, or, to put it a different way, between nature and nurture.

In this chapter, we comment on how the environment has been studied by developmental psychologists. We point out that this interest has been either very specific or very abstract. As a result, we understand quite well how some environments function and we have a set of rich ideas about how one might begin to think about environments. Nevertheless, a general understanding of how environments actually work to affect development has not emerged. We then argue that the recent study by Kerr, Stattin, and Kiesner (this volume) is a compelling departure from this situation. Theirs provides a model of how an environment and the effects of an environment can be studied.

BACKGROUND

In spite of the purported interest of developmental psychologists in the environment as a critical factor in developmental processes, discussion about the environment *per se* has been infrequent. This infrequency is probably accounted for by limitations in the theories and methods we use and by the practical challenges of studying development. In regard to theory, developmental psychologists have typically set out to explain particular phenomena by seeing them in the context to which they are most typically associated. The primary emphasis in most models of development has been on psychological process. Although this primary emphasis is entirely appropriate, it leads to a minimum concern with environmental factors broadly defined. When the environment is studied, we choose the one that we see as most proximal to the child. Practical concerns have minimized our attention to the environment also. It is hard enough to observe individuals in one place or context; observing them in two or more often brings more than twice the cost and aggravation. To make matters more complicated, having observations of persons in multiple contexts places has, until recently, put greater stress on our methods and statistical procedures. It's no wonder that 'place may be one of the lesser angels that watch over the racing hand of developmental psychology'.

The result of these limitations is that we do not yet have an understanding of how place affects development. To be sure there has been quite a lot of interest in the environment among developmental psychologists and it would be an error to say that developmental psychologists are not almost universally interested in assessing the effects of the 'environment'. Interest in the environment has happened at two very different levels of analysis, one very focused and is domain specific, the other is at the level of meta-theory and is concerned with broad abstract ideas about the properties of environment/person interaction. The middle ground between these levels is, for the most part, vacant. In our opinion this gap needs to be filled.

The first level helps us to understand the features and the effects of the specific environments in which children are typically situated. These contexts are often 'proximal' or closely surrounding the child but they can be very broad. Examples of this approach include research domains concerned with family environments, school environments, daycare, neighborhood, and specific cultural contexts. The ultimate goal of these research programs is to understand how these specific contexts work. Research programs at this level often follow similar strategies. These strategies include (a) an interest in identifying and describing the basic features and processes of the environment of interest, (b) working out ways of measuring individual differences between contexts, and (c) developing and testing ideas about how they have their effects.

It is clear that the interest in particular environments has generated many new ideas, concepts, insights and important findings according to their significance for development. These research areas interested in specific developmental domain or contexts have, to some extent, drawn upon some common ideas or concepts, but otherwise each of them has been focused on itself and has treated itself as conceptually distinct from the others. That is, concepts, measurements, and research questions have been developed to explain a particular environment (e.g., the family) rather than environments in general. As a result, these research areas have not contributed many ideas to the understanding of environments in a more general sense. As a result research in each of these areas has shed light on how a particular environment or context works but as a group they have not informed us of how social environments work in general.

The second level of analysis regarding the environment that has captured the interest of developmental psychologists is at a much higher level. These models consist of ideas and concepts about how an environment as a whole can be organized and how its components fit together. The best example of this approach is the ecological systems theory proposed by Urie Bronfenbrenner (1979; Bronfenbrenner & Evans, 2000; Bronfenbrenner & Morris, 1998).

Bronfenbrenner's model is best known for it topological analysis of the environment that distinguished between levels according to their proximal or distal location relative to the child. All students of developmental psychology know about the micro-system, exosystem, and the macrosystem. The doughnut like depiction of this organization scheme appears in nearly every text book. The basic organizational principles of this approach there are less well known. The model consists of four dynamically integrated dimensions: *time* (social-historical period of a specific community, past and present society; history and individual time, stage in life course development), *person* (an active human being, with biological and social characteristics), *process* (proximal processes – day-to-day experiences, peers and other persons to whom the focus person interacts and his/her interpretation/meanings of these experiences) and *context* (physical and social environment, places where the socialization occurs as well as the contact with values, culture, ideologies and so on).

Although Bronfenbrenner was initially regarded as, or even accused of being an environmentalist, he aimed to emphasize the essential processes that defined the interaction between person and context without giving different value or attention to any of the two dimensions. Like Lewin (1939), Bronfenbrenner claimed that during the life course, a person's interactions with environments become more complex and the number of contexts/environments that a person would participate on a daily basis becomes larger (Bronfenbrenner, 1979/1996). The richness of Bronfenbrenner's approach derives from its consideration of the dynamic complexity of person/environment interactions. Instead of expecting directional effects, Bronfenbrenner assumes bi-directionality in which individuals, groups and cultures are influenced and influence each other reciprocally. The impact of Bronfenbrenner's model has been broad. It can be seen in studies of classroom effects during early childhood (Pellegrini & Perlmutter, 1989), genetics (Wachs, 1995), and extracurricular activities (Mahoney & Cairns, 1997).

In spite of these advantages, Bronfenbrenner's model remains aloof from the actual events that underlie development. The model tells us how to think about and how to study the environment in a very general and abstract way. It does not, however, tell us the specifics about development and what environments do to affect development. Even in the many postulates and hypotheses that Bronfenbrenner proposed (1978), one can not see a clear description of how the features of environments work to affect development and how it is that the person environment interaction begins and ends. In this way, the model tells us how to think but it does not tell us exactly what we are supposed to think about.

PEERS AND PROBLEM BEHAVIOR: FILLING IN THE GAP

Although they may not have done so explicitly, Kerr, Stattin, and Kiesner (this volume) have tried to fill this gap between theories that are focused on the functioning of one context and the broad theoretical sweep of Bronfenbrenner's

model. They do this by following the advice of a theorist to whom we have
made some quick references in this essay but who is one of the angels of the
past who has been relegated to a place in the shade: Kurt Lewin (1939). Lewin,
one of our most overlooked intellectual ancestors, believed strongly that to
understand a person one needed to understand the person's 'life space', not
just one or two components of it. Kerr, Stattin, and Kiesner were not modest or
bashful in their study: they decided to assess everyone and everyplace.
Specifically, they argued that the study of the effects of peer relations needed
to go beyond the assessment of the usual suspect contexts such as the classroom. They decided to study all of the children in a town and to try to see them
in each of the contexts the town offered. They did so with the recognition that
the major places, such as the classroom, had been studied quite thoroughly and
quite well already but that much of the story about the effects of peer relations
might lie in the contexts that had not been given much attention. So, in an effort
to determine whether God and the devil could be found in what had been seen
as 'the details' they decided that all contexts deserved and needed to be
considered.

It is tempting to say that the basic premise of their approach is that
relationships are developmental contexts. There is no doubt that Kerr, Stattin,
and Kiesner believe this. But it seems to us that they make an even stronger
claim and one that qualifies or refines the views of Lewin (1939). The claim
that seems to be at the implicit heart of their approach is that context of
development is relationships. In other words, it is not that relationships are a
subclass of the environments in which children function, but instead it is the
case that all contexts of importance need to be studied according to the
relationship experiences they promote or limit. In this way, contexts should
be studied as affordances for relationships.

Aside from their emphasis on relationships, another critical feature of their
study is the distinction between what can happen and what does happen.
Their concern was not with isolated associations but is instead with understanding the specific antecedents and consequences of relationship experiences. So, it is one thing to know that associating with one type of peer can
lead to a particular outcome. Kerr, Stattin, and Kiesner wanted to go beyond
this concern. They wanted to know which peers would get themselves into a
particular relationship experience and what that experience would do to them
especially in regard to antisocial behavior. In other words they wanted to take
an ethological approach, following the antisocial duck from one relationship
context to another so as to watch how the level of 'antisocialness' would go up
or down as a result.

Perhaps the most critical findings of their study are as follows: first, they
show the effects of relationships with older antisocial peers that necessarily
were not classmates. Most of us don't capture this sort of information in our
studies. Second, they show the value of delineating the overlap between one's
relationship experiences to find when one's experiences are conjoint. These
conjoint effects, i.e., when the school and outside of school group are
overlapping, appear to be especially important. Third, the relative lack of

sex differences in peer group constellations is notable. Only two differences were seen: boys were more likely to be peerless than were girls, and some girls showed more overlap between their in-school and out-of-school peer groups. Fourth, they show the power of continuity in experiences across the peer contexts. Specifically, the only time they observed an effect of peer experience was when the in-school and out-of-school group overlapped. The explicit significance of this finding is perhaps less significant than the processes it implies: when a child functions in many groups the negative effects of any one group is substantially diminished. This buffering effect of variability in experience should not be overlooked.

This ambitious study is commendable in another way. It provides further evidence of the intersection of the biological and the social. Whereas there is no reason to think that early developing girls would associate with older peers in school, there is reason to expect that they would have experiences with older peers outside of school. These out-of-school experiences for maturing girls early turned out to differ from in-school experiences. The out-of-school relationships included a higher number of older peers, more delinquent peers and more participation in antisocial behavior than were seen with school-based peers. Someone once said that biology is destiny. These findings show that early maturation affects one's social context and one's social behavior. This particular finding may not have been what the Viennese gentleman had in mind when he made said that biology is destiny, but they show that he might have been at least a little right.

One final comment might be in order here: on some occasions, a big event can sadly confirm the findings of an empirical study. Kerr, Stattin, and Kiesner's report that older peers can lead a younger person to be more antisocial was tragically manifested in the obscene terrorist event that occurred in London on July 7, 2005. Although one will never know for certain, it appears that three of the criminals who detonated the bombs on that day had been influenced by the fourth bomber. It is believed that he was an older 'peer' whom they had met at a community centre. Here, outside their usual social contexts, these young men were influenced by him to the extent that they were convinced of the value of destroying others and themselves. We don't mean to blame killing on an out-of-usual-context peer relationship, but in this case this interpretation may be unavoidable.

CONCLUSION

It would be unfortunate if this essay were to end on such a negative note. The study by Kerr, Stattin, and Kiesner stands as a positive demonstration of how place matters. It is a demonstration on a medium sized scale. It fits Lewin's concept of capturing the life space – that is the place and places where development happens. They show that a set of relationship contexts can and should be studied. Surely many specifics about relationship processes need to be expanded and clarified. But somewhere, Kurt Lewin is smiling.

AUTHORS' NOTE

William Bukowski was supported by grants from the Fonds québécois de recherche sur la société et la culture and the Social Sciences and Humanities Research Council of Canada. The second author was supported by a CAPES Sandwich Scholarship.

REFERENCES

Bronfenbrenner, U. (1979). *The Ecology of Human Development: Experiments by Nature and Design*. Cambridge: Harvard University Press.

Bronfenbrenner, U. & Evans, G.W. (2000). Developmental science in the 21st century: Emerging theoretical models, research designs, and empirical findings. *Social Development, 9*, 115–125.

Bronfenbrenner, U. & Morris, P. (1998). The ecology of developmental process. In W. Damon (series Ee.) & R.. Lerner (vol. ed.), *Handbook of Child Psychology: Vol. 1. Theoretical Models of Human Development* (5th ed., pp. 993–1028). New York: Wiley.

Kerr, M., Stattin, H., & Kiesner, J. (this volume). Peers and problem behavior: Have we missed something? To appear in R. Engels, M. Kerr, & H. Stattin (eds.) *Friends, Lovers, and Groups: Who is Important in Adolescence and Why?* London: Wiley.

Lewin, K. (1939). The field theory approach to adolescence, *American Journal of Sociology, 44*, 868–897.

Mahoney, J. L. & Cairns, R.B. (1997). Do extracurricular activities protect against early school dropout? *Developmental Psychology, 33*, 241–253.

Pellegrini, A. D., & Perlmutter, J. C. (1989). Classroom contextual effects on children's play. *Developmental Psychology, 25* (2), 289–296.

Wachs T. D. (1995). Relation of mild-to-moderate malnutrition in human development: correlational studies. *Journal of Nutrition*, 125–224.

Welty, E. (1957). *Place in Fiction* (essay; limited edition). New York: House of Books.

Index

influence 47
influencer, identity of 40–1
inhibitory control 13
in-school peers *see* classroom studies
interpersonal regulation score 18
intra-ethnic peers 5
intrasex competition 100
introversion 49

juvenile delinquency *see* delinquency

latent growth modeling 22, 23–8
  base models 23–5
life satisfaction 21
life space 171
line-judging paradigm 38
loneliness 34
long-term development trajectories of
    peer influence 42
longitudinal designs 2, 3, 6

marijuana 20, 22, 35
marital violence 63
marriage 62
masturbation 95, 97, 99
matching law 12
median split procedures 87
methamphetamine 20
mixed-sex groups 149
moralistic reasoning 38
motivational factors 34

National Merit Scholarship Qualifying
    Test 108
nature–nurture debate 94
Negative Engagement 17
Negative Physical 16
Negative Verbal 16
neighborhood
  adolescent substance abuse and 9
  effects on behavior 116–18
Neuroticism-Extraversion-Openness
    (NEO) conscientiousness scale 21
non-familial environmental effects 116–18
nonverbal codes 16
normative talk 17

Object Manipulation 16
observational designs 2, 3
older adolescents 4, 138

opposite-sex peers 137–8
orgasm 98
other friends 49
out-of-school contexts 2, 4, 126–7,
    128–9, 140

parental monitoring 120–1
parenting effects on adolescent behavior
    development 118–21
  gene–environment correlations and
    interactions 121
  influences on children 118–19
  as moderators of children's dispositions
    120–1
  parenting measures and adolescent
    substance use 119–20
parent-sanctioned activities 38
peer group studies, limitations of 128–9
peer group membership
  across age and context 140–3
  benefits of 34
  early developing girls 145–6
  in school 140
peer influence 144–5
  comparisons of target and peer
    behavior 39
  conceptualizing and measuring 37–9
  definitions 37
  and development of antisocial
    behavior 33–43
  developmental significance 34–7
  selection and 48
  self-report questionnaires 39
  short-term processes 34
peer pressure
  benefits and drawbacks of 34–5
  definition 37
Peer Process Code 16–17, 18
peer rejection 11–12, 30, 33
peer reports 2
peer-sanctioned activities 38
peer selection 36, 112–13, 113–16
  behavioral similarities among friends
    112–13
  gender differences 113
  peer influence and 48
  twin studies of perceived friendship
    similarity 114
  twin study of actual friendship
    similarity 114–16